MW01223178

Keystone of Democracy

Keystone of Democracy

A History of
Pennsylvania Workers

Howard Harris, Editor
Perry K. Blatz, Associate Editor

Ronald L. Fillippeli
Ken Fones-Wolf
Peter Gottlieb
Mark McColloch

Commonwealth of Pennsylvania
Pennsylvania Historical and Museum Commission
Harrisburg, 1999

Commonwealth of Pennsylvania

Tom Ridge, Governor

Pennsylvania Historical and Museum Commission

ISBN 0-89271-084-5
© 1999 Commonwealth of Pennsylvania

Keystone of Democracy
A History of Pennsylvania Workers

Acknowledgments

The publication of any book marks the conclusion of a long and often time-consuming process. That fact is especially true for this project which began in the early 1980s as an initiative of the Labor Studies Department at the Pennsylvania State University. Along the way we've accumulated debts to a number of people and institutions who have helped make *Keystone of Democracy* possible.

We'd like to thank Donald Kennedy and Peter Shergold for helping to get the ball rolling by recognizing the urgent need for an accessible, one volume history of Pennsylvania's working men and women. Grace Palladino deserves special mention for her contribution to the manuscript in its early stages.

From its very inception, this book was viewed as a collaborative effort. In addition to the chapter authors, a number of people contributed original vignettes which serve to highlight important aspects of the Commonwealth's history. Thanks to Paul Le Blanc, Dale Newman, Richard O'Connor, John Tarka, Russell Gibbons, Maier B. Fox, Robert Wolensky, and Kenneth Wolensky. Two vignette authors, Louis Pappalardo of the Philip Murray Institute for Labor Studies and John Brennan of the United Food and Commercial Workers Union, passed away prior to the completion of the book. Both of them stood in the forefront of the labor movement in Pennsylvania for many years. Also, Perry Blatz would like to thank Andrew Barnes and Michael Weber for their helpful comments and suggestions on his chapter.

The hunt for appropriate illustrative material led us to many helpful individuals, libraries and archives. We would like to thank the following institutions: the Pennsylvania State Archives, the Carnegie Library of Pittsburgh, the Archives of Industrial Society at the University of Pittsburgh, the Heinz Regional History Center, the Urban Archives at Temple University and the Labor Archives at the Pennsylvania State University. Especially helpful to us were Linda Ries of the State Archives and Steve Doell of the Heinz History Center. Also deserving of special thanks are Jim Degan of the Pennsylvania AFL-CIO and Paul Golias of the *Citizen's Voice* in Wilkes-Barre, a newspaper which itself is part of the story told in this book. Finally we would like to acknowledge F. Charles Petrillo of Wilkes-Barre for allowing us to use a photograph from his personal collection.

We are greatly indebted to the Pennsylvania Historical and Museum Commission for its support and faith in this effort. We specifically wish to thank Brent D. Glass, Executive Director, and Frank Suran, Director of the Bureau of Archives and History, for their support. Without the hard work and encouragement of Diane Reed, Robert Weible, Susan Gahres, and Kenneth Wolensky we doubt that this book would have seen the light of day. Diane Reed saw the value of this project for the history of the Commonwealth from the very beginning of our work with the Commission, and she has diligently managed it to fruition. Robert Weible has consistently been a source of good suggestions and advice and we appreciate his vigorous support. Susan Gahres devoted her excellent professional abilities to the design and layout of this book. Finally, but most importantly, Kenneth Wolensky deserves our deepest gratitude. Not only did he assume the demanding task of copyediting the manuscript and shepherding it through its final stages to publication but he also contributed several important vignettes to the volume.

Our greatest debt is to past, current and future generations of Pennsylvania workers. In telling their story in these pages, we honor their efforts to define and sustain the promise of the American Dream for themselves, their families and their communities. They are truly the "keystone of democracy." This book is dedicated to them.

Howard Harris, Editor
Perry K. Blatz, Associate Editor

Introduction

Keystone of Democracy

Howard Harris and Mark McColloch

Pennsylvania's workers have been at the heart of American labor history for over two centuries. From the artisans of Philadelphia giving their ringing support to the cause of freedom and republicanism in the American Revolution, to the steelworkers of Homestead defending their community and their vision of their rights as Americans, to the enormous social and economic transformations wrought by coal miners, laundry workers, and truck drivers in the turbulent twentieth century, the Commonwealth's working men and women have led the struggle for economic and political justice on both the state and national levels.

The story of Pennsylvania's wage earners is representative of the history of all working people in the United States. Given its crucial position, first in agriculture, trade, and artisan production, then as a hub of industrialization in the nineteenth century, the state has always had a large and diverse labor force working at a wide range of trades and occupations. Immigrants and native-born Ameri-

cans, whites and blacks, men and women could all be found laboring in its steel mills, coal mines, textile mills, garment factories,
office buildings, machine shops, hotels, and construction sites. While
the composition of the work force changed over time, its basic concerns remained the same: good jobs at decent wages for both current and future generations. They shared these same concerns with
working people across the country.

Pennsylvanians often took the lead in the ongoing fight for
workers' rights in the United States. Many of the nation's top labor
leaders came from Pennsylvania. Indeed, many unions got their
start here as well. From the protests of Philadelphia cordwainers of
the 1790s to community based efforts to revive closed steel mills in
the 1980s, the working men and women of the Commonwealth
combined a reputation for toughness with a flair for the dramatic
that often pointed the way for fellow workers in other states or
regions.

In the colonial period and Revolutionary War years, Pennsylvania was a center of artisanal labor. Perhaps nowhere else did workers play a more central a role in the establishment of the new republican order. It was no accident that Pennsylvania's first state
constitution was perhaps the most democratic in the young nation.
The Commonwealth industrialized early, rapidly and extensively in
the period from 1800 to 1860. It also led the way in worker organization with the formation of some of the country's first bonafide
trades unions in Philadelphia in the 1820s and 1830s. Irish immigration during the same period swelled the work force, sometimes
bringing the newcomers into direct, bloody conflict with native-born
workers.

The Civil War hastened the pace of industrialization in the 1860s
and 1870s. By the turn of the century the coal, iron, steel, and railroad industries had made Pennsylvania central to the American
economy and transformed the state into a locus for labor conflict as
employers attempted to deny workers the right to organize and
bargain over their conditions of employment. Between the Civil War
and World War I the ethnic composition of the work force continued to change with the influx of new workers from Southern and
Eastern Europe along with an increasing stream of both whites and
blacks from the rural South.

The rise of industrialization combined with immigration would serve as a backdrop for some of the most dramatic incidents in American labor history: the Homestead lockout, the crucial events of the 1877 railroad strikes, the Lattimer Massacre of 1897, and strikes in the coal fields to name a few. These events attracted national attention. The 1919 Steel Strike, centered in Pennsylvania, illustrated more than any other single event the divisions that existed between capital and labor as well as within the internal tensions that divided the state's labor force. A combination of corporate sponsored violence and government repression defeated the strike, setting back the cause of industrial unionism and guaranteeing the continuation of autocratic labor relations in the Commonwealth.

The 1930s and 1940s saw significant changes in the position of workers and their unions as they gained a voice in many areas of labor relations and forged new political and community alliances. The gains of the labor movement during this time laid the groundwork for the enhanced standard of living realized by many Pennsylvania workers between 1950 and 1970. Workers in the public sector mounted an aggressive campaign to obtain the same basic rights as their counterparts in private industry and, by the 1970s, they secured some of the most far-reaching public sector employment laws in the country.

Despite the expansion of both public employment and the service sector, Pennsylvania remained heavily dependent on basic industry in the latter part of the twentieth century. As a result, the nationwide decline of steel production and other types of traditional manufacturing in the 1970s and 1980s hit the state particularly hard. Widespread plant closures, with their subsequent job losses, had a dramatic impact on both organized and unorganized workers and on their communities. The state's labor movement was hard hit by such developments. Initial emotions of anger, frustration, and resignation on the part of labor gave way to efforts to respond to a larger, systemic crisis by placing itself at the head of the working class struggle for economic, political and social change.

The *Keystone of Democracy* offers, for the first time, a history of labor in Pennsylvania in a format designed for a general audience as well as for high school and college students. Although all of the chapters can stand on their own, there are a number of threads which provide a common link. One theme focuses on the nature of work itself with an examination of how various tasks were performed as well as the ways in which they were impacted by technological developments. From the first applications of water and steam power to the introduction of computers and robots, Pennsylvania workers have had to devise ways to adapt to technology to preserve their ability to earn a livelihood.

Another theme is the repeated realignment of the work force in terms of gender, race, ethnicity, and skill level. *The Keystone of Democracy* examines how such changes impacted labor in the state. Internal conflict repeatedly undermined old patterns of solidarity by creating friction among different groups of workers. At the same time, an ever changing workforce helped to lay the basis for new traditions of unity by extending the full status and rights deemed to belong to all American workers.

The role of government and labor's involvement in politics are also examined. From the use of conspiracy laws to the Coal and Iron Police to the passage of extensive labor legislation—especially Act 195—in the post-World War II era, government played a critical role in the history of Pennsylvania workers and their unions. The book offers an analysis of labor's direct involvement in national, state, and local politics and the impact of its defeats and successes in those arenas. Moving from questions of state power to community life, *The Keystone of Democracy* will look at the way working people lived throughout the period covered by the text. Their beliefs and customs are examined in order to present a portrait of the state's working men and women and their families.

The story of Pennsylvania workers is told through text, photographs, illustrations, documents, and vignettes which illustrate significant persons or events in Pennsylvania labor history. It is the hope of the authors and the Pennsylvania Historical and Museum Commission that this book will be read by citizens of all ages now and in the future, so that they might gain a better understanding of the crucial role that workers and their unions have played in building prosperity and extending freedom not only in Pennsylvania, but in the United States.

Chapter One

Colonial Work,
Colonial Workers

Ronald L. Filippelli

The natural environment shaped the lives of colonial Pennsylvanians to a degree that may seem inconceivable to modern
citizens of the Commonwealth. Without tools to alter and
overcome the environment, early settlers were at the mercy of the
physical geography of the colony. Although their lot was hard and
subsistence required constant, often backbreaking labor, Pennsylvanians were among the most fortunate in the colonies, for William
Penn had been granted a benign and bountiful land.

Penn's Woods lay comfortably between the glaciated country of
New England and northern New York and the coastal plain of the
South. Neither the broad beaches and sandbars of the coastal plain
nor the rocky shores left by the glacial age obstructed the safe passage of ships up the broad estuary of the Delaware River to safe
harbor in Philadelphia. There the Piedmont began, the gently rolling, uncommonly fertile plain that stretched unobstructed for nearly

1

a hundred miles to the Appalachian ridges.

The colony sprawled across nearly the entire width of that ancient mountain system. But instead of what might have been a discouraging obstacle, nature had provided the settlers with a broad avenue through the ridges to the west. One hundred miles from Penn's Landing, the core of the Appalachians had eroded away, reducing Pennsylvania's Blue Ridge to a remnant of its former grandeur. Between present-day Reading and Carlisle the mountain had virtually disappeared. Instead of a barrier, settlers found a great valley, called the Cumberland in Pennsylvania and the Shenandoah in Virginia. Pennsylvanians poured through this gap in numbers matched in no other English colony in North America. Some stayed to settle the valleys of south central Pennsylvania, but many more headed toward western Virginia, through the Cumberland Gap to the headwaters of the Tennessee, and on to the West to settle a continent.

Travelers who forsook the relative comfort and safety of the Cumberland Valley and chose instead to journey west toward Fort Pitt and the Forks of the Ohio, had quite a different experience. Standing before them was a succession of seemingly interminable thousand-foot ridges and narrow valleys, like waves in a hostile sea. Not surprisingly, the frontiersmen who braved this trackless wilderness named the range "the Endless Mountains."

Nor, after overcoming this great obstacle, were travelers rewarded with a land of milk and honey. Instead they encountered the Allegheny Front, an escarpment rising some fifteen hundred feet. Behind the front lay the Allegheny Plateau, a vast expanse extending over northern and western Pennsylvania, where twisting streams had sculpted mountains into the high surface and produced a country so forbidding that few who passed through gave much thought to staying. But hidden beneath its harsh soils, out of the reach of the colonists, rich deposits of coal, oil, and natural gas lay waiting.

A variety of river systems drained the Piedmont. But most of the streams were shallow, rocky, and unnavigable. Except for the Delaware below Philadelphia, the streams that flowed to the Atlantic—the Schuylkill, Lehigh, and Susquehanna—could be navigated only at high water and at considerable risk. Ironically, in the heart of the great agricultural belt, no natural avenues of transportation existed.

Early Pennsylvania iron furnace, 1793. (Carnegie Library of Pittsburgh)

This forced Pennsylvanians to employ the arts of road building and canal construction years before other colonists. Later, this marriage of necessity and invention led them to pioneer in the building of railroads.

Western Pennsylvania differed from areas of the Piedmont in its use of rivers. West of the Alleghenies the headwaters of the Ohio, Allegheny, Monongahela, Conemaugh, Beaver, and Youghiogheny Rivers are navigable for long distances and western Pennsylvanians used them as cheap and handy avenues for exploitation of their mineral and lumber resources.

The greatest single factor favoring Pennsylvania's development as an industrial giant was its vast storehouse of natural resources. The bituminous coal fields of central and western Pennsylvania lie at the northernmost extension of the great Appalachian coal field, while one of the world's richest deposits of anthracite coal is to be found in northeastern Pennsylvania. Unknown to the pre-industrial colonists, some 95 billion tons of bituminous and 25 billion of anthracite lay beneath their feet. In the Lehigh Valley vast deposits of limestone would later become the basis of the nation's first cement industry. Rich iron ore deposits at Cornwall in Lebanon County and in the Juniata Valley combined with Pennsylvania coal would launch

3

the iron and steel industries. Abundant timber resources, particularly the white pine and hemlock forests of north central Pennsylvania, would provide the resources necessary for lumber and leather tanning industries. Oil and natural gas would also flow abundantly in the northwestern and western reaches of the colony.

Indeed, Penn's Woods offered its settlers a cornucopia of riches, far more than they had imagined or could immediately use. In more than three centuries since the first European settlement, Pennsylvanians have applied their brains, sweat, and skills—in short, their labor—to the task of realizing the economic potential of the rich land they inherited.

The Colonial Economy

"Fat Pennsylvania," contemporaries called it, describing the bounty of its farms and workshops. For most of the colonial period, William Penn's fortunate province was the economic cornerstone of Britain's American lands, its workshop and breadbasket. Her non-agricultural labor force, both skilled and unskilled, surpassed that of any other colony. These artisans and day laborers were a small minority during colonial times, and for all of the following century.

While agriculture soon came to dominate the economy of colonial Pennsylvania, the first to take a living from the land were the fur traders. The wilderness offered a rich source of deer, beaver, bear, and other animal skins, and, with a seemingly insatiable demand in Europe for furs, these became the first major exports from the colony and laid the foundation for the commercial and financial prominence of Philadelphia. In the early decades of the eighteenth century nearly three hundred traders exchanged guns, rum, cloth, and a variety of trinkets with Native Americans for furs. Philadelphia merchants supplied the trade goods and received, stored, processed, and shipped the furs abroad. Lancaster was the site of one of the earliest trading posts and Shamokin and Sunbury were important centers of the trade on the Susquehanna. In western Pennsylvania, Logstown, near Ambridge on the Ohio River, served as a point of exchange between traders and Native Americans.

By the beginning of the eighteenth century, however, farming had replaced fur trapping as the colony's primary economic activity, providing the livelihood for the great majority of colonial Pennsylvanians. Philadelphia's position as both the largest city and colonial economic capital rested on the efficiency and productivity of the family farm. Jobs for urban workers depended on the processing and transportation of produce from Pennsylvania's rich farmland. The Quaker city's banks, industries, and maritime commerce owed a particular debt to the industrious German farmers of southeastern Pennsylvania.

While immigrants from the British isles—primarily English, Scotch, and Scots-Irish—formed the vast majority of the population, Germans comprised more than a quarter of the total number of residents by the end of the colonial period. The great majority were farmers.

Their peasant backgrounds had taught them to cultivate small holdings through intensive farming and careful management. Prepared to work hard, and with few needs and simple tastes, they depended on the family for the basic labor force, supplementing it with a few indentured servants. Children worked in the fields at an early age. Mothers and daughters worked side by side with fathers and brothers.

The agricultural household economy, whether German or British, was nearly self-sufficient. Someone in the family usually had a hand in making virtually everything that one touched in the course of the day. Much of this work was done during the long winter months when farming activities were at low ebb. Small industries were found on practically all farms including the spinning of yarns and the making of clothing. It is estimated that in eighteenth-century Pennsylvania more than 90 percent of the people wore clothing made from homespun cloth. Along with the looms and spinning wheels operated by women, farms often had their own blacksmith and cooperage shops, grist and aromatic oil mills, tanneries and distilleries, malt houses and mills, brandy houses, and stills. Itinerant craftsmen served smaller farms that lacked their own services. These traveling masons, shoemakers, smiths, and carpenters received payment in kind—corn, wheat or whiskey—for their services, a place at the family table, and lodging for the duration of their contact.

From this solid economic base, and from its fortunate location astride one of North America's great natural harbors, Philadelphia

Colonial era map, Philadelphia, 1762. (Pennsylvania State Archives)

grew to be the largest colonial city in the British empire. By 1750 it was the principal manufacturing center. A large industry turned grain into flour and dressed meat and leather goods for export. Rich timber and mineral resources in the interior provided the basis for wagon and furniture making and for the production of agricultural implements and household wares.

Philadelphia's role as the leading port of the colonies led to the growth of a major shipbuilding industry. There was also a demand for small boats for the fishing and whaling activities in the Delaware Bay. By 1721 the city's shipyards were building twice the tonnage of any other American port, and Philadelphia had become a leading center of naval architecture and design.

Also important among the earliest industries were printing and publishing (see Keystone Vignette, "Printing," p. 33). Pennsylvania's first press was set up in 1686 in the city. By 1775 there were nine newspapers in the colony, all in Philadelphia except for one in Germantown and one in Lancaster. The growth of this industry created a demand for paper, and by 1789 the city had forty-eight paper mills.

Philadelphia's primacy as a manufacturing center extended to the production of spirits as well. Brewing of beer began in the seventeenth century, and as early as 1721, the city's ships carried the beverage as far south as Charleston. The industry flourished in the eighteenth century, and, by the end of the Revolutionary War, the breweries of Philadelphia required more than forty thousand bushels of barley annually. Although the German settlers preferred beer, the Scotch-Irish introduced the manufacture of whiskey in 1720, and Pennsylvania assumed leadership in its production by 1740.

In addition to Philadelphia, other centers of manufacturing were developing in some of the larger settlements of Pennsylvania, the most notable of which were Bethlehem, Lancaster, and York. A visitor wrote of Bethlehem in 1751, "You can scarcely mention any trade which is in the largest city in this country, but what is at this place and carried on after the best manner." In 1760 a meeting of master artisans declared that more than one hundred of the commodities sold in Bethlehem's stores could be produced in the community.

These industries attracted the largest urban labor force in the colonies to Philadelphia and to smaller inland centers of commerce and artisan industry. Like their brethren on the farms, urban workers toiled according to traditions rooted in premodern practices. They knew little of the discipline of the clock and factory—these things were yet to come. Skilled artisans, or mechanics as they were more commonly called, worked at their own pace and their output depended more on the demands of quality than the promise of profit. The employer's or master craftsman's authority rested not so much on the control of capital as on his skill. The master worked beside the journeymen, shared their value system and was, for the most part, their social equal. Master and journeymen cooperated not only at work but also in their civic duties and recreational activities. Theirs was a world characterized by stability and unity in which life knew few distinctions between work and leisure.

Pennsylvania's workers came from England and Ireland, Germany and Africa, and a host of other lands. Most came of their own free will, some in chains as slaves, and a few as convicts.

Many brought skills with them. Of 1,838 immigrants who debarked at Philadelphia during a four-month period in 1709, 706

Rittenhouse Mill, Wissahickon. (Pennsylvania State Archives)

were skilled craftsmen (a surprisingly high figure given that women and children were among them), a good indication of the needs of the colony for skilled workers.

Most of these immigrants became farmers. Others made their way to the iron plantations scattered throughout southeastern Pennsylvania, along the broad Susquehanna and the Juniata.

But most of those who did not take up farming settled in the bustling metropolis of Philadelphia, where, for the first half of the eighteenth century, skilled labor was in great demand and earnings and opportunity were generally superior to those available in the countries from which they had come.

Slavery

Free labor was attracted to Pennsylvania in part because the institution of slavery was relatively weak in the colony. Although slavery had existed in the region even before the coming of William Penn (who was himself a slave owner), on the eve of the Revolution, there were only about ten thousand slaves in Pennsylvania, less than 3 percent of the population.

The prominence of Quakers and pietistic Germans in the population of the colony no doubt contributed to the weakness of slavery. Although many wealthy Quakers owned slaves, the Society of Friends would take measures against its practice. The Germans, who constituted a quarter of the colony's population, rarely owned slaves. One reason was economic. Unlike the plantation economy of the South, Pennsylvania's small, self-sufficient family farms based on grain and livestock production had no need for large numbers of unskilled laborers. In 1790, in the largely German county of Berks, there was only one slave for every 465 whites. The percentage was considerably higher among English and Scots-Irish settlers, but still not high in comparison to Massachusetts and New York— Pennsylvania's two great economic rivals—where one black family on each farm was common. The men worked in the fields and with the livestock, while slave women tended the garden, raised poultry, milked cows, produced cloth, and worked in the fields and as household servants.

A significant number of blacks, both free and slave, lived in Philadelphia and worked in all segments of the growing economy. One estimate puts the number of slaves in the early decades of the colony at between four and five hundred. The number had increased to 1,235 by 1748. Black men could be found among most of the skilled trades, but were more commonly employed as teamsters, porters, carters, and other kinds of day laborers. Black women, like their white counterparts, worked primarily as domestic servants.

Although slavery in Pennsylvania was probably less apparent than in the southern colonies, it was still a cruel, dehumanizing institution. Runaways were common, and Pennsylvania had its own "black codes" under which free blacks found idle could be bound out as servants. It was forbidden to sell liquor to blacks. They were denied the right to trial by jury, could not journey more than ten miles from home without the permission of their masters, and were required to be home by nine o'clock at night. In 1693 the Provincial Council protested against "the tumultuous gathering of the Negroes in the town of Philadelphia on the first days of the week." Shortly thereafter, meetings of more than four blacks were forbidden.

Efforts to eliminate slavery in the colony started as early as 1688. These efforts culminated in 1776 when the Philadelphia Yearly

Meeting of Friends decided to disown any member who refused to free his slaves. In 1780 the Pennsylvania Assembly passed the first law providing for the emancipation of slaves, and in 1787 the Pennsylvania Society for Promoting the Abolition of Slavery became the first antislavery organization in world history.

Indentured Servitude

A major factor in the decline of slavery in Pennsylvania after 1735 was that, instead of chattel slavery, indentured servitude provided the principal answer to Pennsylvania's need for labor. Indentured servants, sometimes knows as "redemptioners," sold their services for a period ranging from three to five years in return for their passage to the new world. The term "indentured" came from the use of a legal agreement to seal the arrangement. These written contracts were usually held by the ship's master who sold them to farmers, merchants, and artisans upon arrival in Philadelphia, or to labor contractors, who marched them into the interior for sale in frontier areas.

Servants came to Pennsylvania for the same reason as free laborers. Two Scotsmen, David Ireland, a smith, and George McCandish, a farmer, chose the Quaker colony because "they were informed that they could live much better and with more ease in the country to which they are going than they could in their country." Similarly, Palatine Germans Jacob and Hannah Duncan were willing to trade four years of service for "a stake in the future." Of course, many others were drawn to servitude more by the need to survive. Wars, famine, and economic depression frequently swept across parts of Europe and contributed mightily to the availability of willing souls for the trans-Atlantic passage.

The system proved to be ideal for Pennsylvania because large numbers of those who wanted to come to the colony, particularly the Scots-Irish from Ulster and the Palatine Germans, could not afford their own passage. As a result, Pennsylvania led the northern colonies in the number of indentured servants. Indeed, the trans-Atlantic servant trade was centered in the Delaware Valley where ships frequently landed human cargoes containing as many as six hundred servants. In the autumn of 1749, twenty-five vessels with

7,049 passengers arrived at Philadelphia. Ten years later a local paper announced that "the ship *Phoenix*, Captain Spurrill, is arrived here from Holland with Palatines. This makes the seventeenth Dutch vessel this Fall, and several more are yet expected." The percentage of unfree labor in Philadelphia peaked at more than 38 percent of the labor force in the early 1750s. In all, some sixty thousand indentured servants entered Pennsylvania between 1735 and 1755, about evenly divided between Scots-Irish and Germans.

The passage, which could last for three months, began the difficult experience. The death rate aboard ship was shocking. From 1750 to 1755, two thousand immigrants bound for Philadelphia found a watery grave instead. In 1732, on one ship alone, no fewer than one hundred Germans perished before reaching Philadelphia. One German gentleman traveling first class on a servant ship described the horrible conditions of the voyage in vivid terms:

> Both at Rotterdam and at Amsterdam the people are packed densely, like herrings so to say, in the large sea vessels. One person receives a place of scarcely two feet width and six feet length in the bedstead. . . . during the voyage there is on board these ships terrible misery, stench, fumes, horror, vomiting, many kinds of sea sickness, fever, dysentery, headache, heat, constipation, boils, scurvy, cancer, mouth rot and the like, all of which come from old and sharply salted food and meat, also from very bad and foul water, so that many die miserably.
>
> Add to this want of provisions, hunger, thirst, frost, heat, dampness, anxiety, want, afflictions, and lamentation . . . the lice abound so frightfully, especially on sick people, that they can be scraped off the body.
>
> Children from one to seven years rarely survive the voyage; and many a time parents are compelled to see their children miserably suffer and die from hunger, thirst and sickness, and then see them cast into the water. I witnessed such misery in no less than 32 children in our ship, all of whom were thrown into the sea.

By the middle of the eighteenth century unfree labor was overwhelmingly centered in Philadelphia. Although the city contained

11

no more than 12 percent of the colony's population, almost 60 percent of bound servants in 1745 had been purchased by Philadelphians. The city's labor market needed skills. In correspondence with their overseas contacts, Philadelphians asked repeatedly for house carpenters, weavers, joiners, smiths, hatters, masons, and others. One of the major reasons for the chronic shortage of skills in the city was the drain of free labor due to the availability of inexpensive land. According to Benjamin Franklin in 1751, "Land being plenty in America, and so cheap as that a labouring man, that understands husbandry, can in short time save money enough to purchase a piece of new land sufficient for plantation."

Conditions for indentured servants could be harsh, sometimes even worse than for slaves. The slave represented a lifetime investment, and there was some natural interest in protecting one's investment. But indentured servants were bound for a limited number of years, usually three, and it was in the employer's interest to extract the maximum amount of work during the period.

The power of the owner was always clear. Although masters and servants worked together, ate together, and often shared the same quarters, they were clearly members of two distinct classes. As the eighteenth century wore on, these divisions became deeper and more codified. Servants had come in much smaller numbers in the seventeenth century, before the harsh trans-Atlantic trade in human labor had been developed. In the small, semi-rural settlement of early Philadelphia, paternalistic relations generally prevailed between master and servant. But servants who came in the eighteenth century were part of a distinct and growing unfree urban working class. As this occurred the incidence of runaways increased. At least 10 percent of the servants indentured in 1745 were advertised as runaways over the next five years, and at least 6 percent of Philadelphia's servants ran away during the late colonial period.

In response, the Pennsylvania Assembly codified the relationship between servants and masters. Fornication, marrying without consent, and purchasing liquor were forbidden. Captured runaways had their terms of service extended. Absolute obedience to their masters was the lot of most who passed through indentured servitude.

Harsh as the system could be, indentured servants did have

rights. They could sue and be sued, and they could testify in court. At the end of their servitude the law entitled them to "freedom dues." As early as 1700, Pennsylvania declared that "every servant that shall faithfully serve four years or more shall, at the expiration of their servitude, have a discharge and shall be duly clothed with two complete suits of apparel, whereof one shall be new and shall be furnished with one new axe, one grubbing-hoe, and one weeding-hoe, at the charge of their master or mistress."

The economic prospects of freed servants changed dramatically after the middle of the eighteenth century. As the indenture system evolved from being largely benign to more harsh and formal, the likelihood of economic success for ex-servants declined. Servants who arrived in the seventeenth century generally did better than later arrivals once they completed their indentures. Of the 196 servants who arrived in the first wave, almost one-third eventually became landowners and nearly one-fifth acquired enough personal property to leave estates. In contrast, their eighteenth-century counterparts rarely acquired property, and more than three-fourths received some type of public assistance at some point in their lives. Circumstances were particularly difficult for women who had worked off their indentures. They required public assistance at a higher rate than men, as reflected by the fact that almost two-thirds of the residents of the city's poorhouse at any time were female.

Although the system of indentured servitude lasted late into the eighteenth century, it had begun its decline before the Revolution. The economic depression that struck Philadelphia at the end of the French and Indian War left the city with a surplus of free labor, a condition that was to become normal as the century wore on. This made bound labor less attractive because of its expense and inflexibility. By the time of the Revolution the overwhelming majority of freed servants were moving into the growing class of unskilled and semi-skilled wage workers as part of the transformation of labor in the new nation. For many, according to historian Richard Hofstadter, the hardships of the journey across the Atlantic "proved in the end to have been only an epitome of their journey through life."

Apprentices

Aspects of indentured servitude were also present in the apprenticeship system. Colonial Pennsylvania law decreed that "all children within the province of the age of twelve years shall be taught some useful trade or skill, to the end that none may be idle, but the poor may work to live, and the rich, if they become poor, may not want."

Although public officials frequently apprenticed orphans and other wards of the state to less desirable trades or to husbandry (a euphemism for child labor on the farm), the apprenticeship of children to a trade was most often voluntary. Parents saw apprenticeship as a means to provide skills and opportunity for their children, or, in the case of poor families, to lighten their own financial burdens. Not all trades were equally desirable. A hierarchy existed, from silversmith and goldsmith, through printer or ship carpenter, to shoemaker. Apprenticing a child to the more desirable trades was often a privilege reserved to parents who could afford to pay a handsome fee to the master craftsman. Benjamin Franklin's father, for example, apprenticed his son to a printer because he could not afford the payment for the cutlery trade.

In Northampton Town (Allentown), justice of the peace Peter Rhoads registered apprenticeship indentures for twenty-seven boys and sixteen girls from 1785 to 1790. Among the boys, three trained to be weavers, three shoemakers, two carpenters, and one each as a blacksmith, hatter, and tanner. Three learned husbandry, seven became servants, and five others were unidentified. All of the girls were apprenticed as servants to learn "common housekeeping, spinning, sewing, and knitting."

The master artisan, farmer, or merchant agreed to provide training for the children in exchange for service. Frequently the employer took the children into his own home. Conditions of the contract were carefully set down:

> Jonathan Hurst, Jr. by consent of his mother Anne Hutchins, indents himself apprentice to James Gottier, of Philadelphia, for eight years from this date to have six months schooling and six months evening schooling to learn to read, write and cipher, to

be taught the trade of cooper, and at the end of his time to have two suits of apparel, one of which is to be new.

The law required employers to care for their apprentices and retain them in hard times as well as good. The term of service was usually six or seven years, normally beginning at age fourteen. Though, for the most part, the apprenticeship system was humane, it was restrictive and could be cruel, and notices of runaways appeared frequently in colonial Pennsylvania newspapers:

Six Cents Reward

Ran away from the subscriber on Saturday evening, the 29th ult. an indentured apprentice to the cabinet making business, named John Rimbey, between nineteen and twenty years of age. He had on when he went away a new black fur hat, blue coat and corded pantaloons and striped vest. The public is hereby cautioned against employing or harboring said apprentice, as the law shall be enforced against any person doing so.

Free Labor

The importance of the system of bound labor emphasizes the favored position of free white male skilled labor. Particularly up to 1750, skilled tradesmen regularly became employers, purchased land, and constructed substantial houses. Describing his situation in a letter home to England, one anonymous early immigrant declared that "It is a great deal better living here than in England for working people. Poor working people doth live as well here as landed men doth live with you that are worth twenty pounds a year. I live a simple life and hath builded a shop, and doth follow weaving linen clothe, but I have bought 450 acres of land in the wood."

Benjamin Franklin observed that "tolerably good workmen in any of the mechanic arts," if sober, industrious and frugal, soon became masters, established themselves in business, married, raised families, and became respectable citizens.

Not only had Philadelphia prospered as a result of its rich agricultural hinterland, it also became the manufacturing and commercial center of the colonies. The size of its trade with Europe and the West Indies caused the maritime industries to flourish. By 1754 twelve shipyards were located in the city, and the industry's ropewalks, sail lofts, cooperages, blacksmith shops, and dozens of other enterprises created a demand for carpenters, shipwrights, joiners, smiths, caulkers, sail makers, rope makers, and a host of others, both skilled and unskilled. A Pennsylvania poet sang the praises of the industry in 1689:

> Within this six or seven year
> Many good ships have been built here
> and more, some say, will be built yet
> for here is timber very fit.
> Good carpenters who bravely thrive,
> and master builders to contrive
> who can prepare the iron stuff.

The increased specialization of the labor force by the time of the Revolution reflected the increased complexity of Philadelphia's economy. Blacksmiths, who had performed almost all of the metalworking in the early colonial period, now shared the work with ornamental ironworkers, anchor forgers, coppersmiths, tinplate workers, and others. Carpenters had the assistance of joiners, turners, cabinetmakers, carvers, and coach makers. Building tradesmen included roofers, painters, glaziers, plumbers, plasterers, housewrights, stonemasons, and bricklayers.

Naturally, small inland towns could not match this diversity, but by the end of the colonial period some had earned reputations for the quality of certain trades. York, founded in 1741, became a regional manufacturing center as part of a developing agricultural area. By 1789 thirty-nine separate trades employed more than half of the town's 385 taxpayers, including shoemakers, tailors, blacksmiths, hatters, weavers, hosiers, locksmiths, dyers, silversmiths, potters, tinsmiths, and others. Reading's fame for hat making, weaving, cooperage, and brick making spread beyond the borders of Pennsylvania. Lancaster and Berks Counties also became well known as centers for the German craftsmen who created the Pennsylvania long rifle—later inaccurately named the Kentucky rifle—the weapon that played such a critical role in the colonial victory in the Revolution and in the conquest of the frontier. During the early 1700s, wheelwrights, blacksmiths, joiners, and turners in Lancaster began to produce the famous Conestoga wagons that became the principal freight-carrying vehicles until the coming of the railroads.

The drivers of these great wagons, professional teamsters, became recognizable by their full beards, leather or homespun clothes, and flat, broadbrimmed hats. They smoked cheap cigars called "stogies," named after their wagons, and became the mainstays of the many taverns that sprang up along the primitive roads from the interior to Philadelphia.

In Philadelphia the crafts reached their highest development and the "mechanics" played significant economic and political roles. It was also in Philadelphia that the division of labor became most pronounced. Woodworking, for example, was divided into at least a dozen major trades, each of which in turn had its subdivisions and specializations.

The words mechanic, tradesman, artisan, and craftsman denoted both the level of economic activity and the social standing of the practitioner. A mechanic owned his own tools and worked either for himself, in which case he was a master craftsman, or for someone else, in which case he was a journeyman. Many of the trades required long periods of training or apprenticeship before journeyman status was achieved. The mechanics possessed intricate skills.

Cordwainers, for example, made the entire shoe or boot. They cut the leather, stitched the pieces together, bound the uppers and the lowers, and trimmed and polished the final product. Cabinet making, an elite trade, required knowledge of drawing, proportion, current styles, wood texture, and adaptability, as well as expert skill in veneering, gluing, and varnishing.

The term mechanic also referred to social class. The mechanic class was well defined in colonial Philadelphia. It did not include apprentices, bound servants, and slaves. A high percentage were master craftsmen—independent entrepreneurs who worked for themselves and owned their own tools and workshops. Unlike Europe, where certain legal and guild requirements intervened, rising to the level of master in Philadelphia was relatively easy. The general shortage of labor kept the demand for skills high for most of the colonial

17

FORGING ARMS FOR THE MINUTE-MEN.

Pennsylvania artisans toiled in the cause of liberty. (Carnegie Libary of Pittsburgh)

period, thus inducing journeymen to strike out on their own as soon as possible. For most trades capital requirements were low and shops were easily established in the mechanic's home.

Those whose skills were not turned to manufacturing often worked for themselves. Rather than settle into journeyman status for one master, they subcontracted their work. In a Philadelphia shop that manufactured fire engines, for example, parts came from a variety of artisan shops in the city. Shipwrights, who acted as general contractors, also subcontracted a great deal of their work to other master craftsmen. For the building of a ship specialists such as smiths, joiners, sailmakers, riggers, painters, and mastmakers were assembled. This economic interdependence helped to forge a strong sense of community among Philadelphia's mechanics.

Social life and connections also brought the artisan community together. Craftsmen's children generally married within their class. When a mechanic died, a fellow artisan was often the executor of

18

his will and was responsible for helping his family. Moreover, the crowded living conditions of the artisan neighborhoods produced an environment in which family, social, and economic life intertwined in the churches, taverns, small houses, and workshops of the area. So firm were the artisan bonds that many who rose to become successful businessmen continued to identify themselves with their trades and the social ties that they represented. One such success was Benjamin Franklin, who, after a career as revolutionary and statesman, directed that his epitaph record only that he had been a printer.

Certain trades demanded heavy capitalization or a higher degree of skill. Bakers, tanners, skinners, and brick makers, for example, worked at trades which demanded greater investment, and they tended to reap proportionately greater rewards. These trades ranked among the ten wealthiest occupations in Philadelphia in 1775. Other trades, such as goldsmith, silversmith, instrument and clock maker demanded great skill and were closed to all but a few. Other artisans worked at the "low" trades, such as shoe and boot making and tailoring, and they were most often poor. In 1772, 40 percent of all cordwainers and 41 percent of all tailors were assessed the minimum tax. Also at the lower end of the scale were weavers, stocking weavers, and breeches makers.

Although at the bottom of the artisan ladder, these workers enjoyed considerably more status and material comfort than Philadelphia's three largest wage-earner occupations—sailors, mariners, and laborers. By the Revolution, these three groups comprised at least 18 percent of the Philadelphia tax-rated population and made up the core of an increasingly disaffected and restless working class. Thus, a clear social class structure had emerged.

Women's Work

The work of women was essential to the household economy, both on the farm and in the town. The skilled services of wives included cooking, baking, spinning, sewing, gardening, bargaining, and milling. In addition, wives sometimes assumed responsibilities which, more traditionally, might be the within the domain of their husbands. A merchant's wife might keep shop or a cordwainer's wife, who frequently helped in the workshop, might also keep the accounts.

On the farm, the life cycle of women determined their economic roles in the family enterprise. Between the age of five and ten, girls learned to churn, sew, spin, milk, and read. By the age of twelve they were full apprentices to their mothers in the household skills. Some daughters, usually from tenant families, left their own houses at an early age to work for others.

Spinning girls were most common in colonial farmsteads, coming like shoemakers, tailors, and other itinerant artisans to spend several weeks working and visiting.

Indeed, the tasks performed by women made them absolutely essential to any viable agricultural venture. Without a family, economic life was precarious for a man, as one observer noted in 1788 after visiting the farm of a bachelor who farmed on the Schuylkill River thirteen miles north of Philadelphia: "As he is without a family he does not have any poultry or pigeons and makes no cheese, nor does he have any spinning done or collect goos [sic] feathers. It is a great disadvantage for him not to be able to profit from these domestic farm industries, which can be carried on well only by women."

The economic status of women also affected their work cycle. A householder, one who lived on land owned by her own family, usually arranged and supervised her own work, subject only to the demands of the family. Tenant women also arranged their own work, but they often sold part of their labor or the products of their labor to large householders. Women in artisan families in rural areas were also available for work on the farms, especially at harvest time.

Although their economic roles gave women considerable independence and influence in the household economy, their status still derived from their husbands. No matter their contribution to the family, to be a wife was to be dependent. At marriage, any property a woman owned became legally her husband's, anything she inherited became his, and any income she brought into the household was also his. While the law obligated men to make provision for their spouses, land and livelihood were normally transmitted from father to son.

Without question, domestic service supplied the majority of job opportunities for women in the town. Indeed, growth in this occu-

pational category paralleled the rise in the number of female indentured servants arriving in the colony. Women were always in the
minority and never constituted more than 20 to 40 percent of the
indentured servant population. Most were young and unmarried,
and most chose to work in Philadelphia rather than in the rural
areas. As domestic servants their tasks were varied and demanding.
They cooked, sewed, washed, and cleaned. On call twenty-four
hours a day, they spent a great deal of time on child care, both as
wet nurses and baby nurses.

Nevertheless, the demand for female servants in Philadelphia
was never as strong as the demand for young males. For one reason, the market for their services as domestics was generally restricted to the houses of merchants or a small number of prosperous
master artisans.

In addition, women suffered disproportionately from the diseases that ravaged the servants during the Atlantic passage, and
they often required extensive medical care and recuperation time
after they arrived—an expense that many prospective masters were
not willing to assume. In a letter requesting a shipment of servants,
merchant Benjamin Marshall instructed his contact not to send women
because they were "so troublesome" and possessed of "so many
drawbacks."

The major contribution of women to manufacturing took place
in home-based textile production, a major industry in Pennsylvania.
By 1776, some four thousand women and children spun, wove, and
knitted in their homes as part of the "putting out system" for local
textile merchants. Although most tailors, furriers, and stay makers
were men, women filled most of the jobs for milliners, menders,
dyers, and wool scourers.

Entrepreneurial opportunities for women were very limited. In
only three occupations, shopkeeping, innkeeping, and crafts making, could they be found in significant numbers. Shopkeeping and
innkeeping were obviously an extension of the traditional household duties of women, because most of the early retail stores and
taverns were located in private dwellings. Between 1762 and 1776,
Philadelphia women owned between 17 and 22 percent of all taverns. Fragmentary evidence also shows that at least ninety-four female shopkeepers operated in Philadelphia between 1720 and 1776,

and that in 1717, 28 percent of all shopkeepers were women.

Although craftswomen often sold their products directly from home, as did their male counterparts, the work was not necessarily related to domestic tasks. Thus, Philadelphia women engaged in roughly thirty different trades ranging from essential to luxury service. In addition to trades already mentioned, there were female silversmiths, tin workers, barbers, bakers, fish picklers, brewers, tanners, rope makers, lumberjacks, gunsmiths, butchers, harness makers, potash manufacturers, upholsterers, printers, morticians, chandlers, coach makers, embroiderers and dry cleaners, woodworkers, stay makers, tailors, flour processors, seamstresses, netmakers, braziers, and founders. Although the variety of activity undertaken by women workers is impressive, it does not reflect the amount of entrepreneurial opportunity. It is likely that many female shopkeepers and artisans were widows who assumed control of the business after the death of their husbands.

Problems in Paradise

Gottfried Mittelberger, a German traveling in Pennsylvania in 1750, described it as a rich, industrious place where "all trades and professions have good earnings, beggars are nowhere to be seen." There was a saying that the colony was the "heaven of farmers and the paradise of mechanics." Benjamin Franklin, describing an earlier period, agreed with Mittelberger's assessment. He wrote of a place where the price of labor was high and nearly all laborers rapidly became employers.

These observations, and countless others like them, conjured up a Pennsylvania populated by sturdy independent, industrious, and prosperous farmers and artisans. Although never totally an accurate picture, this idyllic portrait of the colony came to resemble the truth less and less as the eighteenth century wore on. There is no doubt that many early immigrants could work their way up the economic and social ladders a step or two during their lifetimes, and even become property holders, by taking advantage of the general prosperity and the demand for labor. By the late colonial period, however, the evidence suggests that the climb had become much more difficult.

Even in the prosperous early years of the colony part of the urban laboring classes always lived perilously close to the edge of economic security. The supply of jobs depended on a variety of factors, such as the weather, wars, Indian uprisings, the cycles of nature that affected the shipbuilding and construction industries, and recurrent smallpox and yellow fever epidemics which sometimes resulted in mass evacuations of the city. Of course, cyclical variations in the economy had the most effect on the availability of work.

For the first half century after its founding in 1682, Philadelphia experienced steady growth and prosperity. Although the city always had its poor, the number was generally small in proportion to the population. The general prosperity of the city no doubt contributed to the optimism among workers that led to the popularity of Benjamin Franklin's best sellers *Father Abraham's Speech, The Way to Wealth,* and *The Art of Making Money Plenty.*

While it is doubtful that most of Philadelphia's mechanics were ever able to capitalize on Franklin's advice, most managed to live comfortably up to the middle of the eighteenth century. Between 1720 and 1740, only about 2 to 3 percent of the city's taxpayers lacked the ability to contribute their share to the public coffers, a much lower percentage than in either Boston or New York. But by 1772 the situation had worsened considerably. In that year some three-fifths of the mariners, one quarter of the laborers and weavers, one-fifth of the carters, breeches makers, brick makers, bricklayers, and cordwainers, and one-eighth of the gardeners, blacksmiths, barbers, and joiners were identified as poor. By the end of the colonial period the bottom 60 percent of the city's wealth holders earned less than 6 percent of the community's resources. At the other end of the scale, the top 10 percent of the wealth holders had increased their share to 70 percent.

After the middle of the eighteenth century a series of economic fluctuations, including progressively deeper recessions, struck Philadelphia. The French and Indian War had brought prosperity to the city in the 1750s, but when the war ended, the military spending that had fueled the boom ended. To make matters worse, large numbers of discharged and unemployed soldiers congregated in the city. To this pool were added many new arrivals from Germany and Ireland.

The result was a city, according to Benjamin Rush, "full of sailors who cannot procure berths" and artisans who were beginning "to grow clamorous for want of employment." To the tensions brought about by economic decline were added those brought about by the growing dispute between the colonies and Great Britain.

The dramatic increase in poverty that accompanied the redistribution of wealth put a severe strain on the city's resources. Whereas in 1750 only eight Philadelphians in a thousand received poor relief, that figure had jumped to thirty per thousand on the eve of the Revolution. In the face of this increase the old system of caring for the indigent in their homes or in small almshouses broke down, and taxes increased in order to build institutions to handle the city's "wandering" poor.

Many of the poor were laborers who formed the second largest occupational group in the city, second only to mariners who accounted for as much as 20 percent of the free male workforce on the eve of the Revolution. Laborers officially composed between 5 and 14 percent of taxpayers during the second half of the century, but their percentage was undoubtedly greater than that because many poorer citizens were excused from paying taxes, and many taxpayers with undesignated occupations were also probably unskilled laborers. Laborers' earnings placed them at the bottom of the tax hierarchy. In 1772, assessors appraised nine out of every ten laborers at the minimum rate. Many worked in construction and shipbuilding or hauled goods to and from ships, warehouses, and stores; others found jobs in breweries and distilleries or as street pavers, haymowers, potato diggers, dung spreaders, whitewashers, swamp drainers, sawyers, chimney sweeps and the like—at the bottom of the city's occupational ladder. They formed Philadelphia's unskilled, propertyless class.

Although unmarried males generally found it easy to support themselves, most Philadelphians were married and had at least two children. For them the work of the entire family was necessary for subsistence. As we have seen, women often worked. Opportunities for children were more limited, but they gathered twigs to sell as firewood, tended cattle, and carried dairy produce from the countryside. Poor parents often apprenticed their children at an early age to the less desirable trades to lighten their financial burden.

As a result of these circumstances, private and public aid to the poor rose dramatically during the late colonial period. Increasingly not only the old, infirm, widowed, and orphaned, but also able-bodied men and women found themselves on the charity rolls. Both municipal and Quaker almshouses provided shelter for the homeless as well as food, firewood, and medical care for the indigent. Several private benevolent societies aided the needy along ethnic lines, notably the St. Andrew Society (Scottish), the *Deutsche Gesellschaft von Pennsylvanien* (German), the Friendly Sons of St. Patrick (Irish), and the Society of the Sons of St. George (English). Other charities were occupational, such as the Society for the Relief of Distressed Masters of Ships, their Widows and Orphans.

The rise in poverty, not surprisingly, was accompanied by a rise in the incidence of crime. Philadelphia had always had its criminal classes—sailors without berths, discharged soldiers, insolvent debtors, prostitutes, petty criminals, and a few convicts transported from England. But a severe crime wave followed the economic downturn after the French and Indian War. City prisons were at capacity. The years before the Revolution witnessed an alarming increase in robbery and violent crimes. Accounts of holdups on the highways and stories of seaport gangs roaming the streets—along with reports of housebreaking and pilfering—appeared frequently in the newspapers.

Class tensions also produced a series of crowd actions, some of which turned violent. Some of these were multiclass affairs, such as mass meetings in protest against the Stamp Act in 1765 and 1766, which played a role in pushing Philadelphia merchants to agree not to import British goods. Others, however, were decidedly working class, and reflected the growing hostility of the "lower orders" to increasingly harsh control from the authorities. Such was the case with conflicts between crowds of sailors and customs officials that took place between 1769 and 1774. Sailors had traditionally been allowed to unofficially import small amounts of goods that they sold to augment their incomes upon arrival in Philadelphia. When customs officials began to seize these goods as contraband, sailors and crowds of supporters responded with beatings, tar and featherings, and public humiliation of customs officials.

25

One Philadelphian, noting these disquieting trends, commented on the growing disparity between the classes in the city in 1767: "One half of the world are ignorant how the other half lives . . . while the slightest inconveniences of the great are magnified into calamities: while tragedy mouths out their sufferings in all the strains of eloquence, the miseries of the poor are disregarded; and yet some of the lower rank of people undergo more real hardships in one day than those of a more exalted station suffer in their whole lives."

Protest

The maldistribution of wealth and the accompanying shift of political power to the wealthy led to friction and even conflict. "A poor man," lamented a resident of Philadelphia, "has rarely the honor of speaking to a gentleman on any terms and never with any familiarity but for a few weeks before the election." Such social division prompted another observer to warn that "the community cannot be pronounced happy in which from the lowness and insufficiency of wages, the laboring class . . . are reduced to beggary, whenever employment fails them, or age and sickness oblige them to give up work."

Sentiments such as these were widespread among the city's working classes and gave rise to a political movement aimed at restoring the rough political and economic equality that had characterized society up to the middle of the eighteenth century. "An enormous proportion of property vested in a few individuals," argued one radical tract, "is dangerous to the rights and destructive of the common happiness of mankind, and therefore every free state hath a right by its laws to discourage the possession of such property." This expression of radical republicanism underpinned a movement that believed that great wealth undermined democracy. Inherent in this philosophy was both an emphasis on social equality and a rejection of the materialism and sanctification of commercial values that an unfettered market economy spawned. According to one artisan, rather than riches, most of his fellows wanted to "live decently without acquiring wealth," and to be "useful and necessary members" of the community.

26

So rapid was the growth of the artisan political movement after 1760 that what had been a disunited and ineffective group of individuals had grown to a position of considerable power by the eve of the Revolution. The movement's political goals were broad-based, and somewhat contradictory, reflecting a membership that included master craftsmen, journeymen, small merchants, and common laborers. They advocated a curb on the concentration of wealth, enhanced opportunity, regulation of competition to the advantage of the artisans, and the recovery of political power from the elite. "Our great merchants [are] making immense fortunes at the expense of the people," wrote "a friend of liberty" in April 1776: "They will soon have the whole wealth of the province in their hands, and then the people will be nearly in the condition that the East India Company reduced the poor nations of Bengal to."

The class interests of the radicals coincided with their resentment of British rule. They identified the commercial spirit that they believed was corrupting America with a decadent and materialistic mother country. Thus, the Revolution became not only an opportunity to throw off the colonial bonds, but also to return society to a virtuous republicanism. In the spring of 1768, Philadelphia's artisans exerted themselves as an independent political force for the first time by attempting to spur reluctant merchants to follow their counterparts in Boston and New York and adopt a policy of nonimportation of English goods. Class tensions in the ranks of this movement became clear in 1770 when the merchants ended their action and criticized the artisans as a "rabble" that had no right to involve itself with such issues.

The break with the merchants produced an artisan movement that was successful in the Pennsylvania Assembly elections of 1770 when their votes helped to elect a tailor as one of the city representatives. This election became the impetus for the formation of a new party, the Patriotic Society, formed in 1772. The party opposed excise taxes on liquor because of its imposition on "the middling and poorer classes of inhabitants." It likewise declared that the Leather Act which increased the price of skins "oppresses the poor, by shoes being considerably advanced in price." Believing that government should not be conducted in private, the Patriotic Society won legislative approval for the erection of public galleries in the Assembly and for the weekly publication of Assembly dates and roll calls.

The increased power of the mechanics became clear in their response to the closing of Boston Harbor by the British in 1774. When Philadelphia merchants tried to head off another non-importation movement and prevent the power in the revolutionary movement from falling into the hands of radicals, an angry crowd of some twelve hundred artisans rallied at the Statehouse on June 9, 1774. Their sympathizers took control of the Committees of Inspection of the Continental Congress which oversaw the enforcement of the boycott of British goods.

With the outbreak of the Revolution, the locus of working-class power shifted to the Philadelphia militia which had been drawn largely from the lowest ranks of the laboring population—mariners, common laborers, and those in the less remunerative trades such as cooperage, cordwaining, and tailoring. This signaled a further step toward the radicalization of the mechanics' political movement. The militia urged voters in the elections for the constitutional convention to shun "great and overgrown rich men [who] will be improper to be trusted, [for] they will be too apt to be framing distinctions in society, because they will reap the benefits of all such distinctions." Through its Committee of Privates, the militia pressured the Pennsylvania Assembly to take a more assertive stand on independence, and played a major role in writing the radical Pennsylvania Constitution of 1776.

The Constitution was a testimony to the strength of the artisan political movement in the colony. While voices had also been raised in New York and Boston for the rights of those without property, only in Pennsylvania—where an alliance of Philadelphia mechanics and small shopkeepers had captured control of the political process and then been pressured by a radicalized militia—was the right to vote given to all taxpayers regardless of whether or not they owned property. This was an enormous break with the past, and alongside other democratic reforms, made the Pennsylvania Constitution of 1776 the most radically egalitarian political document the world had yet seen.

Workers' Organization

Although the availability of cheap land, the difficulty of com-

28

munication, the chronic shortage of skilled labor, and British common law all militated against mechanics forming organizations resembling modern trade unions, a number of craft organizations were formed.

Sometimes these associations were linked to issues affecting a particular segment of the community and sometimes they assumed the guise of craft guilds. Unlike European craft guilds, however, the few Philadelphia trade organizations were not established to restrict the supply of journeymen, of whom there were seldom enough to meet the demand. Instead, most were loose-knit assemblages of master mechanics formed in an attempt to maintain the prices of their products and reduce the price of supplies. This was crucial in Philadelphia, because mechanics' prices were governed not only by their own costs, but by a market dominated by imported wares. This factor, coupled with the high price of skilled labor, made economic life for most mechanics extremely competitive.

One of the earliest records of a formal union among mechanics concerned eleven coopers who joined together in 1742 to defend themselves against accusations that they had conspired to fix the price of oil. In 1763, the city's wheelwrights organized to capitalize on a city ordinance that required all wagons on the streets to use wheels with seven-inch rims to protect the streets from damage. Hoping to profit from the wholesale conversion from narrow to wide wheels, the wheelwrights unsuccessfully joined in non-competitive pricing. The association crumbled, however, when a few of their members undercut the agreed-upon price. Other crafts tried to regulate practitioners for various reasons. Sixty-eight tailors formed the Taylors Company of Philadelphia in 1771, hoping to come "under proper regulations" respecting the trade by controlling prices and the wages paid to journeymen. The attempt failed due to easy access to trade in the city. There were simply too many master tailors in Philadelphia who did not belong to the association. Members were also difficult to control. When the association accused William Mann of overpaying his journeymen, he simply withdrew and continued as before.

Resentment against merchant capitalists who controlled raw materials also gave rise to artisan organization for the purpose of lobbying. Philadelphia's rope makers organized in 1776 to petition the Assembly to regulate the quality and price of hemp sold by the few merchant dealers who controlled the trade. Cordwainers also had to deal with merchants—leather brokers—who monopolized available supplies. Along with saddlers, harness makers, and other leather tradesmen, they petitioned the Assembly for relief. When, in the 1760s, Philadelphia silversmiths joined to petition the Assembly for regulations and standards "as to the fineness of the silver and gold to be wrought," to end inferior work by shoddy craftsmen, the Assembly denied the petition, as it had in all of the cases noted above. Market control by master artisans in Philadelphia's competitive economy was impossible. Only in the building trades, where craftsmen did not have to compete with imported wares, was there any success. The Carpenters' Company of Philadelphia was chartered in 1724 for the purpose of "obtaining instruction in the science of architecture, and assisting such members as should be in need of support." The Company, comprised of master mechanics, regulated prices for carpentry, architecture, and construction. It also arbitrated disputes between masters and journeymen and regulated relationships with apprentices. As a mutual aid society, it provided benefits for widows and orphans and furnished carriages for the funerals of members.

Other trades organized into volunteer fire companies, although they seem to have had only a minor interest in fighting fires. The most notable company, the Cordwainers Fire Company, organized in 1760, became the forerunner of the first trade union in the United States. Founded by thirty-nine master shoemakers, the company regulated indentured servants and apprentices and set standards for work quality. In addition to the usual benefits, the cordwainers issued traveling papers signifying good standing in the trade for shoemakers leaving Philadelphia. By 1776 there were seventeen such companies in the city.

The descendants of these Pennsylvania artisans lived and worked in a world in many ways unrecognizable to their parents and grandparents. As the Revolution approached, signs of change were beginning to appear. In the small artisan workshops, the master, operating with limited capital, would soon come under pressure to become a contractor and work for wealthy merchants who supplied raw materials and set the price of the finished product in advance.

His journeymen, in turn, would become wage workers rather than independent craftsmen.

As relations at work began to change, some skilled workers in the seaboard cities turned to trade unions to protect their interests as wage earners. Strikes began to occur. Philadelphia shoemakers struck for higher wages at least three times between 1786 and 1800. And, when the union of cabinet and chair makers fought an attempt by employers to blacklist union members in 1790, they were able to call for support from unions of hatters, shoemakers, house carpenters, tailors, goldsmiths, saddlers, coopers, painters, printers, and others.

Signs of the factory system began to appear even before the Revolution. The enterprise established in 1775 by the United Company of Philadelphia for Promoting American Manufacturing turned out cotton goods and employed four hundred women under one roof. It was a harbinger of things to come. In addition, patterns of work that had characterized the colonial, preindustrial period were slowly altered as a result of changes in the organization of production, marketing, and new technology. Later, as a result of this industrial revolution, Pennsylvania was to become one of the great industrial centers of the world. For more than two centuries its workers searched for ways to protect themselves and to reap their fair share of the benefits of this transformation. The following chapters are the story of that search.

Ronald Filippelli is professor of labor studies and industrial relations at Penn State University. In addition to a number of articles and book chapters, he is the author of *Labor in the USA: A History; American Labor and Postwar Italy, 1943-1953;* and *Cold War in the Working Class* (co-authored with Mark McColloch). He is also editor of *Labor Conflict in the United States: An Encyclopedia.*

Keystone Vignette

Printing

Ronald L. Filippelli

Part of Philadelphia's primacy as the center of colonial commercial and intellectual life resulted from the work of its skilled printers. When the young journeyman printer Benjamin Franklin arrived in Philadelphia from Boston in 1723, the Quaker city was already the center of the American printing industry. Its craftsmen produced the greatest variety of printed material and displayed the highest quality of artisanship in the colonies.

The actual printing presses came mainly from Britain or Holland, as did the ink. Finer book papers also came from Holland, though lightweight stock used for newspapers and magazines was most often made in Pennsylvania paper mills which had produced such products since 1690 when William Rittenhouse set up the first mill near Wissahickon creek. After the Stamp Act in 1765, which placed high duties on paper, the colonial industry grew rapidly. So crucial was the shortage of paper and the deterioration of equipment during the Revolutionary War that the Continental Congress passed a resolution on July 18, 1776, forbidding Pennsylvania printers from joining the army. Of course, the military's needs for cartridge paper for muzzle-loading rifles and currency to pay troops were also important reasons for keeping printers in their shops.

Although inventories preserved from late eighteenth-century printshops suggest that the total value of the equipment and furnishings required for a well-organized printing establishment was about $5,000, most printers started with one press and a limited inventory of type, at a considerably lower investment. With these assets they competed to print the thousands of blank forms, tickets, vestry notices, advertisements, certificates, promissory notes, receipts, and bills that were needed to keep Philadelphia commerce going. In the more successful shops these staples were supplemented by the more lucrative printing of newspapers, hymnals, sermons, school primers, almanacs, and magazines. In 1776, seven newspapers were published in Philadelphia. It was through the Philadelphia newspapers, beginning with printer Benjamin Towne's *Pennsylvania Evening Post*, that on July 4, 1776 the news was first learned that "This day the Continental Congress declared the United Colonies Free and Independent States."

One observer noted of Philadelphia citizens in 1772 that their taste for books was so great "that almost every man is a reader." Yet book publishing was the most challenging of all tasks. Not many were produced. Whereas an apprentice could learn quickly to produce invoices, tickets, and the like, only an experienced journeyman printer could make a book. The task involved design, typesetting, printing, and binding. Because of their piety, Germans created a great demand for religious books and a large part of the book printer's output was made up of hymnals, bibles, and other devotional books in German. Philadelphia printers also played a major role in the revolutionary movement. Pamphlets served as the chief public forum for political debate during the eighteenth century. Often in the guise of "letters," they invariably appeared in times of controversy.

Philadelphia printers produced the essays of protest against the Stamp Act and the *Letters from a Farmer in Pennsylvania* that earned John Dickinson the title of "Penman of the American Revolution." Printer and bookseller Robert Aitkin hired Thomas Paine to revive the faltering fortunes of the *Pennsylvania Magazine,* and Paine used the pages of the journal to argue for the revolutionary cause. Paine's greatest revolutionary tract, *Common Sense,* was also printed in Philadelphia. And, not surprisingly, it was a Philadelphia printer, John Dunlap, who produced the official version of the Declaration of Independence for distribution throughout the colonies.

Readings for Chapter One

Bining, Arthur C. "The Iron Plantations of Early Pennsylvania," *Pennsylvania Magazine of History and Biography* 57 (1933): 117-137.

Bridenbaugh, Carl. *The Colonial Craftsman.* New York: New York University Press, 1950.

Herrick, Chessman A. *White Servitude in Pennsylvania: Indentured and Redemption Labor in Colony and Commonwealth.* Philadelphia: J.J. McVey, 1926.

Hofstadter, Richard. *America at 1750: A Social Portrait.* New York: Random House, 1971.

Jensen, Joan M. *Loosening the Bonds: Mid-Atlantic Farm Women, 1750-1850.* New Haven: Yale University Press, 1986.

Jernegan, Marcus W. *Laboring and Dependent Classes in Colonial America.* Chicago: University of Chicago Press, 1931.

Kriebel, Martha. "Women, Servants and Family Life in Early America," *Pennsylvania Folklife* 28 (1978): 2-9.

Maier, Pauline. *From Resistance to Revolution: Colonial Radicals and the Development of American Opposition to Britain, 1765-1776.* New York: Knopf, 1972.

McCusker, John, and Russell Menard. *The Economy of British America 1607-1789.* Chapel Hill: University of North Carolina Press, 1985.

Morris, Richard B. *Government and Labor in Early America.* New York: Columbia University Press, 1946.

Nash, Gary B. and Jean R. Soderlund. *Freedom by Degrees: Emancipation in Eighteenth Century Philadelphia.* New York: Oxford University Press, 1991.

Nash, Gary B. *Forging Freedom: The Formation of Philadelphia's Black Community.* Cambridge: Harvard University Press, 1988.

_____. "Slaves and Slaveowners in Colonial Pennsylvania," *William and Mary Quarterly* 30 (1973): 222-256.

_____. *The Urban Crucible: Social Change, Political Consciousness, and the Origins of the American Revolution.* Cambridge: Harvard University Press, 1979.

_____. "Up From the Bottom in Franklin's Philadelphia," *Past and Present* 77 (1977): 58-83.

_____. "Urban Wealth and Poverty in Pre-Revolutionary America," *Journal of Interdisciplinary History* 6 (1976): 545-584.

Olton, Charles S. *Artisans for Independence: Philadelphia Mechanics and the American Revolution.* Syracuse: Syracuse University Press, 1975.

————. "Philadelphia's Mechanics in the First Decade of the Revolution, 1765-1775," *Journal of American History* 59 (1972): 311-326.

Parker, Peter J. "Rich and Poor in Philadelphia, 1709," *Pennsylvania Magazine of History and Biography* 99 (1975): 3-19.

Parsons, William T. and Vibbard, Phyllis. "Be It Remembered That These Indentured Servants and Apprentices. . ." *Pennsylvania Folklife* 28 (1978): 10-24.

Rosswurm, Steven. *Arms, Country and Class: The Philadelphia Militia and "Lower Sort" During the American Revolution, 1775-1783.* New Brunswick: Rutgers University Press, 1987.

Ryerson, R.A. "Political Mobilization and the American Revolution: The Resistance Movement in Philadelphia, 1765-1776," *William and Mary Quarterly* 31 (1974): 565-588.

Salinger, Sharon V. "Send No More Women: Female Servants in Eighteenth Century Philadelphia," *Pennsylvania Magazine of History and Biography* 107 (1983): 29-48.

————. *"To Serve Well and Faithfully": Labor and Indentured Servants in Pennsylvania, 1682-1800.* New York: Cambridge University Press, 1987.

Secor, Robert, ed. *Pennsylvania 1776.* University Park: Penn State University Press, 1975.

Smith, Billy G. *The "Lower Sort": Philadelphia's Laboring People, 1750-1800.* Ithaca: Cornell University Press, 1990.

————. "The Material Lives of Working Philadelphians," *William and Mary Quarterly* 38 (1981): 163-202.

Soderlund, Jean R. "Black Women in Colonial Pennsylvania," *Pennsylvania Magazine of History and Biography* 107 (1983): 49-68.

Young, Alfred, ed. *The American Revolution: Explorations in the History of American Radicalism.* DeKalb: Northern Illinois University Press, 1976.

Chapter Two

An Industrial Giant Takes Shape, 1800-1872

Ken Fones-Wolf

P ennsylvania workers began the nineteenth century having contributed mightily to the American Revolution. The state was the most prosperous in the union and served as the crucible of politics and a thriving economy. It was from Philadelphia's artisans that Americans had found their republican voice in Tom Paine's *Common Sense*. By the 1790s, skilled wage earners had established the voluntary craft societies which exemplified a free, independent citizenry. These societies maintained wages and conditions, pressed grievances with their masters, and sustained members or their families when injury, sickness, or death occurred.

Within the first decade of the century, however, the status of Pennsylvania's wage earners appeared in jeopardy. Growing divisions between masters and journeymen threatened the unity of craft societies. A fair day's pay became more contentious as wage-earner status seemed ever more permanent. When Philadelphia shoemakers combined to demand higher wages in 1805, they were indicted on conspiracy charges. The Federalist judge's instructions to the jury charged:

> A combination of workmen to raise their wages may be considered in a twofold point of view: one is to benefit themselves . . . the other is to injure those who do not join the society. The rule of law condemns both.

Could this be the same rule of law which just a generation earlier had brought artisans to the battlefield? The shoemakers thought not, and so they appealed to the public:

> These masters, as they are called, and who would be masters and tyrants if they could, or the law would allow them, have their associations, their meetings, and they pass their resolutions; but as they are rich and we are poor—they seem to think that we are not protected by the constitution in meeting peaceably together and pursuing our own happiness. They suppose that they have a right to limit us at all times . . . they think they have the right to determine for us the value of our labor. . . . If the association of men to regulate the price of their own labor, is to be converted into a crime . . . the prospect is a very sad one for Pennsylvania.

The economy, as these comments attest, was in the process of a long transformation. Journeymen found their paths to master status blocked; employers subdivided tasks and moved production to ever larger shops and factories; manufacturers imported cheap immigrant labor or exploited the labor of women and children. By mid-century, capitalist wage labor dictated the conditions for three of every ten Pennsylvanians. The rule of law, for which workers had sacrificed in the Revolution, was arrayed against organizations of workers for most of that time, preventing wage earners from sharing equally in economic growth. In fact, the state's economy thrived on the labor of immigrants, women, blacks, and children at wages which undermined the sturdy artisans.

Nevertheless, by 1870 Pennsylvania workers had learned much about organization and power. They had challenged the domination of employers in setting the wages and conditions of work; they had forged political alliances to assert the rights of the "common man" and, despite the rule of judges like the one who condemned the shoemakers, they had fought in the Civil War to rescue the republic from the "Slave Conspiracy." Workers were fiercely committed to the principles—as they understood them—handed down from the struggles of 1776. A century later, wage earners were still fighting to see them fulfilled.

The Early Industrial World of Work

On the surface, it would appear that Philadelphia shoemakers were something of an anomaly in 1805. Nine of every ten Pennsylvanians still lived in the countryside. Most production in early nineteenth-century Pennsylvania took place either in small workshops or in households. The major exception was the growing iron industry, where manufacturing was concentrated in village plantations. Iron plantations even utilized various forms of unfree labor—either slaves or indentured servants—like their Southern counterparts.

In most manufacturing, however, handicraft production predominated and work routines were governed by task rather than time restraints. This meant that most producers alternated bouts of hard work to finish, for example, a chair, a suit, or a pair of shoes for a customer with a more relaxed pace at such activities as gardening or fishing.

The vision of independent farmer-artisans, is deceiving however. Already, Philadelphia's growing industrial base had penetrated an ever-wider area to find consumer markets and to produce that which could not be manufactured efficiently in the city. By the 1820s, the nearby Brandywine Valley included more than sixty mills producing paper, iron, stoves, wood, and agricultural produce for the great home market comprised of Philadelphia and its environs.

Beyond Philadelphia, rural counties also belied the popular image. Less than half of Berks County household heads were farmers; nearly one-third of the rural labor force engaged in some form of manufacture. In Reading, hatmaking, brewing, and various types of milling employed growing numbers of people; in Lancaster, busi-

*The growth of transportation opened rural areas to economic development—
Huntingdon, 1862. (Pennsylvania State Archives)*

nesses employed more than 600 artisans in 1819, building a thriving
handicraft trade in shoes, furniture, hats, clothes, leather, and iron-
work. The scattered iron plantations brought industrial work to even
the most remote areas and smaller manufacturing hamlets emerged
where sufficient water power existed, as in the Rockdale area located between several creeks in Delaware County. Finally, Pittsburgh's
ideal location as the gateway to the West foreshadowed its industrial development as early as 1803. Over the succeeding two decades, its population tripled (to seventy-five hundred) while its brass
and tin production increased tenfold and its iron and textile production eightfold. Visitors to the city complained already that "the constant volume of smoke preserves the atmosphere in a continued
cloud of coal dust."

It was in Philadelphia, however, that entrepreneurs pioneered
American industrialization. In the 1790s, the city benefited as the
national capital and became the site of the First Bank of the United
States. The city also had a populous and fertile hinterland, stimulat-
ing a domestic trade isolated from the instability of international
commerce and unsettling world events. This domestic market in
turn attracted large numbers of skilled workers.

The availability of capital, labor, and markets spurred additional
components of growth, particularly new forms of transportation and

Urban growth is reflected in this early Pittsburgh scene of the terminus of the Pennsylvania Canal. (Carnegie Library of Pittsburgh)

business organization. Between 1790 and 1830, Philadelphia merchants launched innumerable road, turnpike, and canal projects to keep rival cities like Baltimore and New York from competing for their trade. As early as 1818, the Pennsylvania Road carried the old Philadelphia-Lancaster turnpike all the way to Pittsburgh, becoming the most heavily traveled road to the west. Meanwhile, the state chartered fifteen private companies to build canals by 1819, including routes linking Philadelphia to Pottsville, Middletown, and York. During those same years, Pennsylvania businessmen inaugurated organizational advances, including joint stock companies and corporations. These advances led to improved bookkeeping and the separation of manufacturing firms from their owners, two practices which had important ramifications for later business history.

As the center of these developments, Philadelphia was the leading city of American industry, spawning a bewildering variety of manufacturing. At the early stages of the industrial revolution, its technology was at the cutting edge of change. Such local mechanics as Oliver Evans, Nathan Sellers, and Robert Fulton, to name three, transformed machine building. By 1810, Philadelphia was the source of one-third of the state's industrial output.

No one industry dominated the state's economic base. How-

41

ever, economic journalist Edwin Freedley noted, with particular reference to Pennsylvania, that iron manufacture was "the great patron of modern industry." As late as 1856, the Commonwealth produced over half the iron manufactured in the U.S. In eastern counties such as Berks and Lancaster the iron industry flourished, employing more than twenty-seven hundred men in Berks County alone by 1830. It was not coincidental that nearby Philadelphia was the national center for ironworking and machine building. Rural ironmaking and urban iron working were finally joined in Pittsburgh in the 1830s, earning it a reputation as the Birmingham of America for its immersion in every branch of the iron industry.

Textile manufacturing was the other axis of remarkable industrial growth. The state's textile production mushroomed, though it followed a path different from that taken by the great spinning establishments of Massachusetts. Pennsylvania textiles relied far more on hand-loom weaving, due in part to the availability of skilled labor but also because artisans, not capitalists, dominated the small enterprises. The cumulative impact of the abundant opportunities for small-scale, flexible production was considerable; by the 1820s Philadelphia alone counted more than forty-five hundred weavers. In ensuing decades, the mechanization of parts of the industry had by no means reduced the number of hand-loom artisans. Philadelphia was home to nearly eight thousand as late as 1850.

Other industries broadened the state's industrial base. In Pittsburgh, the glass industry had grown to importance by 1840, and Philadelphia was the shipbuilding center of the country well into the nineteenth century. Small consumer goods, like clothing, shoes, hats, and tobacco, were produced throughout the state. Shoes, for instance, employed over six thousand Philadelphians in 1850. During the latter part of the century the city was also becoming an important garment center.

Several factors characterized Pennsylvania's industrial expansion. One was the steady growth of the scale of enterprise. In 1811, Oliver Evans's Mars Iron Works in Philadelphia seemed a huge establishment when it employed thirty-five workers. Yet, just twenty years later, the city's Globe textile mills had 304 men, women, and children on its payroll. The driving force behind the increased scale of production was the merchant capitalist. In nearly all spheres of

Canal basin at Towanda. Canal boats being loaded with coal from railroad cars, c. 1860. (Bradford County Historical Society)

industry, the entrance of merchant capitalists, with dreams of tapping new markets opened by roads and canals, signaled the abandonment of old artisan shops in which personalized relationships between masters, journeymen, and apprentices ruled production. In their place, capitalists built factories housing ever-larger numbers of workers, aided by extensive networks of cottage production: thread spun in factories was woven into cloth by the wives and daughters of farmers. Merchant capitalists—often with no knowledge of manufacturing but with access to capital for wages, equipment, and raw materials—exerted control over new modes of production.

Alongside the shift to factory production came the division of labor. In furniture manufacturing or shoemaking, capitalists took advantage of large numbers of workers laboring under one roof to assign specialized tasks and exploit the cheap labor of unskilled workers.

Where in artisan shops a craftsperson made the entire product from start to finish, factory production substituted unskilled workers for routine jobs, leaving artisans free to do only the most demanding work. Apprentices increasingly learned only one facet of pro-

43

Throughout the nineteenth century children performed a surprising variety of jobs. Young girls skimmed crude oil from creeks and ponds in northwestern Pennsylvania—Oil Creek, 1863. (Pennsylvania State Archives)

duction as bosses utilized numerous specialists to replace the well-rounded mechanic. Well before the adoption of power machinery, for instance, the making of bedsteads was divided among seven different workers. Output rose dramatically and labor costs fell. In this way, the industrialization of many crafts preceded the use of new technologies.

The continued expansion of industry also depended upon tapping new sources of labor power. In Lancaster County ironworking villages, local ironmasters frequently recruited African American workers, first as slaves, but after 1800 as free workers who had either been emancipated by the state constitution or had escaped from nearby slave states. Immigrants provided another source of labor—both skilled and unskilled—particularly before the Napoleonic wars slowed their steady arrival. Entering through a process of indentured servitude, immigrants helped keep labor costs in Pennsylvania low, at least until their indenture period expired. Nearly four of every ten Philadelphia wage earners in 1850 were immigrants. In more remote areas like Reading, the proportion was about one of four. Until the 1840s the vast majority of immigrants were English, barely altering the ethnic composition of the workforce.

By far the largest source of new labor power came from the countryside. Women and children—although still only a fraction of the wage-labor workforce—provided much of the labor power necessary for the pioneering factory-based industries such as textiles and shoes. Similarly, married women, confined to the home with children, also contributed to manufacturing output by weaving, stitching clothes, and braiding hats. But rural-born men, squeezed off farms by land shortages or lured to towns by wage-earning opportunities, made up even larger proportions of the emerging manufacturing workforce in Pennsylvania.

Since many of these workers labored in environments without long-established production techniques, concerns arose over managing large workforces and imposing tighter discipline. Before 1800, John Nicholson's hosiery and textile manufacturing complex in Manayunk delegated power to a new class of superintendents to facilitate close control of the works. Rural iron villages required workers to give up periodic hunting trips and holidays. Rules prohibiting smoking or breaks for beer—traditional artisan privileges— emerged with increasing frequency as did factory bells which regulated comings and goings in manufacturing towns and neighborhoods. As the factory system advanced, workers found themselves subjected to fines or dismissal when they followed older workplace customs.

The regimen of disciplined wage labor resulted in astoundingly high rates of absenteeism and turnover. Early labor-capital relations were fitful, made worse by irregular wage payments and the instability of an ever-widening market. Stricter rules broke traditional work rhythms or tended to impose a consciousness of time on men, women, and children who often lacked such reference points. Workers were simply not accustomed to the newly emerging patterns of highly regulated workplaces. As one historian of early industrialization reminds us, many workers "voted with their feet" and deserted factory jobs with alarming regularity.

Flight, in most cases, failed to improve conditions for workers without skills. Highly irregular employment in trade centers like Harrisburg or Pittsburgh typically meant chronic poverty. Cartmen, teamsters, dockhands, and others who performed tasks where physical strength was the only criterion were easily replaced. A common unskilled wage at the bottom of the pay scale rarely provided for even a small family. Similarly, few female occupations paid anything close to a living wage for households headed by widows or deserted women. Early in the nineteenth century, both small towns and large cities faced welfare crises, particularly in an unstable economy susceptible to speculators and financial panics. A depression in 1819 put perhaps one of every five Philadelphians on some form of relief at a time when municipal almsgiving was noted for its severity and stinginess. Although wages had generally improved in the early nineteenth century, the material standards of Pennsylvania's laboring poor were spartan.

Stricter work discipline and low wages took on a more ominous significance for artisans steeped in the traditions of autonomy. Organizations of journeymen began to appear, particularly in those trades in which factory production progressed most rapidly. By 1810, printers, shoemakers, and curriers had established permanent organizations in Pittsburgh and Philadelphia. In part, journeyman societies were benefit organizations protecting members and their families against sickness, death, and irregular employment. Increasingly, however, they sought to regulate wages and working conditions. To add to their power, journeymen attempted to control entry to the craft—through apprenticeship requirements which forced youths to learn all the secrets of the trade—and entry to the shop, through closed-shop agreements with employers.

Almost from the beginning, employers challenged the legality of journeymen associations with the aid of conservative friends in the courts. Drawing upon English common law, even during the height of Jeffersonian democracy, Federalist judges handed down a number of important decisions between 1805 and 1815 that made combinations of workers subject to the law of conspiracy. The first of these cases resulted in a guilty verdict and fines for eight Philadelphia shoemakers. Five other cases were decided in the next decade, the final two involving Pittsburgh cordwainers. Although the five subsequent cases somewhat softened the harsh antiunionism of the Federalist judge in the Philadelphia case, and remarkably few combinations were prosecuted, the weight of the law remained clearly against labor combinations. The court recorder at the 1815 trial boldly asserted: "The verdict of the jury is most important to the manufacturing interests of the community for it puts an end to these associations which have been so prejudicial to the successful enterprise of the capitalist in the western country." Consequently, the first steps of Pennsylvania labor were made on an uncertain terrain. Conspiracy laws were not the only impediments to labor, however. Workers were hindered even more severely by an economic depression which began in 1819.

Serious conflict, however, was limited to relatively few trades. In most of Pennsylvania, the artisan workshop or the household, not the merchant capitalist, governed production. Artisans were a respected political presence in Pennsylvania. Indeed, the 1790 state constitution extended suffrage at least to all white males who paid taxes, and wage earners agitated successfully for amendments to the property qualifications. Mechanics also joined the Jeffersonian opposition to conservative Federalist rule and appeared at the forefront of the crusade for free public schools and libraries.

Where workers could not abolish inequalities, they sometimes engaged in rituals which ridiculed social distinctions. There emerged a rich culture of folk drama poking fun at the elite. One example of this were protests against unequal militia obligations. Elites frequently purchased release from compulsory militia service, something few workers could do. In 1824, however, Philadelphia's working class mocked the militia by electing a half-witted stable boy, John Pluck, as colonel of one of the neighborhood companies. During periodic public drills, Pluck's company appeared in outlandish dress and performed farcical drills. Colonel Pluck's company attracted widespread attention to the unjust militia system prior to its reform by working-class political parties in the 1830s. The week between Christmas and New Year's Day also elicited elaborate folk rituals as workers dressed in costumes and harassed local elites known for unfair business dealings.

Working-class life demonstrated a resiliency despite the poverty of many urban workers. Informal community networks based on kin or the exchange of services assisted wage-earning families with child care, neighborhood sharing, and help during illness. Working-class celebrations and block parties punctuated the routines of the laboring poor as well as more prosperous artisans. Of course, there were negative aspects of this culture—gangs roamed the streets, rival volunteer fire companies frequently engaged in pitched battles while buildings burned, and families suffered strain and violence as a result of poverty. This behavior often flourished amid conditions that made life itself tenuous for the urban working class. Outbreaks of communicable diseases, such as the cholera epidemic of 1832, struck disproportionately among wage earners and infant mortality rates were astounding.

Culture, however, was far from a unifying force among the working class. While many wage earners chose to continue habits of drinking, rowdy behavior and violence, others attempted to follow a path emphasizing religious piety, self-improvement, and hard work. These workers hoped that their deference to wage labor's new disciplines would persuade employers to provide them with greater security and opportunities. Another tendency also emerged among the working class stressing respectable behavior but tracing a radical lineage back to the free thought, popular democracy, and collective economic struggle. Although workers rarely conformed to only one tendency, these cultures helped shape internal working-class strife.

Making and Unmaking a Working Class

The protective tariff of 1824 signaled a recovery from the depression of 1819. Pennsylvania's factory system was now expanding at an unprecedented rate. Although Philadelphia was the leading manufacturing city in the state, the most dramatic growth was in Pittsburgh. In 1815, the city's population was around six thousand; by 1860 it reached nearly fifty thousand. Its 1,191 workshops employed 20,500 workers. The value of its glass manufacture quadrupled between 1815 and 1850.

Cities were not the only locus of manufacturing. In two tiny hamlets along the banks of Chester Creek in Delaware County, the population climbed to over two thousand by 1850, nearly three-fifths comprising wage earners in local cotton factories. In Lancaster, steam-powered cotton mills replaced older handicraft manufacturing, employing nearly four hundred persons by 1849 with the largest mill yet to be completed. Such growth spurred competitors; by mid-century Allentown and Reading vied with Lancaster for local manufacturing dominance. Capitalist wage labor arrived in the rich anthracite fields of the Pottsville basin in northeastern Pennsylvania with the perfection of a process that substituted anthracite coal for charcoal. Anthracite miners in Schuylkill County increased five-fold in the 1830s, and two-and-one-half times in the next decade.

One reason for the tremendous economic growth in the 1820s was the cheap cost of labor following the depression. With more than twenty thousand workers unemployed in Philadelphia alone, competition among wage earners was intense and wages plummeted despite a longer workday. The wage rates for carpenters declined from $1.75 per day in 1817 to $1.25 per day in 1836. William Ramsey, a Chester County shoemaker, earned $2.87 per pair of boots in 1822, $2.75 per pair in 1823, but only $2.12 per pair in 1824. Artisans, however, suffered less than factory operatives. During the 1820s, operatives at Whitaker's Mill in northeastern Philadelphia saw their rates cut by one-quarter.

The return of prosperity in the mid-1820s enabled workers to mobilize opposition to the deteriorating labor conditions. Beginning in 1824, labor organizations began to re-emerge, demanding predepression wage rates. In the space of a year, Philadelphia's ship carpenters, weavers, and cabinetmakers struck for higher wages, while millwrights and machinists introduced a relatively novel demand, the ten-hour workday. In large part, the attempt to regulate the hours of labor was a response to the harsher work discipline of the factory. Employers no longer allowed for alternating hard work with breaks for beer or grog, nor did they tolerate days off for hunting and fishing. Instead, assisted by the high unemployment caused by the depression, employers demanded longer hours as a condition of employment and had lines waiting for each available position. When conditions improved, labor organizations sought to impose limitations on a workday increasingly under the control of the manufacturer.

Employers, of course, were not about to capitulate to renewed labor demands, particularly so long as they had the favor of the courts. In two cases, Pennsylvania manufacturers successfully pursued indictments against shoemakers (1821) and tailors (1827) for conspiring to raise wages. However, judicial interpretation began to change in the 1820s. Unlike the earlier cases, the convictions in the 1820s rested less on the application of conspiracy doctrine to labor combinations and more on the illegal intimidation and coercion of innocent third parties by strikers. In some measure, these two cases cleared the way for more systematic trade union action after 1827.

The awakening of labor occurred first among Philadelphia's artisans in the building trades. Carpenters demanded a ten-hour workday in 1827, inspired by an anonymous pamphlet asserting that mechanics could not "make the inestimable blessing of universal suffrage worth something" until they gained "sufficient knowledge." For labor to attain that knowledge, it needed a free press, libraries, lectures, and most importantly a shorter workday. The carpenters' strike failed, but in its wake left a weekly newspaper, *The Mechanics' Free Press*, a Mechanics' Library Company, and a Mechanics' Union of Trade Associations (MUTA), a federation of unions representing workers in fifteen trades. For the next four years, the MUTA coordinated the struggle of shoeworkers, tailors, weavers, printers, cabinetmakers, and building trades workers to improve their wages and working conditions.

From its inception, the Mechanics' Union was concerned with politics reflecting the working-class belief in the principles of republicanism, the founding fathers' Revolutionary faith.

In the broadest sense, republicanism stood for equality of opportunity (for white males, at least) and for freedom from arbitrary rule. However, the republican faith had become fractured since the founding of the new nation. Its tenets were subject to numerous interpretations. For upwardly mobile mechanics and master craftsmen, "republicanism affirmed a fluid and culturally homogeneous social order," says historian Bruce Laurie. To them, the ideals of the Revolution were evident in the opportunities provided by the new economic order and needed protection from foreign powers, typically through tariffs. For another segment of the working class, represented by volunteers in Colonel Pluck's militia company, republicanism meant, simply, freedom from too much government interference.

For the artisans and mechanics in the Mechanics' Union, however, republicanism demanded more than protection from external threat. Journeymen, for instance, were finding their path to the achievement of master status blocked, a development that coincided with a period of growing economic inequality. In trades in which merchant capitalists and manufacturers had taken greater control of the market, threatening the independence and prosperity of journeymen, republicanism itself became the object of dispute. In the words of the *Mechanics Free Press,* the real threat to republicanism came from the social privilege accorded to capitalists through "injudicious legislation" and the granting of "charters for monopolising companies."

Therefore, to the MUTA it seemed that growing economic inequality had political roots and that political activity would be necessary to complement trade union struggle. Journeymen harkened to traditions of craft "corporatism," in which masters and subordinates shared common interests. The MUTA argued that the intervention of the state—through laws, charters, and courts—had tipped the scales firmly in the direction of employers. However, to the journeymen's mind, it was not master craftsmen who posed a threat, but the growing power of bankers and merchant capitalists. Consequently, the Mechanics' Union in 1828 formed the first Working Men's Party in the United States. The party's outlook was republican rather than class conscious, as demonstrated by leader William Heighton's comment: "If an employer superintends his own business (still more if he works with his own hands) he is a working man," eligible by implication, for membership in the Working Men's Party.

The platform of the Workeys (as they were known) testified to artisanal republicanism. As "children of the Enlightenment," the leaders of the Working Men's Party made education the cornerstone of their program. Free public schools were a necessity not only to prepare children for participation in the "land of opportunity," but to distribute power more equally. An educated electorate was needed to relieve unfair burdens on the poor such as imprisonment for debt, compulsory militia service, poll taxes, and anti-labor court injunctions. Politically astute workers could also prevent the chartering of monopolies, like banks, which squeezed wage earners and block the selection of candidates by party caucus systems which excluded broad, democratic participation. As good republicans, suspicious of powerful government, the Working Men's Party asked for few positive interventions from government on behalf of the working class. Its program called principally for the elimination of special privilege.

The Working Men's Party idea spread rapidly throughout Pennsylvania. Pittsburgh, Harrisburg, Lancaster, Carlisle, and other locales had parties representing workers by the summer of 1829. The party's program briefly galvanized an artisan political consciousness between 1828 and 1831, before it succumbed to internal tensions, political intrigues, and the superior electioneering of the established parties. Most important for its demise, the Working Men's Party was an urban phenomenon in a state dominated by rural voters. Thus, alliances were difficult to achieve.

Even in cities, however, independent political action by workers had many barriers to overcome. Already in the 1820s, workers were attracted to the rituals of partisan politics. In the manufacturing villages of Manayunk and Roxborough, Democrats had a strong following among factory workers who enjoyed the culture of the saloon and popular democracy. Whigs appealed more to master craftsmen and property-holding artisans, particularly those who advocated temperance and religious piety. For both groups, the expected gains from their earlier partisanship appeared to outweigh the prospects of a united working-class politics. Cultural differentiation among workers continued to impede the labor movement.

Nevertheless, the first independent working-class party left a legacy longer than its brief existence. In elections in Philadelphia, Pittsburgh, and Dauphin and Mifflin Counties, it garnered some impressive totals and shifted the political balance. More importantly, the Working Men's Party highlighted issues that led, eventually, to state legislative action. These included public schooling (1834), reform of the compulsory militia system (1837), abolition of imprisonment for indebtedness (1835), and a lien law which protected the mechanic's right to be paid for work completed in case of bankruptcy (1854).

Failed fortunes only briefly stymied an emerging working-class industrial movement. In late 1833, Philadelphia labor veterans revitalized their trade unions, seeking to win at the workplace what they could not win at the polls. Moreover, while the Working Men's

Party principally represented artisans, the rise of the General Trades' Union (GTU) reflected a broader alliance. Between 1833 and 1836, the GTU grew from two thousand to ten thousand members and included blacks, women, and unskilled workers in addition to skilled craftsmen. They formed a democratic organization aiming to avoid the pitfalls of partisan politics while uniting on cultural issues that had previously proved divisive. For instance deeply religious workers, concerned with temperance and propriety, shunned association with free-thinking radicals. However, on Independence Day, 1835, working-class temperance advocates astonished religious leaders when they sang:

> Some strike for wages, some for hours,
> Shall we refuse?—O never!
> For time and cash we pledge our powers,
> And strike for both for ever!
> Then strike who will for "6 to 6,"
> We flinch not in the war;
>
> For temperance and for Seventy-Six
> We strike—hurrah! hurrah!

The song captured the euphoria of workers fresh from the first general strike in the United States, fought for the ten-hour workday. Begun by unskilled coal heavers on the Schuylkill docks in late May 1835, their parades through the city inspired cordwainers, smiths, leather workers, cigarmakers, weavers, and building trades workers to throw down their tools and shout: "We are all day laborers!" The shared experience of capitalist wage labor expressed in that slogan overshadowed, for a time, the great differences of situation separating skilled workers and common labor. Similarly, judicious and skilled radical leaders of the GTU toned down their partisan support for Andrew Jackson and their opposition to temperance and religious evangelicalism. Finally, the assertion of working-class power swelled the ranks of the GTU, bringing in new recruits, many of whom had no trade-union experience. By June 22, thousands of Philadelphia workers had secured either a reduction of working hours or an increase in wages.

53

News of the victory of Philadelphia's working class stirred wage earners throughout the state. Norristown railroad workers struck for the ten-hour workday in late June; Pottsville miners and boatmen joined them in July. Before the end of the year, skilled tailors in Reading, shoemakers in Pittsburgh, and bookbinders throughout the state had asserted their right to shorter hours. Even in the tiny manufacturing hamlets along Chester Creek, resistance to employers was growing. In February 1836, the textile operatives of Rockdale, Lenni, and Knowlton struck for higher wages and against the overworking of children. Few of these strikes were as successful as the Philadelphia general strike, but over a two-year period labor historian William Sullivan recorded seventy-two strikes in the state. Never had the power of capital met such staunch opposition.

The potential of the working-class movement of the mid-1830s, however, was never quite realized. In the spring of 1837, a large number of banks failed, specie payments were suspended, and a general economic panic ensued. With thousands of workers unemployed, trade-union discipline collapsed. Workers took whatever work they could find at whatever wages the employer offered. By 1839, estimates of unemployment ranged as high as one-third of the workforce in some cities. Wages dropped by anywhere from 30 to 50 percent while several anthracite mining villages had become little more than ghost towns. Even in Philadelphia, "streets seem deserted," wrote the conservative Sidney George Fisher as late as 1842; "the largest houses are shut up and to rent, there is no business . . . no money, no confidence."

Competition among workers for the dwindling number of jobs destroyed whatever solidarity remained from their shared status as wage earners. Hard times particularly heightened racial tensions. As early as 1834, animosity between blacks and whites exploded during a summer carnival in Philadelphia. Again in 1838, working-class whites disrupted an abolitionist meeting in Pennsylvania Hall and burned the building to the ground. At least partly underlying these episodes was a desire to exclude blacks from certain skilled occupations. Attacks took on a new importance during the depression. In 1839, a race riot rocked Pittsburgh's black community and resulted in the torching of Negro dwellings. Then, on August 1, 1842, periodic scuffles between blacks and whites competing for common labor on Philadelphia's docks turned ugly when blacks paraded in commemoration of Jamaican Independence Day. Prowling white mobs used the spectacle of the parade as a pretext for brutal acts of violence intended to muscle blacks out of unskilled dockwork.

In the early 1840s, a new ingredient was added to intra-class violence. Large numbers of Irish immigrants, fleeing famine in their homeland, flooded an already oversupplied urban labor market. In Philadelphia resentment mounted, especially in the textile-producing neighborhoods of Kensington and Moyamensing where native-born handloom weavers feared displacement by immigrant labor. When Catholic immigrants intruded into hard-pressed but tightly-knit Protestant weavers' communities, the mixture became volatile. After several minor episodes, full-blown hostilities erupted in May and again in July 1844 as nativist artisans battled Irish weavers and then turned on the state militia when it tried to restore order. Similarly, nativism became one of the most salient features of working-class attitudes in Pittsburgh and other Pennsylvania cities in the 1840s.

Finally, working-class organizations dealt poorly with the growing participation of women in the workforce. At times men and women made common cause, but in most cases craft organizations excluded females. During strikes, unions typically cast demands in terms most favorable to skilled male workers, ignoring the problems unique to lower-paid women. Even in the street parades which were such a crucial part of working-class communication, female participation met with scorn, scandal and near riot. In part, men excluded women because they accepted the middle-class Victorian ideal of female domesticity. But working-class families gave this a slightly different twist. They emphasized that wage-earning men should be paid a "family wage" or a wage sufficient to enable them to provide for an entire family so that their wives and children would have the same opportunities as the wealthy. As interpreted by unions, the family wage appealed principally to men and ignored the needs of women who were on their own such as daughters and widows forced to provide for families. All too often, the family-wage argument became merely an excuse to reduce labor competition by excluding women, with little or no concern for their circumstances or desires.

Wage-earning women increasingly had to take matters into their own hands and form their own organizations. In Philadelphia, the Female Boot and Shoe Binders Society conducted several militant actions culminating with a dramatic victory in 1836. Female factory workers often organized protests and petitioned legislatures. In cases where women were already firmly established in an occupation, such as in garment making and cigarmaking, strikes even obtained support from men who felt they would gain by the organization of everyone in the trade. Yet the labor newspapers of the 1830s—the *National Laborer* or the *Mechanics' Free Press*—spoke more forcefully for keeping women in the home rather than helping them achieve economic independence or equality.

Consequently, the working-class movement of the 1830s was, a decade later, in disarray. The floundering economy had exposed the most vulnerable aspects of working-class unity. At the same time immigrants, African Americans, and women were altering the composition of the industrial labor force particularly as technological change and the factory system encroached on more industries. The working class crossed a chasm in the 1840s; it had a startlingly different composition thereafter, acquiring new leadership and new strategies.

The Era of Reform

Immigration dramatically changed the American working class in the two decades prior to the Civil War. From the time of the Constitution to 1845, slightly more than one million immigrants arrived in the United States. The ensuing decade brought approximately three million immigrants and their percentage of the urban labor force rose from roughly 10 percent to over 30 percent. Between 1847 and 1853, the number of common laborers increased from 36,000 to 83,000. Famine in Ireland and war and revolution in continental Europe sent Irish and German peasants and European radicals to the U.S. by the thousands. Many landed in Pennsylvania's cities. Philadelphia's population increased from 360,000 in 1840 to 670,000 in 1860 and Pittsburgh's jumped from slightly over 21,000 to more than 50,000. Even towns like Reading grew rapidly, nearly tripling in size in just two decades.

At the same time, American industry was recomposing the

workforce. In the second third of the nineteenth century, many crafts-men experienced a long-term decline. The traditional manner of acquiring a trade—through apprenticeship—declined as the market economy, cash wages, and the ability to get by with semi-skilled labor changed the rules for both master and apprentice. Masters had difficulty requiring apprentices to finish their training and, on the other hand, apprentices often found themselves without mar-ketable skills. For young workers, apprenticeship meant a continual struggle against machines and factory foremen.

By 1850, more than one-fourth of Philadelphia's wage earners worked in settings utilizing either steam or water power; about four of every nine worked in firms employing more than fifty workers. The factory setting allowed for greater exploitation of the unskilled immigrants entering Pennsylvania and of growing numbers of women and children, especially in textiles, clothing, shoemaking, printing, and hatting. For instance, in Lancaster, the steam-powered cotton mills of engineer Charles Tillinghast James increased manufacturing employment for women and children to nearly one-third of the workforce between 1845 and 1860.

Still, it is easy to overestimate the declining fortunes wrought by industrialization. If wages stagnated or declined, so did prices, at least over the long term. If factories employed growing numbers of workers, most still labored in small shops untransformed by mecha-nization. Outside of urban settings, industrial transformation occurred at an even slower pace (Even gathering timber for market on the rivers of central Pennsylvania led to conflicts like one described in Keystone Vignette: "The Batle of Clearfield Creek," p. 75). It was more the apparent future than the existing reality of industrial soci-ety that most alarmed Pennsylvania's citizens.

Factory production also offered many opportunities for some less skilled workers to move into a range of new industrial crafts, or skilled occupations, which evolved alongside mechanization. Due to lagging technology, worker resistance, or the need for skills re-gardless of machinery, some workers in the factory system estab-lished an autonomy and status resting on superior knowledge and craftsmanship. Glass blowers, iron molders, stationary engineers, and boilermakers, for instance, were not preindustrial artisans; their numbers expanded with the growth of industry in the mid-nineteenth

Veteran logger Miles King. Born in 1847, photographed at a twentieth century lumbermen's reunion, Lock Haven, Clinton County. (Pennsylvania State Archives)

century. Young men (and most were indeed white males) like John Fritz, who learned the machinist's trade in a rural Pennsylvania shop, could look forward to plentiful employment at wages typically well above the average.

Despite the varying effects of industrialization, the ravages of the depression of 1837 had triggered a re-evaluation of the political and moral consequences of economic change. At the beginning of the depression, the Pennsylvania senate investigated the conditions of working-class life and was horrified at what it discovered. The documentation of poorly clad families living in crowded, ill-ventilated tenements with no sanitary features shocked the senators. Even more unsettling were the arbitrary discipline and harsh conditions under which factory operatives labored. Employers routinely docked workers half a day's pay for lateness and the use of the lash on children was not uncommon. George Low, a thirteen-year-old boy, complained of a foreman who pulled his ears "until they bled." The workers' plight worsened during the depression; factory operatives routinely worked seventy-two hour weeks and inflated prices easily outstripped meager wages.

Reformers feared a permanent underclass would plague American cities. Chronic unemployment, children without access to honorable trades, mothers working long hours, and unsupervised children roaming neighborhoods in gangs, committing violent crimes or engaging in petty vice could be the consequences. Actions of factory operatives, like the female textile workers in Pittsburgh who walked off the job in September 1845 pleading for a ten-hour workday, stirred the sympathies of such prominent spokespersons as Orestes Brownson, Horace Greeley, and Philadelphia economist Henry Carey. These men criticized capitalist wage labor and its inability to provide the independence and self-sufficiency American workers needed to sustain the republic.

Some employers sought to reverse the declining conditions of wage earners through paternalism. Carey, in particular, inspired employers to apply a Christian spirit in their factories, "To substitute true Christianity for the detestable system of Malthusianism," which argued for the lowest possible wages. Indeed, the "cotton lords" of Chester Creek and Philadelphia locomotive builder Matthias Baldwin, among others, attempted to put Christian industrialism into practice.

They provided churches, hospitals, housing, and other material benefits for their workers and families while rewarding loyal employees with bonuses or pensions. In addition, they enabled some workers to rise to moderate prosperity through managerial positions or skilled specializations.

A more far-reaching avenue of reform concerned legislation for a ten-hour workday. Following the 1845 walkout by the factory girls of Pittsburgh, workers in many cities formed ten-hour leagues to petition and agitate for a state law fixing the hours of labor. Like the factory operatives of New England, Pennsylvania's workers described the debilitating effect of twelve- or fourteen-hour workdays:

> We see the laborer in the morning approach his toil with dread. . . . We see him as the day progresses with wearied limbs, gloomy thoughts, and cheerless spirits . . .
>
> We see him in ignorance, servility, and degradation, deprived of the time, the taste, the energy necessary for his elevation and improvement.

Unfortunately, social legislation conflicted with the English common-law doctrine of freedom of contract. Although laws were passed in several states (including Pennsylvania in 1848), the laws were filled with contractual loopholes, making avoidance easy. In Delaware County, for instance, employers simply ignored the law; in Pittsburgh, employers drafted twelve-hour contracts and laid off some two thousand operatives who refused to sign.

More radically inclined reformers proposed sweeping changes in the organization of production. Influenced by European experimenters like Robert Owen, Charles Fourier, and Charles Brisbane, American utopians established communities for cooperative production (called phalanxes) as a potential alternative to wage labor. Although the most famous were Brook Farm in Massachusetts and New Harmony, Indiana, one of the first and most successful phalanxes was called Sylvania and located in western Pennsylvania.

Few wage earners joined these communal experiments, but phalanxes did impart the notion of cooperative production and distribution. In 1848, Horace Greeley even attempted to help cotton-mill workers in Allegheny County set up a profit-sharing factory following an announced wage cut by Pittsburgh manufacturers. In several other trades, cooperation advanced further; shoemakers in Pittsburgh, tailors and bookbinders in Philadelphia, and molders in Sharon and Allegheny City were among the craftsmen asserting their right to the "full product" of their toil. Particularly among the molders, cooperative production had a pragmatic appeal lasting for decades. Even more enduring were cooperative stores, where wage earners could buy food, clothing, medicine, and other goods without the high markups of retail shops. Pennsylvania became a thriving center for all sorts of working-class cooperatives, including banks and building and loan associations. If they failed to transform or even to enlist a majority of the burgeoning working class, cooperatives nevertheless were important symbols of the efforts of wage earners to assert their dignity.

Throughout the 1840s, trade unionism remained on the defensive, made timid by internal divisions, a flooded labor market, and memories of political failures. Reformers concentrated their efforts on unskilled factory operatives, mostly women and children who were the most visible victims of industrialization. In some trades, however, the craft worker's skill remained critical to the production process even after the introduction of factory production. In 1844, a young man named William Sylvis learned the craft of molding in a stove-making establishment in sparsely-settled Clearfield County. Although the days of profitable, small rural shops where Sylvis might aspire to artisanal independence were passing, his skills were highly desirable and amply rewarded in the large factories of Philadelphia or Pittsburgh.

It was from craft workers like Sylvis that the desire for trade unionism reemerged. When prosperity returned after 1845, tailors, compositors, cabinetmakers, metal workers, and building trades workers reasserted their control over craft labor markets. By the 1850s, workers were rebuilding the labor movement. Miners in Schuylkill County, molders and shoemakers in Philadelphia, printers and cigarmakers in Reading all struck to raise wages and establish the closed shop. Moreover, several crafts had formed national unions. Printers, cigarmakers, shoemakers, molders, and machinists, among others, attempted to impose uniform wage scales, working conditions, and apprenticeship regulations on a nationwide basis.

One unfortunate by-product of the craft union movement, however, was the association of some artisans with nativist sentiments. For the decade after 1845, Pennsylvania's labor movement divided into two major groups, one organized around native-born or British Protestant craftsmen for whom unionism was at times an expression of hostility to immigrants and blacks almost as much as to employers, the other dominated by European immigrants who linked unions to a radical political agenda. Attempts at unity rarely survived the political hostilities generated by campaigns of the nativist American Republicans or the Know-Nothings, the anti-immigrant political parties which flourished during the era.

In the 1850s, one issue began to forge some unity among labor's diverse factions: the support for "free labor." In part, the slogan harkened back to earlier artisan radical traditions which asserted that labor created all wealth and that workers were thus entitled to the full product of their work. Just as importantly, the republic could not long survive if workers were deprived of their independence and reduced to mere "wage slavery." To many northern workers, the existence of slavery threatened to undermine the wages, status, and independence of white workers. German radicals took the lead in articulating antislavery arguments in the labor movement. After 1850 opposition to slavery surged in Pennsylvania. In 1851, the citizens of Lancaster County defended local blacks who repelled southerners attempting to recapture runaway slaves under the Fugitive Slave Law. By the mid-1850s, many of the craftsmen who had formed the backbone of the Know-Nothings in Harrisburg and Pittsburgh were joining former Whigs and German immigrants in the emerging Republican Party because of its support for free soil and free labor.

As the election of 1860 approached, northern labor divided over whether or not to support Abraham Lincoln. For Irish Catholics, joining a party harboring so many of their former enemies was onerous. William Sylvis, for one, clung to the Democratic Party, resisting Lincoln's attempt to court wage earners with promises to protect workers from slave competition and to pass a homestead law which would open land to free settlement.

Many northern workers also feared competition from emancipated blacks. Economic depression had struck again in the mid-1850s, creating unemployment and threatening the fragile labor movement. The Democratic Party charged that Lincoln's victory would unleash thousands of free Negroes who would contend for northern jobs. The Irish, at the bottom of the occupational scale, appeared most vulnerable to such competition and were, consequently, most resistant to the slogan, "free labor." German and native-born workers, on the other hand, helped carry Lincoln to victory in 1860.

The era that had inspired so much sentiment for labor reform closed with the shots on Fort Sumter, April 12, 1861. Secessionist rumblings in the South had already evoked protest demonstrations from the Pittsburgh Typographical Union ("No Compromise with Traitors"), mechanics in Easton and New Castle, and workers at the Pennsylvania Steam Engine and Boiler Works in Philadelphia who were "moving forward for the Union." Near Chester Creek, on April 15, workers flocked to Lincoln's call for enlistments and organized the "Delaware County Union Rifles," among several other volunteer companies, nearly vacating Rockdale. Even Sylvis, who voted against Lincoln, raised a company of Philadelphia workers to defend the Union. Yet, the shared free-labor vision of northern workingmen and their employers did not long survive; by 1863, Pennsylvania wage earners were again organizing against the disproportionate sacrifices demanded of the working class in the conduct of the Civil War.

War and Labor's Revival

Thousands of northern working men marched off to war with enthusiasm for what they viewed as a great crusade against the system of slavery. Many expected the first show of force to cower the secessionists. But when Robert E. Lee's forces invaded Maryland in the fall of 1862, the North understood that it would not be a brief conflict. Enlistments no longer met the military requirements of the war and Lincoln ordered an unpopular draft in August 1862. Meanwhile, wartime prices skyrocketed, creating untold hardship on workers who thought manufacturers were taking advantage of the war and unfairly profiteering. Philadelphia machinist Jonathan Fincher asserted that "the laboring millions will accept the wages of peace if they be accompanied by peace prices; but if we must pay war prices, we must have war wages." Finally, confusion reigned over the war itself. Slavery had not been abolished despite the clamoring of northern reformers, and opponents of the war, like the western Pennsylvania newspaper, *Indiana Democrat*, published false reports that runaway slaves were taking the places of white workers at the Cambria Iron Works.

Not surprisingly, opposition to the war manifested itself first in those places where pro-Republican sympathy was weak. In the anthracite fields enlistments were far below expectations. Irish miners remembered vicious nativist attacks by Republicans prior to the war and they resented draft regulations that allowed the sons of wealthy mineowners to buy their way out of service. In Pottsville, armed mobs stopped a train full of draftees and assisted the escape of reluctant recruits; in Cass Township, a commissioner handed over false enlistment affidavits to circumvent conscription.

Resistance spread far beyond the coal fields, however. Philadelphians attempting to avoid the draft were assisted by the Catholic Church. In Crawford County, citizens pelted enrolling marshals with eggs and vegetables. In particular, the enlistment of African Americans touched off heated disputes like the near riot against such recruits which shook Pittsburgh. Although there was no disturbance in Pennsylvania rivaling the New York City draft riots of 1863, a secret Irish organization in the anthracite region—the Molly Maguires —reputedly engaged in sporadic violence in part against the unequal burdens carried by the working class for the duration of the war.

In general, opposition to the draft and encouragement from the Copperheads (northern opponents of the war) did not reverse worker support for the North and free labor. The Emancipation Proclamation and the Homestead Act clarified the Republican Party's free-labor program. Working-class support for Lincoln remained strong in Pittsburgh and actually increased in Philadelphia. Nevertheless, such important labor leaders as Jonathan Fincher (Machinists and Blacksmiths) and William Sylvis (Molders), among others, advocated revitalizing unions so that workers might better protect themselves against unjust exploitation in wartime industry. In 1863, Sylvis reorganized the molders locals in Philadelphia and Pittsburgh and then left for a nationwide organizing tour. Fincher, that same year, began publish-

The rough character of extractive industries is clear in this 1863 photograph taken near Titusville. (Pennsylvania State Archives)

ing *Fincher's Trades' Review*, one of the three most important labor weeklies of the time. In Philadelphia and Pittsburgh, even the Irish moved closer to the free-labor ideology of their working-class comrades as the Fenian Brotherhood started a vocal opposition to the alliance between Britain and slavery.

The actions of the Republican administration severely tested the loyalty of men like Fincher and Sylvis. Beginning in 1863, several states passed laws limiting labor's rights after workers struck against wartime exploitation. More galling was the use of federal troops to break strikes. The most dramatic incident occurred in Tioga County where, in December 1864, mine operators determined to rid the region of the American Miners Association. Operators posted notices of a wage reduction and declared that they would no longer tolerate union interference. When miners refused to comply with these terms, a surprise raid by three hundred soldiers brought the arrest of union leaders and the eviction of some four thousand people from company housing. Household goods of miners' families were dumped in the streets of Blossburg. Operators then slashed wages by 50 percent and the state legislature legalized the action by passing the so-called Tioga County Law. Fincher wrote: "Shame. Eternal shame on the men who can be guilty of such an outrage on honest labor!" Sylvis added, "What would it profit us as a nation were we to preserve our institutions, save our constitution, and sink the masses into hopeless poverty and crime?"

The Civil War, in short, spurred an aggressive labor upsurge. In Pittsburgh, skilled iron and glass workers established a "craftsmen's empire" in which they dominated the social, cultural, and political life of the city with leaders like Thomas Armstrong who melded craft pride with the Radical Republicanism aroused by the war. In the anthracite region, John Siney's Workingmen's Benevolent Association (WBA) won concessions from the mine operators while the secretive Molly Maguires carried on clandestine warfare against the powerful Reading Railroad. In Philadelphia, Sylvis captured the tone of labor's new aggressiveness when he warned: "Let those who would trample underfoot the rights of the working people of the nation, beware!"

One of the most significant developments to emerge from the Civil War was working-class support for a labor-reform movement. Government legislation and strikebreaking during the war, at both the state and federal levels, revealed to workers the importance of government. Union leaders and the labor press called for a new political awareness by working men and women. The labor-reform movement of the postwar era, however, did not reflect the narrow or parochial perspectives of white, male artisans as in earlier times, nor was it a movement led by middle-class intellectuals. Instead, labor reform was a genuine working-class phenomenon blending both economic and political objectives. In February 1866, Sylvis, the leading trade unionist of the day, and his Philadelphia comrade Jonathan Fincher issued a call to convene a national labor federation, named later that year the National Labor Union (NLU), to respond to the new conditions of post-war industry.

The 1860s continued a long period of expansion in the United States economy. The rise of the factory system, which subdivided labor and exploited the unskilled, together with new sources of power and a tremendous swelling of the labor force in the persons of immigrants, women, and children, provided the ingredients for unprecedented growth. Although conditions appeared threatening

66

Rolling rails, 1863. Iron manufacturing expanded dramatically across the Commonwealth in the mid-nineteenth century. (Carnegie Library, Pittsburgh)

to the workers of 1870, in fact most occupations remained relatively untransformed by technology. In textiles, shoes, and garment making, to be sure, mechanical advances made a significant difference, but production still relied on manual operations which could be speeded only to a limited degree. In metal making, construction, machine building, glassmaking, and other industries central to Pennsylvania's economy, production methods and pace remained in the hands of skilled workers. Most metalworking industries, for instance, still relied on an outdated system of inside contracting in which manufacturers provided the equipment and raw materials but skilled workers controlled production and reaped a part of the profits. Such conditions prohibited a dramatic increase in productivity and the profit margins of American manufacturing either leveled off or declined, especially when a reinvigorated labor movement pushed up wages in the postwar era.

Constraints on industrial expansion hampered some segments of the workforce more than others. A new influx of women seeking employment during the Civil War outpaced the number of new jobs just as mechanization impinged on the labor markets where women were concentrated. The sewing machine and the McKay stitching machine for binding shoes squeezed female employment opportunities. Male-dominated crafts rarely provided new avenues, as unions feared that the entrance of women into a particular trade would drive down wages. Even so progressive a labor leader as Jonathan Fincher harkened instead to middle-class ideals of domesticity rather than make room for women. Fincher cautioned that workers in the army "will esteem it a poor reward for all their sacrifice, to find every [employment] avenue choked up by their wives and daughters at half paying prices." Many unionists likewise ignored the plight of women who needed decent wages to support either themselves or an entire family.

African Americans fared little better than women in postwar Pennsylvania. Following a decade of bitter race relations in the 1840s, this population leveled off in cities like Philadelphia. In the 1850s and 1860s, African Americans were increasingly segregated into poor neighborhoods and banned from better-paying jobs and men, in particular, fled the cities, leaving households headed by women. In Philadelphia's African American community there were more than seven women for every five men by 1860. Furthermore, violations of civil rights were widespread despite the recent constitutional changes for which northern soldiers had fought. In 1871, one of Philadelphia's most prominent Negro leaders, Octavius Catto, was murdered by a gang of whites. White Democratic Party mobs routinely prevented blacks from voting and their industrial opportunities continued to shrink, a trend that would not be reversed until the turn of the century. Although a small percentage of the northern workforce, African Americans remained a reserve army of labor,

Philadelphia political leader Octavius Catto, murdered in 1871. (Pennsylvania State Archives)

highly useful to employers in cracking the citadels of trade-union control.

Immigrants, unlike blacks and women, reaped some of the benefits of the last decade of prosperity before the long economic decline which began in 1873, but not all groups benefited equally. Irish-American sons gained entrance to new industries like machine building or thriving old industries like construction, while Germans, who had dominated older artisanal crafts like handloom weaving or furniture making, witnessed a decline. Still, Germans and Irish enjoyed the benefits of industrial employment. As the ratio of immigrants in Pennsylvania's workforce approached one-third, the foreign-born superseded both women when it came to better-paying factory employment and African Americans when it came to employment on the docks and in cartdriving. Yet, even as they gained a toehold, manufacturers were maneuvering to assert full control over the labor process, to strip away the remaining vestiges of craft autonomy.

Amid these developments, there were many native-born white males who wished to close ranks and maintain the craft exclusiveness of organized labor. This tendency was revealed most strikingly in the anti-Chinese movement of 1869-70. Although this movement had its greatest impact on the West Coast, it also appeared in cities like Philadelphia when some eastern manufacturers imported Chinese as strikebreakers. Fearing both deskilling mechanization and competition from cheap labor, many Philadelphia workers latched onto the anti-Chinese crusade as a racist solution to unsettling changes at their workplaces and in their communities.

Despite the unsavory aspects of craft-union culture, the labor-reform movement by and large advocated a truly radical departure. The appeal of the National Labor Union (NLU) reached far beyond the parochial interests of skilled white males. Although Pennsylvania's NLU leaders, Sylvis and Fincher, did not challenge middle-class domestic ideals or the sexual division of labor, they did argue for organizing female unions, admitting women to existing unions, paying equal wages for equal work, and they supported female suffrage as they built an alliance with Susan B. Anthony and Elizabeth Cady Stanton. The NLU also attempted to overcome the most visible forms of racism and organize black workers—nine of the 142 delegates to the 1869 NLU convention were African Americans. Moreover, the NLU contained large numbers of Irish and German unionists, and Sylvis encouraged an internationalist labor perspective by joining in the International Workingmen's Association.

Pennsylvania labor's participation in the NLU did not end racial, ethnic, and gender hostilities within the working class, but at least the leaders were on record as condemning them.

The program of the labor-reform movement matched its changing class composition. Of course, the NLU supported the Radical Republicans' campaign to ensure equality before the law for all men, but labor's demands did not stop there. Workers demanded that the political system address a growing inequality in the economic sphere. One concern focused on making the Homestead Law operative by preventing the federal government from giving land to railroads and monopolies. Taking up another concern, Pennsylvania workers, particularly in the west, joined in the clamor for a "people's currency" that would relieve the deflationary pressures of the gold standard. Such labor leaders as Sylvis and Tom Armstrong believed that a paper currency was needed to ease working-class debt. Greenbacks were also a component of the renewed working-class interest in cooperative production, advocated by such men as Philadelphia shoemaker Thomas Phillips, to enable easier credit.

No part of the NLU platform, however, galvanized Pennsylvania workers like the eight-hour workday. A genuine working-class issue with appeal for all wage earners, it became a rallying point for labor. The eight-hour movement seemingly begged for a political strategy. Trade unionists understood that female, black, and unskilled workers had little bargaining power to force the issue at the workplace. In addition, they believed that an eight-hour workday for white men was unattainable without it becoming a "legal day's work" for all. Consequently, the eight-hour campaign demanded a broad political and legislative coalition.

Amid protest from workers and reformers, the Pennsylvania General Assembly enacted a weak eight-hour law in 1868, encouraging trade unions to seek rapid enforcement. The first tests came in the anthracite region where the miners' WBA struck for the eight-hour day. Shortly thereafter building trades workers in Pittsburgh and Philadelphia followed suit. But a law without teeth had little impact on the powerful coal companies or thriving construction contractors. By the summer of 1868, union leaders like Ben Johnson of the Coachmakers realized the law was a "glaring fraud."

The coalition making up the NLU also began to unravel, in part due to issues more pressing to the agenda of radical Americans. Although Elizabeth Cady Stanton trumpeted the suffragists' participation in the 1868 NLU convention, tensions flared between trade unionists and suffragists. Stanton's associate, Susan B. Anthony, deserted the NLU and formed the Working Women's Association, which openly criticized trade unions for their exclusion of women from the crafts. Anthony then incurred the wrath of trade unionists, both male and female, by encouraging women to act as strikebreakers so that they might obtain better paying skilled trades. Meanwhile, female trade unionists, unhappy with labor's pace in including women, began organizing their own unions in the shoe, cigar, and garment industries.

Similarly, the importance of keeping civil rights before the public encouraged African American workers to form the National Colored Labor Union. Like women, blacks had difficulty obtaining entry to craft unions and access to industrial jobs more generally. Forming their own national labor congress enabled them to combat exclusion from trades as well as to support Republican Reconstruction and urge assistance for former slaves.

Meanwhile, the NLU's leader, William Sylvis, died in 1869. Sylvis had been a powerful force for labor unity. Furthermore, labor's political campaigns in several states were disastrous failures. Combined with the collapse of the eight-hour law, this series of setbacks dispersed working-class interests among aspects of the NLU's sweeping program.

Increasingly, the emergence of powerful national trade unions attracted the attention of white, male craft workers. A more parochial national craft interest supplanted the broader, but more localized, classwide perspectives for cigarmakers, molders, printers, and machinists. Workers represented by the International Typographical Union or the Cigarmakers National Union won improvements in wages and working conditions through direct negotiations with employers. The advancement of skilled workers appeared related less and less to the fates of their less fortunate sisters and brothers.

In Pennsylvania, however, the eight-hour movement and labor reform persisted through 1872. The Workingmen's Benevolent Association was a strong political force in Schuylkill and Luzerne Counties, lobbying successfully for a mine inspection act in 1869 (the original act did not prevent the horrifying "Disaster at Avondale," see Keystone Vignette, p. 78). In Scranton, Philadelphia, and Pittsburgh, political parties openly courted labor organizations, granting concessions to workers in city ordinances or political appointments. One young Scranton machinist, Terence V. Powderly, began to acquire skills as both an urban politician and labor leader. Finally, in June 1872, Philadelphia workers from several industries joined a citywide effort to obtain the eight-hour workday through trade-union methods. While few wage earners gained the shorter workday, employers acknowledged labor's growing power with wage concessions or other compromises.

Philadelphia was also the birthplace of the Noble and Holy Order of the Knights of Labor. Part fraternal order, part benevolent association, and part labor federation, the Knights would skyrocket to importance over a decade later. In 1872, the Order was little more than a Philadelphia amalgam of craft locals just beginning to spread to the anthracite region. But the Order's leaders aspired to organize all workers, regardless of skill, religion, politics, race, or gender.

The Knights had a powerful vision, one that grew out of the experiences of Pennsylvania workers nourished by participation in workingmen's parties, trade unions, labor-reform organizations, and the National Labor Union. It was also an elusive vision, attenuated by craft parochialism, political intrigues, partisan loyalties, and suspicions of new groups or new ideas. In the early 1870s, Pennsylvania wage earners were still searching for a language of class formation that would recognize both the exploitation inherent in capitalist wage labor and the potential for radicalism in a democratic society.

The Unyielding Rule of Law

When the century began, combinations of workers were considered illegal. In a series of cases through the 1830s, judges upheld the English common law doctrine of conspiracy, used successfully to impede the growth of organized labor. Still, in the first half of the century, the state was a small, unimposing force. Prosecutions for conspiracy were remarkably infrequent between 1819 and 1842 given the scale of trade-union activity. *Commonwealth v. Hunt* (1842), the famous Massachusetts case that held that labor unions were not illegal conspiracies, further diminished the legal barrier to organized labor. However, labor-capital conflict at mid-century and activist state and federal government during the Civil War returned the issue to public discourse. Pennsylvania workers asked: How, in a republic largely created and defended by workers, could the voluntary association of wage earners to improve wages and working conditions be illegal?

As the Reading Railroad prepared to rule in southern portions of the anthracite coal fields after 1868, the WBA spearheaded a drive to have the state legislature remove the legal barrier to organized labor. In 1869, the WBA obtained an act legalizing trade unions only to find that it did not protect unions from prosecution for conspiracy. Again, in 1872, the miners turned to the legislature, this time securing a law eliminating criminal penalties for striking, nearly seventy years after the prosecution of the Philadelphia shoemakers.

Unfortunately, the legalization of organized labor in Pennsylvania did not reduce government involvement in industrial disputes, nor did it help the miners avoid prosecution in their battle against the Reading. Instead, the state became an ever greater presence in labor conflict as workers struggled for the dignity and honor they felt labor deserved. Over the next quarter century the labor movement would make considerable headway toward reclaiming for workers the heritage of American republicanism.

Ken Fones-Wolf is associate professor at the Institute for Labor Studies and Research, West Virginia University. He is the author of *Trade Union Gospel: Christianity and the Labor Movement in Industrial Philadelphia, 1865-1915*, (Philadelphia: Temple University Press, 1989).

Keystone Vignette

The Battle of Clearfield Creek

Howard Harris

Although far away from the textile mills of Philadelphia or the iron furnaces of Pittsburgh, the timber raftsmen of the Allegheny Plateau experienced firsthand the power that Pennsylvania corporations had gained over the lives of working people in the years before the Civil War. A growing demand for wood led to the development of an extensive lumbering industry near Williamsport along the West Branch of the Susquehanna River by the 1830s.

Local farmers cut white pine during the winter months, moving the felled trees to the banks of local streams and rivers. The logs were squared by hand or in small, water-powered sawmills and then lashed together to form rafts. Taking advantage of high water in the spring, highly skilled six man crews navigated rafts downstream to market. According to a local newspaper nearly five hundred rafts were on the river at one time near Lock Haven alone.

Thousands of Pennsylvanians earned a living or supplemented their incomes by working as timber cutters or raftsmen.

In the mid-1840s two Maine lumbermen, John Leighton and James Perkins, joined with a number of their Williamsport counterparts to form the Susquehanna Boom Company. Their plan was to float unfinished logs downstream to a sorting pen composed of logs anchored to stone cribs with heavy chains that stretched across the entire river. Once the drive was completed, the logs would be sorted according to owner and hauled to nearby sawmills to be turned into lumber.

By 1851 three permanent booms were in place near Williamsport, Lock Haven, and on Pine Creek. Not only did the booms interfere with the passage of rafts but drivers often took logs belonging to the raftsmen. The great masses of logs floating downriver often did considerable damage to boats, rafts, and property lying along local

Rafting Pennsylvania lumber. (Carnegie Library of Pittsburgh)

rivers and creeks. As their anger at the log drives increased, local lumbermen took action. They "ironed" logs by driving metal objects below the bark which created havoc when they reached area saw-mills. Rafters also initiated petition campaigns to pressure legislators into permanently banning log drives and booms. An anti-driving bill actually passed the House and failed in the Senate by one vote late in 1852.

Subsequent attempts to eliminate log drives or place limits on the further incorporation of boom companies also failed. As the number of floating logs increased in the mid-1850s, rafters and their allies became increasingly frustrated. Public meetings in Clearfield and other communities passed resolutions and issued statements in the newspapers warning log drivers that they would be prosecuted for creating a public nuisance if they continued to use area water-ways to transport timber. An article in the *Raftsman's Journal* of May 6, 1857 reflected the feelings of many people in the region.

> Log Floating is regarded in this country in the lights of a nuisance, and many efforts have been made to have it restricted by law . . . but the Legislature has been so tardy in acting upon the bill before it that our raftsmen have been subjected to this

annoyance another season. Heretofore they have born it meekly as they could, but it seems with some "forbearance has ceased to be a virtue," and they have determined to apply a corrective measure themselves.

Local raftsmen had actually taken such action on May 1, 1857. Two armed groups headed up Clearfield Creek to prevent a reported log drive. When the drivers refused to cease operations, the anti-boomers attacked, chasing them from the woods and totally destroying their boats and equipment. Three of the defeated loggers received gunshot wounds. Soon after the confrontation warrants were sworn out against the attackers. They responded by having complaints issued against some of the loggers for blocking local waterways. In subsequent trials a small number of raftsmen and loggers received fines. Not one of the attackers served a single day in jail.

Although rafters continued to operate in the region throughout most of the nineteenth century, it was the booms and an ever-increasing number of large mills which came to dominate the timber industry of north central Pennsylvania. When conflicts between the two groups did occur, they were settled in the courts or through other legal channels rather than through direct action. As Williamsport grew into the world's largest lumber producing center, a small number of Susquehanna raftsmen carved out a niche for themselves, supplying producers with special types of timber. Although they didn't fully know it at the time, the battle that took place on Clearfield Creek in May, 1857, marked the beginning of the end of a colorful chapter in the history of the Commonwealth.

For additional information see Thomas R. Cox, "Transition in the Woods: Log Drivers, Raftsmen and the Emergence of Modern Lumbering in Pennsylvania." *The Pennsylvania Magazine of History and Biography* 104, no. 3. (July 1980): 345-364.

Keystone Vignette

Disaster at Avondale

Howard Harris

On Monday, September 6, 1869, miners at Avondale in Luzerne County were happy to be back at work; for over three months they had been on strike. The relatively new Steuben Shaft owned by the Delaware, Lackawanna, and Western Railroad had just reopened the previous Friday, and the underground workforce of 108 men began sending up coal early that Monday morning. At around 8:45 A.M., however, the head house at the top of the breaker began to fill with smoke. Fifteen minutes later, the house was so full of smoke that the engineer could not enter, but the superintendent dismissed the problem, suspecting that the underground fireman was starting up the ventilation furnace with wood. Shortly after, flames began shooting into the head and engine houses, quickly setting the entire wooden breaker afire and forcing men and boys to leap to safety.

For the men underground, there was no escape. The shaft had only one entrance; there was no fire equipment on the premises; the level of gases in the improperly ventilated shaft was so high that the fire raged for several days. Ten hours after the fire began, rescue efforts had to be halted when the first two rescuers lowered into the shaft were promptly asphyxiated. Not until September 8 (two days later) could rescue teams finally begin to remove the bodies of the 110 men who died in the most grisly coal-mining disaster that had yet occurred in America.

Popular magazines presented graphic descriptions with sketches forever etching the horrible episode into the popular memory.

Immediately, related parties looked to assign the blame. Miners' leader John Siney, President of the WBA, gave inspired speeches against the callousness of the mine operators. The state Democratic and Republican parties exchanged accusations concerning the political reasons that previous mine-safety laws were both insufficient and had exempted Luzerne County altogether. Furthermore, rumors circulated that the disaster was caused by the ongoing enmity between Irish and Welsh miners, and that the origins of the fire might be traced to the Molly Maguires, a notion that was soon dismissed. But whatever the cause, the disaster pointed to the need for improved safety measures. The miners' union appointed a committee to lobby for a new safety law in Harrisburg.

Meanwhile state senator Samuel G. Turner, the man principally responsible for ensuring that earlier mine safety laws did not apply in Luzerne County, feared that his political future would be in doubt if he did not take an active role in promoting safety legislation. Thus, but a year after he opposed safety laws, Turner engineered the passage of a law that expanded previous legislation and implemented several new points, banning children under 12 from the mines, ensuring that each mine have at least two entrances, and prohibiting the building of the breaker and engine house directly over the shaft. In other ways, however, the 1870 law provided little more safety than previous legislation. Enforcement remained a problem, standards of ventilation were still inadequate, and mine owners as well as other prominent citizens continued to blame accidents on careless miners rather than callous employers.

The Avondale disaster was nevertheless a catalyst for change in the anthracite region. Indeed, Samuel Turner lost his state senate seat. Secondly, the experiences of violence and injustice typified by such accidents perhaps contributed to a sense of lawlessness in a region where gangs and ethnic groups at times sought their own means of achieving retributive justice.

This argument would be used both for and against the "mythical qualities" of the Molly Maguires in their war with unjust mine operators. Finally, witnessing the disaster and the moving response of union leader John Siney probably inspired many young men and women to lead a life in the labor movement; Terence V. Powderly, for one, experienced a conversion to labor at just such a moment. But more than anything else, the Avondale disaster is a reminder of the terrible costs workers paid for industrial development.

For more on the Avondale Disaster see Anthony F.C. Wallace, *St. Clair.* Ithaca: Cornell University Press, 1987.

Readings for Chapter Two

Arky, Louis H. "The Mechanics' Union of Trade Associations and the Formation of the Philadelphia Workingmen's Movement." *Pennsylvania Magazine of History and Biography* 76 (1952): 142-176.

Broehl, Wayne G. *The Molly Maguires.* Cambridge: Harvard University Press, 1964.

Brown, John K. *The Baldwin Locomotive Works, 1831-1915.* Baltimore: Johns Hopkins University Press, 1995.

Cale, Edgar B. *The Organization of Labor in Philadelphia, 1850-1870.* Philadelphia, 1940.

Davis, Susan G. *Parades and Power: Street Theatre in Nineteenth-Century Philadelphia.* Philadelphia: Temple University Press, 1985.

Feldberg, Michael. *The Philadelphia Riots of 1844: A Study of Ethnic Conflict.* Westport: Greenwood Press, 1975.

Fones-Wolf, Ken. *Trade Union Gospel: Christianity and Labor in Industrial Philadelphia, 1865-1915.* Philadelphia: Temple University Press, 1989.

Grossman, Jonathan. *William Sylvis: Pioneer of American Labor.* New York: Octagon Books, 1973.

Hershberg, Theodore, ed. *Philadelphia: Work, Space, Family and Group Experience in the Nineteenth Century.* New York: Oxford University Press, 1981.

Kenny, Kevin. *Making Sense of the Molly Maguires.* New York: Oxford University Press, 1998.

Laurie, Bruce G. *Working People of Philadelphia, 1800-1850.* Philadelphia: Temple University Press, 1980.

Levine, Susan. *Labor's True Woman: Carpet Weavers, Industrialization, and Labor Reform in the Gilded Age.* Philadelphia: Temple University Press, 1984.

Licht, Walter. *Getting Work: Philadelphia, 1840-1950.* Cambridge: Harvard University Press, 1992.

Miller, Donald and Sharpless, Richard. *The Kingdom of Coal.* Philadelphia: University of Pennsylvania Press, 1985.

Montgomery, David. *Beyond Equality: Labor and the Radical Republicans, 1862-1872.* New York: Knopf, 1967.

_____. "The Shuttle and the Cross: Weavers and Artisans in the Kensington Riots of 1844." *Journal of Social History* 5 (1972):

441-466.

Palladino, Grace. *Another Civil War: Labor, Capital, and the State in the Anthracite Regions of Pennsylvania, 1840-1868.* Urbana: University of Illinois Press, 1990.

Pessen, Edward. *Most Uncommon Jacksonians: The Radical Leadership of the Early Labor Movement.* Albany: State University of New York Press, 1967.

Ricker, Ralph R. "The Greenback-Labor Movement in Pennsylvania, 1865-1880." Ph.D. dissertation, Pennsylvania State University. Bellefonte: Pennsylvania Heritage, 1966.

Schultz, Ronald. *The Republic of Labor: Philadelphia Artisans and the Politics of Class, 1720-1830.* New York: Oxford University Press, 1993.

Scranton, Philip. *Proprietary Capitalism: The Textile Manufacture at Philadelphia, 1800-1885.* New York: Cambridge University Press, 1983.

Shelton, Cynthia. *The Mills of Manayunk: Industrialization and Social Conflict in the Philadelphia Region, 1787-1837.* Baltimore: Johns Hopkins University Press, 1986.

Silcox, Harry C. *A Place to Live and Work: The Henry Disston Saw Works and the Tacony Community of Philadelphia.* University Park: Pennsylvania State University Press, 1994.

Slaughter, Thomas P. *Bloody Dawn: The Christiana Riot and Racial Violence in the Antebellum North.* New York: Oxford University Press, 1991.

Sullivan, William A. *The Industrial Worker in Pennsylvania, 1800-1840.* Harrisburg: Pennsylvania Historical and Museum Commission, 1955.

Walker, Joseph E. *Hopewell Village: The Dynamics of a Nineteenth-Century Ironmaking Community.* Philadelphia: University of Pennsylvania Press, 1966.

Wallace, Anthony F. C. *Rockdale: The Growth of an American Village in the Early Industrial Revolution.* New York: Knopf, 1978.

_____. *St. Clair: A Nineteenth-Century Coal Town's Experience With A Disaster-Prone Industry.* New York: Knopf, 1987.

Winpenny, Thomas R. *Industrial Progress and Human Welfare: The Rise of the Factory System in 19th-Century Lancaster.* Washington D.C.: University Press of America, 1982.

Chapter Three

Titanic Struggles,
1873-1916

Perry K. Blatz

O n the eve of the Civil War, Abraham Lincoln reflected on what made the North different from the South. For him, it was the North's free labor system and the seemingly bound-less opportunities that resulted. He saw such a system as enabling all men to achieve the independence derived from owning their own land or being their own boss. He stated, "If any continue through life in the condition of the hired laborer, it is not the fault of the system, but because of either a dependent nature which prefers it, or improvidence, folly, or singular misfortune." But such indepen-dence was not so easy to achieve in a rapidly changing state such as Pennsylvania where a growing proportion of the population had been working as hired laborers since the first stirrings of industrial-ization in the early nineteenth century. Following the Civil War, Lincoln's assessment became less accurate and more anachronistic. For Pennsylvanians the goal of economic independence would re-

Telephone installer, 1891. (Carnegie Library of Pittsburgh)

cede along with the largely rural life many had known.

In these years, many workers found that a traditional route to economic independence—weaving, shoemaking, or puddling iron—

provided less security. Industrial growth and technological change fed upon one another, requiring workers to perform ever more specialized and limited tasks in the manufacturing process. The skill of workers was being replaced by the design of machines. Consequently, companies preferred unskilled and semiskilled workers capable of tending those machines rather than skilled artisans with the ability to make a product from start to finish. In its eagerness to manufacture more products at the cheapest possible price, the new industrial society cared little about the worker's investment in a craft which often had been handed down from generation to generation.

From the end of the Civil War to the beginning of World War I, Pennsylvania became a "Titan of Industry" in what was, by 1900, the world's leading industrial nation. The growing number of Pennsylvanians who found themselves working for wages, especially the hundreds of thousands who immigrated from overseas, became increasingly dependent on employment by corporations that practiced an especially ruthless form of competitive capitalism. Furthermore, workers faced an economy wracked by depression from 1873 to 1878 and from 1893 to 1897, and by a series of less severe downturns. Such economic volatility robbed workers of what little security they might have achieved during more prosperous times. As industrialists like Andrew Carnegie, Henry Clay Frick, Franklin B. Gowen, Charles Schwab, Thomas A. Scott, and George Westinghouse employed ever larger numbers, workers came to realize that they could achieve little security as individuals.

But efforts by workers to organize in the workplace were met with determined opposition by employers. The men who ran Pennsylvania's rapidly growing industries did their best to avoid dealing in any way with unions, which they consistently viewed as a threat to control of their businesses and property rights. A great many strikes were fought not just over wages and working conditions, but over the recognition of workers' organizations. By refusing to recognize unions, companies sought to maintain full control of their work force. By trying to stop strikebreakers from taking their jobs, workers asserted a right in which they believed most fervently: the right to keep their jobs. Yet, American society showed no more concern for the worker's right to a job than it did for the worker's investment in a craft. In a nation founded on the inviolabil-

Iron mills were located throughout the Commonwealth—Sharon, Mercer County, 1888. (Carnegie Library of Pittsburgh)

ity of property rights, state and local authorities would give legal recognition only to the employer's right to hire whomever he chose to work on his property, not to any right of the employee to his or her job. Pennsylvania's concern for the sanctity of corporate property was reflected in laws passed in 1865 and 1866 that gave railroads, then coal mining and iron enterprises the power to commission their own police. Through most of this period, state government viewed its role as one of protecting the interests of property and leaving individuals and families to take care of themselves.

In the face of such opposition, workers often failed in their early struggles to organize. Pennsylvania witnessed a number of America's most significant labor disputes, such as the railroad strikes of 1877, the Homestead lockout of 1892, the Lattimer Massacre of 1897, and the anthracite coal strike of 1902. Some strikes resulted from lengthy organizing campaigns, but more frequently in the late nineteenth and early twentieth centuries, workers struck over grievances and turned to organized labor for help. Strikers often marshaled community support on the spur of the moment, for example, from local storekeepers who would extend credit to striking workers. Such assistance, along with the incredible ability to self-sacrifice of strikers who could barely make ends meet when working, enabled strikes to go on for weeks and sometimes months. But, as recounted here, such efforts, however courageous, could seldom defeat wealthy corporations backed by government authority.

Depression and Industrial Violence, 1873-1877

As early as the 1870s, agriculture had ceased to dominate the lives of Pennsylvanians. Some three-quarters of the state's labor force was employed outside of agriculture. Within the industry, a substantial majority remained farmers, yet tens of thousands were classified as agricultural laborers in the censuses of 1870 and 1880. Thus, even many rural workers did not own the land that might guarantee the independence that Lincoln saw as so characteristic of the American experience.

Industrial development proceeded apace not only in growing metropolises like Pittsburgh and Philadelphia, but also in many smaller communities. Especially common in Pennsylvania was the "company town." There an industrialist who located in an isolated area—generally because of the availability of raw materials—built a town to house his employees. Workers in company towns found their independence curtailed by the employer, from whom they bought the necessities of life and rented their homes. Such towns would come to dominate the experience of tens of thousands of Pennsylvania workers, most notably in the coal industry. But whether industries built a whole new town or a large plant in a city neighborhood, they dominated their surroundings and the politics, culture, and daily lives of the people who lived there.

The most common occupation for the state's male population in the 1870s was "laborer," which included more than 140,000 in 1870 and more than 230,000 ten years later, or approximately 15 percent of the work force. The leading industrial occupation was mining, followed by carpentry, work in cotton and woolen mills, and work in iron and steel mills. Other leading occupations for males in the Commonwealth included railroad work, blacksmithing, and boot and shoe manufacture, as well as clerking and sales. Among females who reported an occupation, more than half were domestic servants. Others worked as dressmakers, tailors, teachers, and cotton and woolen mill employees. By 1870, a majority of the state's teachers were women. Foreign-born workers composed about one-quarter of the state's work force, with Ireland, Germany, and England the leading countries of birth. In 1870 and 1880, of the leading industrial occupations mentioned above, mining and iron and steel work had the largest proportion of foreign-born workers. In the 1870s, 2 percent of the state's population was African American, with the majority residing in urban areas. Despite the rapidly increasing demand for industrial workers, African Americans were generally excluded from solid employment opportunities. Unfortunately, in the 1870s and for decades to come, strikebreaking provided African Americans the only consistent opportunity for industrial work. For African American men and women, the most common job was far less lucrative and often centered around domestic service, laundering, and working as cartmen and teamsters.

In the decades following the Civil War, child labor still played a substantial role in industrial life. More than 10 percent of Pennsylvanians from ten to fifteen years of age reported occupations, most notably domestic service for girls and mining for boys. Children working in the coal industry were often employed as "breaker boys," separating slate from coal above ground in the massive industrial buildings called breakers that increasingly dominated the landscape of northeastern Pennsylvania's anthracite region. The census figures for child labor should be considered as minimums, since child labor tended to be more casual than adult work and thus was less likely to be reported.

In the years immediately following the Civil War, the rampant inflation of the war years was transformed into prosperity. Workers made gains in the postwar years but struggled to retain them in the depression that began in 1873, which began with the failure of one of the nation's most famous financiers, Philadelphia's Jay Cooke. Cooke badly overextended himself by investing in western railroads. Railroads across the nation sought to avoid Cooke's fate by cutting their losses, often by laying off workers or lowering their wages. The nation's first "big business," railroads employed more than twenty thousand Pennsylvanians in the 1870s. Workers did not hesitate to protest when mammoth enterprises like the Pennsylvania Railroad announced wage cuts soon after the depression began. At the end of December 1873, several thousand engineers and firemen struck that road's lines from western Pennsylvania through the Midwest. Late in March 1874, more than one thousand workers struck the Erie Railroad's shops at Susquehanna Depot in northeastern Pennsylvania in response to that firm's failure to pay wages promptly. The strikers used a tactic that would be utilized frequently in the 1930s, occupying their employer's property. However, they left after several days when eighteen hundred state militiamen were dispatched by Governor John F. Hartranft. As commonly occurred in strikes of this era, the workers' leaders were fired and blacklisted.

Struggling to maintain their wages amidst a declining economy, workers launched similar "defensive" strikes in other industries. Beginning in the 1850s, Johnstown had risen to prominence as the home of the Cambria Iron Works, which employed six thousand workers in the company's coal mines and iron mills. That firm responded to the arrival of the depression not only by cutting wages, but by paying workers in credit at the company store rather than cash. Miners then moved to join the recently established Miners National Association (MNA). The company countered that move by resuming payment in cash and restoring part of the wage cut. However, in March 1874 the miners' agitation grew and the man who ran Cambria, Daniel J. Morrell, closed all of his operations, locking the men out. He would allow them to return to work only if they would sign a contract to stay out of any labor organization. Over the next few months, most of Cambria's workers did so, and those who stuck by the union found themselves replaced.

Some 125 miles northeast of Johnstown, the coal companies that mined beneath the company towns of Antrim, Arnot, Fallbrook, and Morris Run in Tioga County had every reason to expect a similarly favorable outcome when mine workers challenged them toward the end of 1873. Starved for cash as a result of the economic downturn, those firms "paid" their workers in credit at the company store for three months. When mine workers organized an affiliate of the MNA, the companies locked them out and evicted them just before the beginning of winter. However, the workers found allies in the nearby community of Blossburg. Merchants there had long resented the companies' refusal to let them sell their wares in the company towns. Many townspeople so sympathized with the evicted miners that they gave them lodging. During the three-month lockout, the companies had little success luring new workers to their towns and finally accepted the union.

Another group of Pennsylvania workers displayed the extraordinary solidarity needed to win a labor dispute during the depression. In the fall of 1874, iron puddlers in Pittsburgh and their union, the Sons of Vulcan, turned back an effort by the city's Association of Iron Manufacturers to reduce the negotiated wage scale that had governed their earnings since 1865. The work of the puddlers was reminiscent of the mythological god of fire for whom they named their union, as they stirred and melted pig iron in a furnace until, freed of impurities, it "came to nature," ready to be rolled and molded. When the union refused to accept the reductions, the ironmasters locked them out. Skills such as puddling were developed over many years and were practically impossible to replace, although two employers tried to bring a few African Americans from Richmond, Virginia into their mills. Strikebreaking provided the only opportunity for black puddlers to leave the South, since the Vulcans prohibited blacks from union membership. But Pittsburgh's puddlers and their union marshaled sufficient white solidarity following four months of idleness to force employers to end the lockout and maintain the old scale.

Such union successes were rare. Over the next few years, as the depression deepened, the Miners National Association would disintegrate amidst implacable corporate opposition, as would its counterpart in Pennsylvania's anthracite coal fields, the Workingmen's Benevolent Association (WBA). Founded in 1868 by John Siney, the WBA exercised considerable power for the next seven years. In 1869, it reached an agreement with a number of coal companies to set wage levels for most workers according to a "sliding scale" based on the price of coal. Two years later, it engaged employers in one of the first uses of formal arbitration in the United States. But the depression weakened the WBA, even in its stronghold in the Lehigh and Schuylkill coalfields, from southern Luzerne County through Carbon, Northumberland, and Schuylkill Counties. During the fall of 1874, companies prepared for a strike by stockpiling coal. They closed their mines on December 1, offering the WBA reductions ranging from 10 to 20 percent. The union rejected the operators' terms and the "Long Strike" commenced. By April 1875, however, most mines in the area were operating again. In mid-June the union officially abandoned the strike, lacking an agreement with the operators. Until the end of the century, unions would have little impact in the anthracite fields.

The person most responsible for driving unions out of the anthracite coal industry was the president of the Philadelphia and Reading Railroad, Franklin B. Gowen. He had formed the Philadelphia and Reading Coal and Iron Company as a subsidiary to the railroad which, like other railroad corporations in the anthracite fields, controlled the shipment of coal. The Reading dominated the industry in the Schuylkill field by the time of the "Long Strike," but Gowen played an even larger role in discouraging labor organizing. Ironically, it suited his purpose to fortify the legend of a group whose deeds have become a byword for violent action in the cause of the oppressed, the "Molly Maguires."

When more than a million Irish immigrants came to the United States to escape the potato famine from 1846-1854, they brought with them the tradition of meting out revenge secretly to their foes who, in Ireland, had been landowners who had wrung exorbitant rents from an impoverished people. In industrializing America, the foes were bosses and workers of English and Welsh ethnicity, who generally held places higher in the industrial hierarchy than the Irish. The events that have made the Mollies so prominent in the history of Pennsylvania began during the Civil War.

Many Irishmen had little sympathy for the North's effort to forcibly return the Confederate states to the Union. During the war, a mine superintendent and a mine foreman were murdered in Schuylkill County after they had confronted Irish opponents of the draft. In the years following the war, several other superintendents were murdered, but no one could be charged with the crimes.

In the 1870s, others were murdered including a foreman, a mine paymaster, one of Tamaqua's two policemen, and several miners who had had assorted run-ins with Irish miners. In the 1870s, Franklin B. Gowen, who had served for two years as district attorney of Schuylkill County during the war, enlisted the help of the Pinkerton Detective Agency along with his firm's Coal and Iron Police to uncover the roots of what he viewed as a lawless reign of terror. Toward the end of 1873, the Pinkertons sent an agent to infiltrate the Irish groups that Gowen suspected were responsible. That agent, James McParlan, would provide the testimony that led to the conviction and hanging of twenty men between June 1877 and December 1878. While some of the Mollies later convicted of murder had also apparently plotted a variety of crimes against property, few had ever occurred. The crimes of the Molly Maguires were as much rooted in ethnic differences and personal slights as they were class-conscious action against bosses. A number of those convicted were tavern owners—not mine workers—and, of course, the guilt of some of the Mollies has long been questioned. Most important, while several of these crimes did occur in the same years that the WBA was expanding, and while a number of the accused had shown sympathy for the union, no links can be made between the murders and the WBA. However, in numerous public statements, Gowen made the connection and impressed it upon the minds of Pennsylvanians. In his view, at least, unions were synonymous with violence.

The hanging of ten Mollies at Pottsville and Mauch Chunk on June 21, 1877—the infamous "Day of the Rope"—took place less than a month before the beginning of the railroad strikes of 1877. Those strikes unleashed the most widespread labor turmoil in American history, with walkouts, protests, injuries, and deaths occurring from Pennsylvania, New York, and Maryland west to Chicago, St. Louis, and even San Francisco. But no state experienced more violence than Pennsylvania.

On June 1, the nation's largest corporation, the Pennsylvania Railroad, put into effect a 10 percent wage reduction on top of 20 percent in cuts since the beginning of the depression. In the next few weeks, other railroads did the same. On June 2, a group of workers met in Allegheny City, now Pittsburgh's North Side, to form the Trainmen's Union, an organization to include all railroad workers. The union experienced surprising growth, especially since management had fired a number of its members. One member visited Martinsburg, West Virginia to organize. The men responded by walking out on Monday, July 16 when the Baltimore and Ohio Railroad put its 10 percent cut into effect. A militiaman who turned a switch to enable a train to depart a freight yard was shot by a striker on Tuesday, prompting the governor of West Virginia to ask President Rutherford B. Hayes for federal troops. The strike came to Pittsburgh on Thursday, July 19. Robert Pitcairn, boyhood friend of Andrew Carnegie and his successor as superintendent of the western division of the Pennsylvania Railroad, did what many other rail managers had done during the depression. To save money, he ordered all eastbound freight trains to go out as "double-headers," as westbound trains had been doing for some time. With two engines pulling twice the usual number of cars over the mountains, some brakemen would be laid off, while others would face the increased risk of handling twice as many cars in one of railroading's most dangerous jobs. Workers refused to run the trains.

Few Pittsburghers had much love for the Pennsylvania Railroad, whether or not they worked for it. Along the tracks crowds gathered at switches to make sure no freights would leave the city. On Friday, railroad officials called on Allegheny County Sheriff Robert H. Fife to restore order or request troops from the state. Receiving a hostile reception wherever he told the crowds to go home, Fife signed a request for troops prepared by a company lawyer. The adjutant general approved the request for Governor Hartranft, who just that week had begun a tour of the West on a railroad car provided by none other than Pennsylvania Railroad President Thomas A. Scott. Pittsburghers had plenty of reason to doubt the impartiality of state officials, just as those officials and representatives of the railroad had every reason to doubt whether militia based in Pittsburgh would move against their neighbors to protect the railroad's property. While calling out local regiments on Friday evening, state officials worked with the railroad to obtain a special train to bring more militiamen from Philadelphia.

As the Philadelphia troops traveled from the east, their train was stoned in Harrisburg, Johnstown, and Altoona. When they arrived at Pittsburgh's Union Depot on Saturday afternoon, July 21, hundreds of rail cars were stranded due to the strike. At the urging of rail officials, the troops moved to clear the crowds from the tracks so double-headers could leave the city. The Philadelphians in particular drew the taunts of the crowd, now numbering several thousand, and those taunts were soon accompanied by rocks, bricks,

93

and bottles as the troops moved into defensive formation at approximately 5 P.M. No one knows who fired the first shot, but the Philadelphia regiment soon peppered the crowd with bullets, killing at least ten and wounding twice as many or more.

This carnage was the opening act in a horrifying drama that showed just how much ordinary Pennsylvanians felt threatened by the economic and political power of the state's major railroad. Thousands of Pittsburghers gathered outside railroad buildings into which the troops—fifteen of whom had been wounded—had retreated after they fired into the crowd. Intent on revenge, later that evening some in the crowd ignited freight cars filled with oil and coal and pushed them down the grade along the Allegheny River toward the besieged troops. When several railroad buildings were ablaze, the Philadelphia troops fired occasionally to hold the crowd at bay. Some in the crowd helped to spread the fires while others prevented the small city fire department from saving railroad property. Still others began to loot freight cars and nearby warehouses and businesses. Amidst this chaos on Sunday morning the militiamen evacuated their burning bivouac to march to the safe haven of Sharpsburg across the Allegheny.

Word of the carnage and inferno reached Governor Hartranft in Utah on Saturday night. He hurried east and requested federal troops from President Hayes. On Tuesday evening, July 24, the governor reached Allegheny City, where he stopped to meet with several state officials. The violence had not spread across the Allegheny from Pittsburgh, as members of the Trainmen's Union had helped maintain order and had even directed train operations there for a time. At the station, a large crowd of strikers called on Hartranft to speak. Addressing them briefly, the governor stated how much he regretted the recent lawlessness and destruction across the river and expressed his confidence that the strikers deplored it too. He further complimented them on their role in protecting railroad property.

As violence abated in Pittsburgh, it erupted elsewhere in the state. On Sunday and Monday, as the entire state militia tried to deploy throughout the Commonwealth, units were delayed or halted at Columbia, Altoona, Meadville, and Harrisburg. Reading, headquarters of Gowen's railroad, experienced violence that rivaled

Ruins of the Pennsylvania Railroad roundhouse—Pittsburgh, 1877.
(Carnegie Library of Pittsburgh)

Pittsburgh's. Just three months before, Gowen had turned back a brief strike by the strongest railroad union, the Brotherhood of Locomotive Engineers. Reading workers were showing increasing interest in the Trainmen's Union, especially since cash-flow problems had caused the railroad to fall behind in paying them. The Reading did not pay for May until Saturday, July 21, and apparently that grievance, when coupled with the news from Pittsburgh, induced some townspeople to act. On Sunday evening, a crowd tore up some track and set fire to the railroad's bridge across the Schuylkill River. On Monday, crowds stopped one train and tried to stop another, and that evening, they faced a militia unit sent from Easton to restore order. Events paralleled those in Pittsburgh just forty-eight hours before, as some in the crowd threw rocks and even fired shots, wounding many of the militiamen. The soldiers opened fire indiscriminately, killing six and wounding more than twenty, including several police struggling vainly to keep order. The tumult in Reading ended on Tuesday, July 24, with the arrival of federal troops.

Some brief disorder had occurred in Philadelphia on Sunday,

but that had been halted by the vigorous action of Mayor William S. Stokley at the head of his police force, much larger than Pittsburgh's. The arrival of federal troops the next day insured order. Still, Philadelphia was one of several cities in which the Workingmen's Party of the United States, the nation's most prominent socialist organization, struggled to exert some influence despite its small membership. The news from Pittsburgh offered an opportunity for organizing, and the Workingmen's Party planned a series of mass meetings in Philadelphia for the following week. But Stokley, a businessman sympathetic to the railroads, ordered his police to break up the meetings, which they did with brutal efficiency. On Wednesday the twenty-fifth, Governor Hartranft arrived in Philadelphia and conferred with General Winfield Scott Hancock, commander of federal forces and hero of the Battle of Gettysburg some fourteen summers before. On the next day, the governor left Philadelphia by rail with a force of militia, followed by another force of federal troops. By the weekend those units had crossed the state, made sure the Pennsylvania Railroad's main line was clear, and camped in Pittsburgh.

The last eruption of violence occurred in Scranton. Although striking railroad workers set it off, it also involved anthracite mine workers who, throughout the depression, had faced severe underemployment. When workers struck the Delaware, Lackawanna, and Western Railroad on Tuesday, July 24, they were joined by mill workers of the Lackawanna Iron and Coal Company and railroad workers from the Delaware and Hudson Company. All sought to restore cuts they had received earlier in the depression. Mine workers employed by the railroads, who owned large amounts of coal land like the Reading, walked out beginning on July 26th, and their strike spread across the entire Wyoming or northern region of the anthracite fields, from south of Wilkes-Barre to north of Scranton. The railroaders gave up their walkout within a few days, but the mine workers stayed out. In Scranton on August 1, a crowd of strikers moved to close down the railroad shops and, in the ensuing confrontation, Mayor Robert H. McKune was injured. Then the hastily organized "Scranton Citizens' Corps," led by William W. Scranton, superintendent of the Iron and Coal Company and son of one of the town's founders, fired on the strikers, killing six and wounding more than fifty. This brought state and federal troops, but the mine workers remained on strike. To force a settlement, they resorted to the unusually militant tactic of barring pump runners, firemen, and other maintenance workers from performing their duties, essential to preserving the mines. However, the companies were able to carry on these tasks with supervisors, and this strike ended in defeat in October.

Few workers won tangible gains from the strikes of 1877. Mine workers and iron and steel workers in cities across the state had struck along with the railroad workers, but one group after another returned to work if they retained their jobs at all. Not surprisingly, one institution that had considerable success in protecting itself from loss was the Pennsylvania Railroad. Through legal maneuvering, it avoided liability for freight that had been destroyed and made Allegheny County responsible for approximately $1.5 million in company property destroyed by riots. The county paid the railroad through a bond issue that would not be retired until 1906.

But dollars and cents gained and lost tell us little about the strikes of 1877. For a time it seemed that the nation was on the brink of revolution. At no time before or since was such a revolution as likely. While strikes and violence between labor and capital would occur in succeeding decades, nothing would rival the scope, spontaneity, and violence of these strikes.

Pragmatism or Solidarity? 1878-1886

To assess and provide information regarding work, wages, and industrial conditions, the Commonwealth established the Bureau of Industrial Statistics in 1872. Hampered by insufficient appropriations and suspicious employers reluctant to provide data, the bureau surveyed workers by sending them questionnaires. The data they furnished falls far short of a comprehensive statistical portrait. Only a little more than one hundred workers were surveyed annually, and it is likely that those who responded were better educated than the average worker and had a better income. Still, the information offers a useful glimpse of wages at a time when a family of five required $600 to maintain a decent standard of living in urban areas and somewhat less rural areas. Skilled workers did reasonably well, with surveys revealing average earnings of approximately $700 for iron puddlers, $600 for carpenters, and a little over $500 for miners.

These averages hide many interesting details. A coal miner surveyed in 1882 earned only $451.20, but the other nine members of his family earned a total of $1,026, giving the family the substantial income of nearly $1,500. Of course, quite a few miners earning $450 or less reported no additional income. Most of those surveyed were skilled workers, but figures for laborers give some sense of the struggles faced by the less skilled. A forty-six-year-old laborer from Huntingdon County reported an income of only $240 in 1882, while a thirty-six-year-old Northumberland County laborer earned only $312. A laborer from Fayette County reported $450 in earnings which was supplemented by $855 in additional income from his wife and six children. More than a quarter of the families surveyed had income in addition to the father's which often provided the necessary margin for survival. Unskilled and semi-skilled workers would become an ever-larger proportion of Pennsylvania's work force in the closing decades of the nineteenth century. These workers could only obtain a secure income by sending their children or wives to work in tedious, low-paying jobs.

The insecurities faced by American workers led many to join the first nationwide labor organization with a mass following—the Noble and Holy Order of the Knights of Labor. Founded at the end of 1869 by a handful of Philadelphia garment cutters, the Knights offered a vision that transcended boundaries of race, sex, occupation, and skill. It would grow in the early 1880s until, in 1886, it had reached almost three-quarters of a million members.

The Knights viewed the increase in hired laborers throughout American society just as negatively as had Abraham Lincoln, and they railed against the demoralizing dependence fostered by the wage system. Still, their vision was not one of violent revolution. They advocated cautious cooperation and unity among workers. Especially under their first leader or "Grand Master Workman," Uriah S. Stephens, the Knights maintained secrecy. They gradually expanded beyond Philadelphia to the rest of the state during the depression of the 1870s. Groups of locals formed district assemblies in Reading, Scranton, and Pittsburgh by 1875. While workers in a wide variety of trades formed Knights' locals, coal miners and railroad workers in particular joined the organization. At the Knights' first national meeting or General Assembly in January 1878, approximately two-thirds of the delegates were from Pennsylvania.

Though pioneering in its inclusiveness, the Knights recognized craft divisions. Indeed, most locals were organized by craft. Yet, in the 1870s, the Knights did not see themselves as competing with craft organizations. Workers, eager to achieve more comprehensive organization, joined both the Knights and a union of their craft. Only a few national craft unions survived the depression. Perhaps the most important for Pennsylvania was the Sons of Vulcan, who joined with other crafts in the iron industry in 1876 to form the Amalgamated Association of Iron and Steel Workers (AAISW).

Fully cognizant of how difficult it was to win a strike, the Knights and other labor groups looked to mobilize workers outside the workplace. They encouraged cooperative stores for workers and manufacturing and mining cooperatives and, for several years, operated a mine in Ohio. While these efforts experienced little success, they show the Knights' interest in finding alternatives to working for wages. More important to the Knights was political action. After the strikes of 1877 had been suppressed, a great many Pennsylvania workers expressed their frustration with the Democratic and Republican Parties. Along with a number of the Knights' leaders, they joined with the recently organized Greenback Party to form the Greenback-Labor Party. The Greenbacks blamed the depression on the federal government's decision to retire the greenback or paper money used to finance the Civil War and replace it with a currency convertible to gold. With the infusion of worker support in the fall of 1877, the Greenback-Labor Party became a formidable third party for the next two years, especially in its strongholds of Pittsburgh and Scranton. In the fall elections of 1877, the party received nearly 10 percent of the vote statewide and more than 20 percent in Allegheny and Luzerne Counties, with stronger showings in steel and coal towns. The party built on this strength in 1878, obtaining more than 10 percent of the state vote. Its totals exceeded 30 percent in the anthracite mining counties, and the party reached similar levels in several northern counties where bituminous coal and oil dominated the economy. Yet, despite this promising beginning, the Greenback-Labor Party declined rapidly thereafter, winning less than 5 percent of the state's vote in 1880 and 1882.

Most workers who had abandoned the Republicans and Democrats returned as the economy emerged from depression after 1878.

Under the leadership of Pennsylvanian Terence V. Powderly (see Keystone Vignette: "Terence V. Powderly, p. 149), who became Grand Master Workman in 1879, the Knights of Labor took advantage of the improving economy. Powderly gradually succeeded in persuading his fellow Knights to curtail the secrecy and quasi-religious ritual which had characterized the order in its first decade. These features had made organizing very difficult and roused the suspicions of most Catholic clergymen against the Knights which was damaging since more and more of Pennsylvania's work force consisted of Catholic immigrants. With the decline of secrecy in 1882, the Knights began a slow and steady growth, reaching one hundred thousand members nationwide by 1885.

The growth of the Knights in the early 1880s contrasted with efforts by craft unions to form a national federation. The American Federation of Labor (AFL) dates its birth to a gathering in Pittsburgh in November 1881. There 107 delegates from craft unions and groups affiliated with the Knights founded the AFL's predecessor, the Federation of Organized Trades and Labor Unions. However, until December 1886, when this group reorganized as the AFL, it did little more than hold annual meetings. Through the 1880s, the Knights and trade unions philosophically differed—the first becoming more inclusive and the second focusing more narrowly on the needs of members, primarily through collective bargaining with employers. The basic difference was that the Knights challenged the wage system, however meekly, and saw an all-inclusive organization as crucial to that challenge, while the trade unions limited themselves to mobilizing their members to demand a better deal from the wage system.

One reason for the uncertainty of labor leaders as to how to organize workers was the hostility of the state judiciary toward organizing. Until the 1840s American courts viewed organizing efforts as illegal conspiracies. Gradually they accepted the idea that labor unions were not conspiracies in and of themselves. Yet, employers usually succeeded in persuading judges that any action by a union beyond enrolling members—encouraging a strike, discouraging strikebreakers from replacing strikers, or telling workers to disregard contracts in which they had promised to avoid unions—still constituted conspiracy against their property rights. In 1875, organizer Xingo Parks of the Miners National Association received a sentence of one year in state prison for persuading strikebreakers in a Clearfield County walkout to return to their homes. The judge in the case agreed that workers had the right to withhold their labor, but he said that concerted action to hinder others from working constituted an illegal conspiracy. Fortunately for Parks, the labor movement was not without some influence—Governor Hartranft pardoned him two months into his sentence.

Unions successfully lobbied the state legislature to enact a law in 1876 to permit peaceful efforts to maintain a strike. However, the courts interpreted this law narrowly and prosecutions continued to hinder organizing through the 1880s. The lengths to which the Commonwealth would go to limit support for a strike are best shown in the conviction of mining organizer David R. Jones and fifteen others who, in November 1880, attempted to persuade the workers of the Waverly Coal Company in Westmoreland County to join a strike which had begun several weeks before at area mines. Among the owners of the firm was Judge Thomas Mellon, patriarch of what was fast becoming one of nation's largest fortunes in banking and industry. The Waverly workers' contracts required that they give sixty days notice before any strike or lose 10 percent of their annual wages, but Jones told the workers that the local Miners' Association, affiliated with the Knights of Labor, would compensate them for the loss. Before the workers could walk out, Jones and his associates were arrested. For their alleged offenses against property, Jones and his associates received a far lighter sentence than Parks—one day in jail and court costs and fines, which were paid by the union. Ironically, the workers at Waverly did strike one year later after giving the required notice and refusing to sign new contracts, but their employer broke that strike in two months by bringing in immigrant strikebreakers.

The rising entrepreneur Andrew Carnegie also used "ironclad" contracts to try to keep his workers from joining the Amalgamated Association of Iron and Steel Workers. In 1875, Carnegie opened the J. Edgar Thomson Works on the Monongahela River in Braddock to refine pig iron by the recently developed Bessemer process which

Producing Bessemer steel at the Pennsylvania Steel Company in Steelton, Dauphin County c. 1895. Refined in the pear-shaped Bessemer converter, molten steel would be poured into the vessel below. (Hagley Museum and Libary)

refined iron through a series of chemical reactions spurred on by blasting cold air through the massive Bessemer converters which held the metal. The product of that transformation, steel, was not only more malleable than the puddler's product of wrought iron, it could be produced in much larger batches by workers far less skilled than the puddlers. The use of anti-union contracts spread along with the Bessemer process throughout the Monongahela Valley. Manufacturers found it much easier to dispense with the AAISW in their new mills, which increasingly could be operated by unskilled workers. The Pittsburgh Bessemer Steel Works at Homestead demanded an ironclad contract from its workers soon after that plant opened in February 1881. But in Homestead, after a strike of three months in the following year, the result was different. Community solidarity made victory possible, as unskilled members of the Knights of Labor united with the skilled workers of the AAISW, and townspeople made sure that strikebreakers were not welcome.

That success was the only one for organized labor in the mines and mills of western Pennsylvania in 1882. Some eighteen hundred members of the Miners' Association west of Pittsburgh left their jobs that spring over management's demands for a wage reduction. The four-and-a-half-month strike was gradually broken, as coal operators replaced workers with hundreds of African Americans and European immigrants. In the iron mills, some twenty-two thousand workers from Pittsburgh to Erie had no more luck in their attempt to secure an advance in their wage scale. The AAISW struck on June 1, but by September disharmony among the various occupations of the union led to a settlement at the old rates.

Philadelphia had a very different mix of industries than Pittsburgh and the Monongahela Valley. By the 1880s, Philadelphia had some sixty thousand workers in the textile industry, over 60 percent of whom were women and children. These textile workers were split into numerous lines of work carried out at hundreds of factories. A great many strikes had occurred in the 1870s over rates of pay. But these were generally settled quickly, since workers had little formal organization and walkouts seldom extended beyond a few factories. However, management demands for wage reductions prompted resistance in 1884, particularly in carpet mills in the Kensington district. One walkout lasted nearly the entire summer of 1884, and another lasted from August 1884 until February 1885. While both of these disputes were settled by compromise, the key element in their length was the bitterness of employers over the workers' decision to join the Knights of Labor.

From summer 1884 to spring 1886, the Knights experienced

electrifying growth across the nation from approximately a hundred thousand to seven hundred thousand members. This resulted from an improving economy, the Knights' willingness to enroll practically any worker of any occupation, and surprising victories in four railroad strikes in the Midwest and Southwest. But the Knights' national headquarters lacked the resources and the militant spirit needed to manage this success. In March 1886, overwhelmed by the thousands of workers clamoring to join, Terence Powderly suspended organizing for forty days and vigorously condemned a growing strike wave.

The Knights' growth occurred at approximately the same time as another element of the "Great Upheaval" of 1886. The Federation of Organized Trades and Labor Unions, at one of its least well-attended meetings in October 1884, had called for a mass movement of American workers on May 1, 1886 to achieve an eight-hour day. Craft unions, however, were quite weak, and Powderly had no interest in supporting their effort. Thus, only a few thousand workers in Philadelphia and Pittsburgh joined the strike for the eight-hour day.

Still, more than twice as many strikes and lockouts occurred in the state that year as in any of the decade's previous years. Overall, Pennsylvania had ninety-five thousand members of the Knights when the organization was at its peak, second only to New York. More than fifty thousand, half of them textile workers, belonged to Knights District Assembly 1, which governed workers in some seventy trades in and around Philadelphia. In February and March 1886, textile workers won gains in disputes at mills making curtains, carpets, upholstery, and woolens. These successes spurred employers to organize the Philadelphia Manufacturers Association in May. Meanwhile, the Knights became less militant as their leaders tried to take control of the ongoing wave of walkouts. District Assembly 1 had responded to Powderly's attempt in March to discourage strikes by prohibiting any walkout it did not sanction. But textile workers continued to strike, increasingly over workplace control issues like hiring, firing, and union membership that tended to be even more bitter than wage disputes. In September, ninety weavers struck at the Wingohocking mills in Philadelphia's Frankford district, claiming that their boss had failed to comply with an agreement to hire

104

only Knights. That dispute expanded during the next few weeks, as the mills tried to operate with strikebreakers, workers called sympathy strikes at nearby mills, and mill owners threatened a lockout throughout the city. National leaders Powderly and John Hayes, frightened by this threat, came to Philadelphia and, without consulting local workers, ordered the Wingohocking weavers to call off their strike, even though their employer refused to rehire most of them. Workers found that they could not count on the Knights and by mid-1887 membership in District Assembly 1 had declined by 80 percent.

Many workers, especially the unskilled, would abandon unionism altogether as the Knights collapsed in the next few years. Others would find a new home in craft unions. The chaotic growth of the Knights in 1886 had caused one battle after another over the organization of workers. That rivalry culminated in the formation of the American Federation of Labor in December 1886. The policy of craft unions and the AFL was more pragmatic but far more restrictive than that of the Knights. Workers' first loyalty would be to their craft union and its own success. Organizing would concentrate on skilled workers, thus tending to exclude the growing numbers of women, African Americans, and eastern and southern European immigrants in the work force. In the next thirty years, the AFL would provide a core around which more and more workers could demand a better deal from the wage system. But its restrictive philosophy, regardless of the pragmatism at its roots, would keep the promise of unionism from a great many Pennsylvanians.

Coal, Steel, and Class War, 1887-1892

Coal fueled the industrial transformation of the United States in the nineteenth century. Steel, made in part from coal, provided, the foundation for the transformation. The United States assumed world leadership in the production of coal from Great Britain in 1902. In steel production, the United States became the world leader in 1886, and by 1901 it exceeded the combined production of Germany and Great Britain. In terms of employment, coal mining was Pennsylvania's leading industry by a substantial margin. In 1900, almost 10 percent of males in the work force were employed in anthracite and bituminous coal mines. The iron and steel industry employed less than half that much or a slightly smaller number than the textile and railroad industries. Pennsylvania was the nation's leading producer of coal and steel for decades and would retain that leadership for most of the twentieth century. Although its dominance slowly began to slide by the end of the First World War, Pennsylvania still produced more than 40 percent of the nation's iron and steel, about one-third of its bituminous coal, and practically all of its anthracite. The state also led in the production of coke, obtained by cooking bituminous coal. Soon after the Civil War, coke replaced anthracite as the most effective fuel for smelting iron ore into iron and steel.

These industries set two important trends for the work force. First, coal, steel, and coke had a large proportion of immigrant workers, reflecting not only the steady increases in immigration to the United States in the 1880s and 1890s, but also the fact that immigrants, many of whom were from eastern and southern Europe, had little choice but to take the dirtiest and most dangerous work. In 1900, almost 60 percent of the mining work force had been born overseas, giving the industry the highest proportion of foreign-born of any in the state and making it the only major occupation in the state where the foreign-born formed a majority. By the middle of the 1880s, about one-third of the work force in the coke industry was Hungarian, Polish, Slovak, or Czech. About 30 percent of iron and steel workers in 1900 had been born overseas, a figure among the highest in Pennsylvania industries. Second, coal, steel, and coke continued the trend toward contentious labor relations and labor conflict, as they had since the end of the Civil War. But while many of Pennsylvania's coal miners would become effectively organized in the 1890s and early 1900s under the United Mine Workers of America (UMWA), organization in the coke industry and in steel would ebb, especially in the wake of the bitter labor dispute at Homestead in 1892.

Steel's demand for coke transformed Westmoreland and Fayette Counties, whose forests and farmland covered a massive field of the world's finest coking coal. The biggest coke proprietor was Henry Clay Frick, whose dominance in that industry was recognized by Andrew Carnegie in 1882 when he began to buy large amounts of stock in the Henry C. Frick Coke Company. Frick's interests grew especially profitable during the 1880s, as he and his fellow producers cooperated in restricting production, supporting prices, and apportioning among themselves the market for coke. Carnegie soon owned most of Frick's company, and Frick had become immensely wealthy. To cement their relationship, Carnegie gave Frick an interest in his steel firm early in 1887.

Coal mining was hard, dangerous work, but in some ways it was preferable to the intense heat and foul smoke a worker encountered tending coke ovens. Whether employed above or below ground, workers in rural southwestern Pennsylvania's coke industry generally lived in company towns. In January 1886, workers sought a wage increase. Immigrants vigorously supported the ensuing strike and joined a new union, the Miners and Laborers Amalgamated Association (MLAA). Violent clashes with sheriff's deputies took place, as strikers marched from mine to mine to induce those who had not walked out to join the strike. After a month's idleness, employers granted an advance. This success caused the MLAA to try to perfect its organization, often bringing it into conflict with the Knights of Labor, which had enrolled a number of native-born workers in the area. As the price of coke increased and the profits of the operators swelled in 1887, the unions called for an additional advance larger than the operators were willing to offer. Both parties agreed to settle the issue before an arbitration board but, when that board decided in May against any increase, the unions could not keep disappointed workers at their jobs. The employers, with Frick in the lead, maintained a united front and appeared to be winning the walkout. But in June, Frick was forced by Carnegie to offer an advance to his striking workers to prevent Carnegie's mills from shutting down due to a lack of coal. This led Frick to resign as president of his coke company, only to return several months later at Carnegie's urging.

On the opposite side of the state, both the MLAA and the Knights experienced defeat in a walkout by mine workers and railroad men in the southern and middle anthracite fields from the fall of 1887 to the spring of 1888. But in the coke region, those workers not employed by Frick were eventually able to obtain an increase similar to the one Frick had granted so reluctantly. By 1891, Frick and his fellow employers united to resist workers' demands for a further advance, causing a walkout of some sixteen thousand. The dispute developed in a familiar way, as strikers tried to force workers who remained on the job to join the strike, while companies turned to local authorities to protect their operations. As more plants opened for work, the level of violence increased. On March 30, more than one thousand strikers coordinated an attack on Frick's Morewood coke works near Mount Pleasant. Sheriff's deputies protecting the property fled and considerable damage was inflicted. The Westmoreland County sheriff requested state militia from Governor Robert E. Pattison who responded that local resources for keeping order had to be exhausted first. On the same day, a crowd of immigrant women drove strikebreakers away from the coke ovens at Leith in Fayette County, injuring several. Early on the morning of April 1, a crowd of eight hundred moved on Morewood again. Both the deputies and the strikers claimed they did not fire the first shot, but when the smoke cleared, seven strikers had been killed by the deputies. This event convinced Governor Pattison to send state troops. Additional violence occurred as the coke operators took advantage of their position as landlords in the company towns to evict strikers. By the end of May the strike had collapsed completely. Some two thousand had been evicted. The deputies charged with shooting the strikers were acquitted.

Henry Clay Frick had shown his antagonism toward labor unions long before he provoked a violent confrontation at Homestead in July 1892. Andrew Carnegie struggled for years to keep the Amalgamated Association of Iron and Steel Workers (AAISW) out of his mills, despite occasional statements in his voluminous writings supporting the right of workers to join unions. Although many workers at the Edgar Thomson works had been forced to accept ironclad antiunion contracts in the 1870s, the AAISW and the Knights had made inroads there early in the 1880s. Eager to cut costs, Carnegie had taken every opportunity to replace skilled workers as new equipment was installed, and he had long wanted to get rid of more workers by eliminating the eight-hour day. In December 1887, Carnegie locked out workers, offering them lower wages, a twelve-hour day, and an ironclad contract as conditions for their return. After more than four months of idleness, he arranged for skilled workers to vote for one of two unpalatable choices—significantly reduced wages with the eight-hour day or a twelve-hour day and somewhat better wages tied to the price of steel according to a sliding scale. Eager to return to work, the men chose the latter and the ironclad contracts that went with it.

Carnegie planned a similar strategy to eradicate unionism in Homestead in 1889, before he went off to Scotland for his annual visit to his homeland. But most of Homestead's workers were loyal unionists. The AAISW there had even enrolled some unskilled immigrant workers, Slovaks in particular, despite questions from the national union as to their eligibility. Other unskilled men belonged to the Knights of Labor, and in Homestead the Knights and the AAISW worked closely together, as opposed to the bickering which generally characterized their relations. Consequently, workers were determined to resist the company's terms—a sliding scale that would reduce wages for many, a twelve-hour day where it was not in force, and an end to unionism in Homestead. Without agreement on a contract, the works shut down on July 1. On July 10 the company sent thirty-one strikebreakers into town by train, escorted by the sheriff, but a crowd of almost two thousand stopped them, assaulting several. Two days later, the sheriff returned to deploy some 125 deputies but, facing an even larger crowd, nearly all of them decided to return to Pittsburgh. The Carnegie executive in charge, William Abbott, fearing further violence and the possibility of sympathetic strikes at Carnegie's other plants, negotiated a three-year agreement with the AAISW that resulted in wage cuts for skilled workers and a sliding scale. Elsewhere in the state, the AAISW fared even worse. In July 1891, rolling mills in Reading, Norristown, Harrisburg, Pottsville, Scranton, and Catasauqua refused to recognize the union any longer. The resulting strikes ended in failure.

With the contract at Homestead due to expire on June 30, 1892, Carnegie placed Frick in charge of negotiations to prevent another compromise like 1889 and then left for Scotland. Noting recent price declines in steel, Frick demanded substantial reductions for many skilled workers by lowering the floor to which the sliding scale could fall and insisting that any new contract expire, not at the end of June as contracts traditionally had, but at the end of December. Both the union and the company understood that a strike in winter presented special perils for workers. At the end of May, Frick made it clear that if the AAISW did not accept the company's terms by June 24, the company would impose its terms and no longer deal with the union. To emphasize his point, Frick then ordered the construction of a massive fence around the plant with barbed wire and lookout towers, which locals dubbed "Fort Frick." It became increasingly clear to the people of Homestead that the company's goal was to destroy the union.

On June 28, the company locked out most of its skilled workers, and in response the AAISW held a meeting of all workers, who agreed to strike. Union leaders and the town's officials, some of whom were the same individuals, mobilized the populace to watch for strikebreakers. On June 25, Frick requested three hundred armed guards from the Pinkerton Detective Agency as security at the plant. The Pinkertons received five dollars a day and agreed to wear the company's uniform. While the Pinkertons traveled toward Pittsburgh, on July 5 the sheriff of Allegheny County, William McCleary, came to Homestead with twelve deputies and warned union officials of his duty to protect company property. That night the Pinkertons began their journey in two roofed barges, towed by tugboats, from west of Pittsburgh on the Ohio River through the city, where union men spotted them and telegraphed a warning to Homestead.

In the early hours of July 6th, the barges proceeded up the Monongahela to Homestead, now towed by a single tug. When they arrived they faced several thousand men, women, and children, arrayed along the river bank to prevent entrance into the plant. The crowd ignored the warnings of the AAISW not to trespass on company property. Union official Hugh O'Donnell called for the Pinkertons to leave. Their commander expressed his determination to enter the plant. As is so common in the history of labor violence, it is unclear who fired the first shot. But, when the Pinkertons tried to come ashore near daybreak, a scuffle ensued and gunfire broke out. Several steelworkers were killed and a Pinkerton captain was wounded. Of nine wounded workers, six were eastern Europeans. Four more steelworkers were killed in another exchange of fire later in the morning, after which the tug evacuated six wounded Pinkertons across the river.

Such carnage made any kind of compromise or disengagement

impossible. When the tug returned to remove the barges from the landing, it was driven away by a barrage from the shore. The enraged crowd, growing larger throughout the day as steelworkers from nearby towns marched to Homestead to join in its defense, tried to set the barges afire. Meanwhile, as the events at Homestead became clear to Sheriff McCleary he telegraphed Harrisburg to request state militia from Governor Pattison. The governor declined the sheriff's request, suggesting that he deputize large numbers of citizens to restore order.

The crowd was not about to disperse nor would they allow the barges to be withdrawn. The men in the barges had shot and murdered their neighbors, and the crowd was determined to obtain vengeance. Earlier in the day, William Weihe, national head of the AAISW, had made a futile effort to persuade the company to reopen negotiations with the union. Now Sheriff McCleary and political boss Christopher L. Magee suggested he go to Homestead to persuade the workers to let the barges depart. The crowd would not agree but seemed willing to allow the Pinkertons to surrender if the sheriff would come to arrest them. The Pinkertons were ready to give up, and when Hugh O'Donnell guaranteed their safety, they gave their arms to workers who came aboard the barges. But as the Pinkertons clambered up the steep river bank toward the mill at about 5 P.M., the crowd could not contain its hate. Despite the futile efforts of O'Donnell, the Pinkertons were repeatedly beaten by the men and women of Homestead as they walked through the mill grounds and Homestead itself to the town's opera house, where they would be detained until after midnight. They were put aboard a special train which had come from Pittsburgh with Sheriff McCleary, Christopher Magee, and other officials. Once in Pittsburgh, the sheriff decided against charging the Pinkertons and set them free.

For the next several days, the workers remained in control of Homestead. Sheriff McCleary, after a half-hearted effort to assemble a new force of deputies, made a brief visit to Homestead on July 8, where the citizens received him with little respect. Claiming he had done all he could to restore order, he once again requested state militia from the governor. A group of community and strike leaders journeyed to Harrisburg to meet with Pattison and dissuade him from sending troops. Upon receiving a report from a confidential

Strike breakers, Homestead Mill, 1892. (Carnegie Library of Pittsburgh)

agent who had visited Homestead after the battle, on July 10 the governor ordered four thousand troops to the town. At first, most people in Homestead seemed willing to cooperate with the militia and hoped to show them that the Pinkertons had been responsible for the violence. However, militia commanders saw their task as seizing control of Homestead from its citizens. The militia, whose operations had been professionalized in the years following its disastrous service in 1877, quickly established itself in strategic posi-

112

tions overlooking the town and moved to guard Carnegie's plant. Troops were in place on July 12, and the company started putting strikebreakers to work on July 15.

In succeeding weeks, more and more strikebreakers were brought into the plant, including a number of African Americans. Evictions of the families of strikers embittered Homesteaders. Heightening tensions on July 23 was the attempted assassination of Henry Clay Frick in his Pittsburgh office. Anarchist Alexander Berkman shot Frick twice and tried unsuccessfully to finish off the wounded industrialist with a stiletto. The union struggled to maintain a brave front. AAISW workers at smaller Carnegie plants at Beaver Falls and in Pittsburgh's Lawrenceville section struck in sympathy on July 15 and 16. Employees at the non-union Duquesne works organized on the nineteenth and twentieth and declared a strike on the twenty-third. But the strikes at Lawrenceville and Duquesne were broken by early August and, in Beaver Falls, the company closed that plant for four months to quash resistance.

From late July into August, county authorities arrested a number of strikers on charges stemming from the battle of July 6, and late in September, the grand jury indicted 167 Homesteaders for murder, conspiracy, and aggravated riot. Several days later, the state charged more than thirty strike leaders with treason against the state. Strikers filed charges against several officials of Carnegie Steel and the Pinkerton Detective Agency, but could obtain no indictments. On October 13, the militia left Homestead, giving the task of keeping control of the town to Sheriff McCleary and a large force of deputies. Some sporadic violence occurred against strikebreakers, most notably an attack on a number of African Americans in November that left several badly hurt. On October 20th, the union reluctantly voted to end the walkout. Despite the defeat, the men of Homestead retained a great deal of public sympathy. In several trials, juries refused to convict strike leaders, and early in 1893 the company and the union agreed to abandon further prosecutions.

The immediate consequence of Homestead was that the massive steel plants of the Monongahela Valley would operate without unions for the next forty-five years. Homestead shows the determination of employers to eliminate unions. It also reflected the determination of workers to unify across ethnic boundaries. Neverthe-

113

less, in a rapidly expanding national and world economy, workers had no choice but to unite beyond their communities if unions were to survive.

Pennsylvania and the United Mine Workers of America, 1893-1902

The UMWA was established in 1890 as two rival mining unions amalgamated. The union had little success in its early years. The financial panic that occurred in the spring of 1893 and developed into a full-fledged depression imperiled the survival of the UMWA and other labor organizations. At its worst, the depression brought unemployment to approximately 20 percent of American workers. However, the coal strike of 1894 proved important in securing the union's foothold.

Cutthroat competition had long characterized the bituminous coal industry. A great many coal operators were willing to deal with the union, both to dampen competition through wage uniformity and to end recurring strikes. However, the competitive atmosphere that made a settlement with the UMWA appealing also made it difficult to accomplish, since coal operators feared competition from operators who avoided an agreement with the union. During the early 1890s, collective bargaining did occur between some operators and the UMWA at the district and state levels. However, constant concern over how competitors might undercut those who signed with the union made it practically impossible to reach agreement or to enforce such limited agreements as were negotiated. Desperate to stop wage cuts, in April 1894 the UMWA ordered a nationwide strike after yet another conference with operators collapsed.

Although only about thirteen thousand of the nearly two hundred thousand bituminous mine workers in the United States belonged to the UMWA, more than 60 percent of the industry's work force joined the walkout. This success was not sufficient to compel all of the nation's coal operators to negotiate an agreement with the union. As the strike dragged on into June, the UMWA abandoned its goal of a nationwide agreement, instead calling on district and local officials to make the best deals they could. The union did obtain an agreement covering most of the operators in its traditional strong-

Late nineteenth-century coke ovens, Connellsville region. (Pennsylvania State Archives)

hold from western Pennsylvania to Illinois, restoring some of the wage cuts imposed in the early months of the depression. Still, many mine workers in those fields harshly criticized the union for being too willing to compromise, and at some mines disputes continued through July.

Elsewhere in Pennsylvania, few operators would deal with the union. Certainly Henry Clay Frick and his fellow coke barons had no interest in doing so. After the 1891 coke strike, Frick had given his workers higher wages than their counterparts at other firms, perhaps to insure that they would not organize again. When the agreement that still governed the other coke workers expired at the end of March 1894, they demanded an increase and struck. Although the UMWA had not organized the workers originally, it did provide some aid as it had in 1891. Westmoreland and Fayette Counties erupted into violence again, as the strikers directed their efforts toward bringing Frick's men into the walkout. Deputies again confronted crowds of immigrant strikers. A group of several hundred attacked one of Frick's mines on April 4, drove the deputies away, and chased the firm's chief engineer into the coal tipple, where he was killed. Over the next several months the companies adopted the brutal but familiar strategy of evicting strikers from company-owned homes while bringing in large numbers of strike-breakers, many of them African Americans. Despite the UMWA's withdrawal of aid in June, the strike continued through the summer. Nevertheless, coke workers would come to share the same non-union fate as Homestead's steelworkers.

Mine workers in the numerous coal fields throughout central Pennsylvania, from Somerset and Cambria Counties north to Jefferson, Clearfield, and Centre Counties, had joined the nationwide walkout in April. But, while negotiations did take place between operators and the union, they did not result in an agreement. In this area the strike subsided during June, with the most notable clashes occurring near Punxsutawney, where Governor Pattison dispatched units of the state militia to end violence against strikebreakers.

The depression continued to have a severe effect on mine workers. Because mines needed continual maintenance, they seldom closed completely, regardless of how little demand there might be for coal. Thus, relatively few mine workers were actually laid off. Instead, they had to survive on as little as one or two days of work per week. In 1895 and 1896, the nation's bituminous mine workers averaged only 193 days of employment. Consequently, the UMWA faced hard times too. Having few members outside of its Ohio stronghold, it attempted to assemble joint conferences with operators at the local and state level, but with little success. Desperate to halt wage cuts, the UMWA ordered another strike to begin on July 4, 1897. Nearly all of the mines from western Pennsylvania to Illinois ceased operations. The UMWA won a 20 percent increase in September for the strikers in what would become known as the Central Competitive Field. Just as important, it won a promise from operators in that field to participate in further negotiations in January 1898. The resulting joint conference led to a full-scale contract through a collective bargaining process that, continuing for the next thirty years, would stand as the UMWA's greatest achievement. With the coal market continuing to improve, operators agreed to additional wage increases and granted the eight-hour day and check-off of

*Bituminous mine workers outside drift opening—Medix Run, 1904.
(Pennsylvania State Archives)*

union dues, in which operators would deduct dues from the workers' pay and forward them to the union. Such benefits were exceed-
ingly rare in American industry. Still, this contract covered only about
half of the almost ninety thousand bituminous mine workers in Pennsylvania, although continued organizing in the central part of the
state would bring a contract to thousands of mine workers there in
1899. Ominously for the future, the union did not succeed in West
Virginia, which would remain a largely nonunion thorn in the side
of the UMWA and a threat to unionized mines in western Pennsylvania until the 1930s.

It would prove far more difficult for the UMWA to gain a foothold in the anthracite coal industry. In 1897, anthracite employed
some 150,000 Pennsylvanians and, until 1906, it would employ a
larger number of the Commonwealth's workers than the bituminous
industry. Unionism in anthracite had been practically eliminated after initial attempts at collective action met with defeat in the "Long
Strike" of 1875. Unlike bituminous, anthracite was dominated by a

small number of large operators affiliated with major railroads. Throughout the 1870s, 1880s, and 1890s, these companies had taken control of many mines and tried to limit competition, not fully succeeding in doing so until the end of the 1890s, led by America's most powerful financier, J. Pierpont Morgan. Becoming quite adept at working together to control prices and apportion the coal market, the anthracite railroads, in contrast to the bituminous operators, did not have to worry much about competitors or unionized workers.

The UMWA did little to organize anthracite workers until 1897. But, as the bituminous walkout of that year drew toward a successful conclusion, a series of spontaneous strikes occurred in the small coal "patch" towns around Hazleton. Some strikers walked out over an abusive supervisor, others wanted more than the dollar a day so many earned, while others were upset over paying inflated prices for company-store goods. During these walkouts, eastern and southern Europeans showed the greatest militancy, as they had in the coke fields. Many joined the UMWA, but only after the strikes had begun and leaders called for the president of the union's moribund anthracite district, John Fahy, to organize them. Earlier in 1897, Fahy had become so frustrated with organizing that he had spent much of the year in Harrisburg lobbying successfully for several measures, including a tax of three cents per day on the wages of each immigrant worker. Ironically, a number of walkouts occurred in response to the implementation of that tax, which operators deducted from workers' pay. Fahy organized several thousand mine workers in the Lehigh field, but he did not try to take control of the spreading strike wave. The situation came to a tragic climax on Friday, September 10, 1897, outside the patch town of Lattimer when sheriff's deputies killed nineteen and wounded thirty-six unarmed marching strikers in what would become known as the Lattimer Massacre (see Keystone Vignette: "Lattimer Massacre," p. 150).

Some twenty-five hundred state militia were soon ordered to the area by Governor Daniel Hastings. Strikers ended their walkouts during the next two weeks, having obtained few concessions. Many would remain faithful to their new union, but they could not come close to duplicating the accomplishments of their counterparts in bituminous coal. Employers refused to negotiate with UMWA representatives, and the union's strength declined as the underemploy-

118

ment which had plagued the bituminous industry persisted longer in anthracite. For the year 1897, the anthracite mines provided an average of only 150 ten-hour days of work, and in 1898, 152.

No union of mine workers had ever made much progress in the northernmost or Wyoming coal field. Here more than half of the industry's mine workers produced more than half of the coal. Yet, beginning in the summer of 1899, when the anthracite industry finally began to pull out of the depression, workers struck at one mine after another. Their grievances went well beyond concerns such as wages and hours, as they tried to exercise greater control over a work process they viewed as consistently unfair. Miners, who were paid for each car of coal they mined, were penalized or "docked" for not heaping enough coal onto the car to satisfy the company. Even the youngest anthracite workers, "breaker boys" and mule drivers, walked out with increasing frequency. These workers, many of whom were in their early teen years or younger, struck for causes ranging from abusive supervisors to disagreements over promotions.

As the new century began, the UMWA district for the Wyoming field, District 1, had grown to include more than three-quarters of the nearly nine thousand anthracite mine workers who belonged to the union. Yet that total represented less than 10 percent of the industry's work force. The UMWA realized it could not achieve real success until it brought the railroad companies that owned the mines to the bargaining table. By adamantly refusing to bargain, the companies made the rank and file eager to strike, but cautious union leaders looked for the right moment to do so. The thirty-year-old UMWA President John Mitchell knew he might have to call an industry-wide strike to bring most of the anthracite men into the union, but he also realized no strike could succeed unless all three anthracite fields went out together. Fundamentally conservative and tactically shrewd, Mitchell also wanted to do all he could to avoid alienating elected officials and the public who, particularly in the Northeast, depended on anthracite to heat their homes.

Throughout 1900, union leaders tried to rein in a militant rank and file in some places, while struggling to strengthen the organization in others. Formal requests to the railroads to discuss grievances in a bituminous-style joint conference received no response. The

UMWA ordered all anthracite mine workers to strike on September 17. About two-thirds of the work force of 142,500 responded initially, and nearly all of the remaining workers gradually joined the walkout. Relatively little violence occurred, except for a clash between sheriff's deputies and strikers in Shenandoah in Schuylkill County that resulted in one death, and led Governor William Stone to call out two thousand state militia. The strike was aided by state legislation, passed in 1889 and toughened in 1897, requiring anthracite miners to be certified on the basis of their experience and performance on an oral examination before a board of veteran miners. Therefore, the companies could not bring in trainloads of inexperienced men to mine coal and break the strike.

In ordering the strike, Mitchell realized that the fall's presidential election campaign would increase pressure for a quick settlement. President William McKinley and his campaign manager, Senator Mark Hanna, a coal operator whose Ohio mines were covered under the UMWA contract, orchestrated the re-election effort around the return of prosperity. They did not want the anthracite strike to sound a discordant note for the voters. The political climate had become more sympathetic toward unions, and practically all public officials looked to avoid Homestead-like violence. Consequently, Hanna pressured the railroad presidents to settle the strike. The companies would not negotiate, but instead posted notices at their mines offering an increase of 10 percent, consisting for most miners of a decrease in the price they paid for blasting powder. But the workers showed their loyalty to the UMWA by not returning until the union ordered them back to work on October 29, a date which would be celebrated for decades in the anthracite region as "Mitchell Day."

The strike of 1900 represented an important victory for the union. Union leaders were caught between their desire to appear responsible before the public and the ever-growing militancy of an energized rank and file. Mine workers continued to strike at one mine after another over a variety of local grievances, and this only heightened the companies' fear and loathing of the union. The victory of 1900 and the ensuing wave of local strikes brought most anthracite mine workers into the union. By the end of 1901, District 1 had become the UMWA's largest with forty-five thousand members. Overall the three anthracite districts totaled more than seventy-eight thousand.

The union called on the companies to negotiate again in March 1901. When they refused to do so, Mitchell persuaded delegates not to strike. Once more the union pushed for a joint conference in March 1902 and received the same response. However, Mitchell's caution had won him the friendship of Mark Hanna, who influenced Morgan to press the railroads at least to meet with Mitchell and the anthracite district leaders. Several meetings brought no progress, even though Mitchell lowered the union's demands. Mitchell and several other leaders argued against a strike, expressing the hope that future meetings with the rail presidents might eventually accomplish something. But a majority of delegates to a union convention disagreed, and ordered a strike by some 150,000 mine workers, causing practically all anthracite mines to cease operations on May 12.

The UMWA ordered engineers, firemen, and pump runners who maintained the mines to leave their jobs and maintained its solidarity by taking advantage of its national strength. In July, the UMWA decided against a sympathy strike of bituminous workers. Instead, it assessed union members to accumulate a relief fund for the anthracite men and their families. Of the more than $2 million raised, one-fifth of the amount came from donations outside of the UMWA.

The changing national climate of the Progressive Era led many elected officials to view labor disputes as matters of public concern. As early as June, President Theodore Roosevelt, who had succeeded McKinley when he was assassinated in September 1901, called on the federal commissioner of labor to investigate the dispute. Governor Stone sent state militia to quell violence in Shenandoah in August and in Carbon County's Panther Creek Valley in September, but the railroads complained that these steps were not sufficient to provide the "order" they needed to break the strike. With the arrival of autumn, consumers readied themselves to substitute smokier bituminous coal for the unavailable anthracite, but as bituminous use increased fear of a potential coal famine moved the president to act.

At the beginning of October, Roosevelt, several railroad presidents, and Mitchell met. The union suggested that the president appoint a commission to resolve the dispute. The executives maintained that workers would return to the mines if only the militia would play a stronger role. Their arrogance annoyed Roosevelt. Morgan, concerned over public outrage against the railroads, pressed the reluctant presidents to submit the dispute to a commission to be appointed by Roosevelt.

The Anthracite Coal Strike Commission, which included a Catholic bishop, a labor representative, and industry and engineering experts, held hearings for more than three months, mostly in Scranton. It ruled that miners should receive a wage increase of 10 percent. Mine workers had their hours reduced from ten to nine at the same daily wage. The commission also mandated a form of de facto recognition for the union by requiring that grievances arising over its detailed ruling be resolved by a joint labor-management board of conciliation. However, the commission refused to impose greater uniformity on wages and working conditions, even after revelations of differences in wage rates, not only between companies, but at different mines of the same firm and even in the same mine. The commission also refused to force the railroads to recognize the union officially through joint conferences like those that prevailed in bituminous coal. For years to follow the companies would negotiate with union officials but maintained that those officials represented only the mine workers, not the union. Thus the strike of 1902 showed both the growing power of labor and limits to that power. Unions might win acceptance from workers and the public, but corporate America could still refuse to accept them. The public might demonstrate concern for workers, especially if they produced an essential product, but such concern would result in only modest gains. (The struggles of anthracite mine workers after 1902 can be found in Keystone Vignette: "Rinaldo Cappellini, The Knox Mine Disaster and the Decline of the Anthracite Coal Industry," p.154)

Progressive Problems, Progressive Remedies

Like elsewhere in the nation during the Progressive Era, the struggles of African Americans in Pennsylvania at the turn of the century were the product of unremitting discrimination that robbed most of them of the opportunity for a decent job. They continued overwhelmingly in low-income work, particularly in domestic and personal service. Constituting 2.5 percent of the state's population in 1900 and 1910, only a small number of blacks worked in a few of the state's growing industries. Work in coal mines, steel mills, textile mills, and other manufacturing plants was difficult, often dangerous, and paid poor wages. Still, such jobs were steadier, paid more, and certainly allowed greater opportunity for advancement than did work as servants, waiters, barbers, or janitors, the jobs which more than 60 percent of the state's African Americans held at the turn of the century. The opportunities that African Americans needed in the decades after the Civil War had instead been offered to immigrants. By 1909, fewer than 1 percent of workers in the state's principal industries were African Americans, while more than 47 percent had been born overseas. Only in steel did African American representation approximate their overall percentage of the population. In steel the foreign-born, who were less than 20 percent of the state's population, made up a majority of the work force, as they did in coal mining, where less than 1 percent of workers were African Americans. In Pittsburgh and Philadelphia, where more than half of the state's black population lived, only after 1890 were any significant numbers of African Americans hired for jobs on public construction projects for roads, water treatment plants, and other municipal facilities.

As tempting as it may be to blame the lack of opportunity for African Americans solely on the racial prejudice of employers, white workers shared that prejudice. In Philadelphia in 1881, a number of white officers quit the police force after the city hired three black policemen. Forty-eight white nurses signed a petition protesting the Philadelphia Board of Charities' decision to hire an African American nurse in 1890, and several quit when that nurse began work. In 1898, white workers stopped the Philadelphia and Western Streetcar Company from employing two black motormen by striking. Pressed by white locomotive firemen, officials of the Baltimore and Ohio Railroad in Pittsburgh agreed to hire no more blacks and to remove those who had been hired. A great many of the early opportunities for black workmen at steel mills and coal mines came only when employers looked for strikebreakers. But few unions offered alternatives to black workers, instead discriminating as vigorously as they ever had. While the official policy of the AFL was to

Street construction—Pittsburgh, 1908. (Archives of Industrial Society, University of Pittsburgh libraries)

organize workers regardless of race, it made no effort to discipline member organizations that either did not enroll blacks or segregated them in separate locals. One of the very few unions to enroll substantial numbers of African Americans was the UMWA.

Women in Pennsylvania surely had a greater range of industrial opportunities than did African Americans, but were still generally restricted to low-paying positions. Most of the 20 percent of the state's work force composed of females were unmarried and left the work force once they had children. In 1909, women and young girls constituted a majority of the work force in the manufacture of garments, tobacco products, silk goods, and hosiery. Beyond those industries, the range of factory employment for women included work in canneries, candy and cracker making, work in sheet metal and tin-plate plants, and the manufacture of lamps and other electrical equipment. By the turn of the century, increasing numbers of women were entering clerical work or taking such new jobs as telephone operator. But such positions were generally restricted to the native born. Thousands of Pennsylvania's mothers in this era did manufacturing work in their homes, in addition to caring for husbands, children, and often boarders. The manufacture of cloth-

Food preparation for H. J. Heinz and Company—Pittsburgh at the turn of the century. (Carnegie Library of Pittsburgh)

ing was common, but women at home also made at least some part of products as varied as jewelry, gloves, brushes, candy, toys, holiday decorations, and artificial flowers.

After 1900, a growing number of investigations of work and living conditions among the state's workers brought their problems into clearer focus. Workers without marketable skills struggled to support growing families in the best of times, and when they faced layoffs, sickness, or injuries from industrial accidents, their survival was imperiled. More and more steelworkers were employed twelve hours a day, seven days a week for wages of less than two dollars a day. Other industries were less arduous for workers, but they paid less too. Of course, because the vast majority of African Americans were denied the opportunity for industrial jobs, their struggles were even more difficult. All of these pressures forced thousands of Pennsylvania's children into the work force. Elderly Pennsylvanians have commonly recalled in oral history interviews how, in the early years of this century, they started to work even before the age of ten.

Despite a growing understanding of the perils of industrialization, the state of Pennsylvania during the Progressive Era made no effort to address such basic problems as low wages and job discrimination. Businessmen along with a great many other Pennsylvanians viewed any such effort as dangerous government interference. Pennsylvania's legislature enacted laws to protect workers, but only where their problems had become so great and so poignant that they could not be ignored. In 1913, the state reorganized industrial regulatory activities into the Department of Labor and Industry, adding a Bureau of Mediation and Arbitration to help settle labor disputes.

These limited legislative efforts occurred only because of the growing political influence of workers and their unions, whose membership nationwide increased nearly fivefold from 1897 to 1904. Indicative of this trend is the AFL's effort in 1906 to encourage labor leaders to run for political office. Across the nation, six won election to Congress, and two of these were Pennsylvania Democrats prominent in the UMWA—Thomas D. Nicholls of Scranton, president of anthracite District 1, and William B. Wilson of Blossburg, national secretary-treasurer of the union. Other Pennsylvania labor leaders turned to the Socialist Party to achieve economic change. The most notable of these was James H. Maurer of Reading who led the state AFL from 1912 to 1928 and served in the legislature from 1910 to 1912 and 1914 to 1918. A sizable minority of Pennsylvania workers also supported Socialists. Although the state Socialist vote for President in 1912 was less than one percentage point ahead of the national figure of 6 percent, in the same election, Socialists won 25 percent of the vote in steel towns such as Duquesne and McKeesport and in Westmoreland County coal towns. Not surprisingly, the Socialist vote also increased during strikes, like the 1902 anthracite walkout, and after unsuccessful strikes, as in 1911 in New Castle, when workers elected a Socialist mayor and a near-majority of Socialists for the city council. Even if workers' growing political clout seldom resulted in Socialist victories, the clamor for change represented by such votes could not be ignored.

The massive toll of death and destruction in the state's leading industry, coal mining, had induced the legislature to enact safety regulations as early as 1869. The state's program of mine safety inspection was strengthened on several occasions thereafter, and it eventually required certification of mine foremen and miners themselves. Beginning in 1877, the state established a similar program of mine inspection for the bituminous fields, which was strengthened after 109 mine workers died in an explosion in January 1891 at Henry Clay Frick's Mammoth mine in Westmoreland County. To assist injured mine workers, the state even built two hospitals and provided funds to assist in the building of many others.

It was also in coal mining that the state first made a genuine effort to deal with child labor. The 1870 law prohibited boys under twelve from working underground and required that boys obtain a certificate attesting to their age before they could be employed. In strengthening the anthracite mining code in 1885, the legislature raised the age limit for underground work to fourteen and established a minimum age of twelve for work on the surface. At the turn of the century, about one-tenth of the workers in the anthracite industry worked picking slate in the breakers. Most were boys, but some were longtime mine workers or injured men who could no longer perform other work. Also in 1885, the legislature enacted an age limit of twelve for underground work in bituminous mines and prohibited the employment of any female in the state's mines, except in clerical work. Although there is no evidence that women or girls were knowingly employed, anecdotes still circulate in the mining regions of female relatives who worked around the mines without revealing their sex.

The fact that young teens could legally work in the state's mines is appalling from our current-day perspective, but just as disturbing is the fact that the laws to keep younger workers off the job were commonly violated. Working-class families generally believed they had little choice but to send children out to work as soon as possible to add to the family's income. Local officials who issued age certificates showed far more interest in obtaining fees than verifying the child's age. With the certificates on file, the companies who hired young workers could claim that they bore no responsibility.

Progressive concerns about child labor spurred the legislature in 1905 to increase the minimum age for employment outside the anthracite mines to fourteen and inside them to sixteen, as well as to tighten enforcement procedures. It also decided to require documentary proof of age. However, the courts, which consistently sought

Young anthracite mine workers underground—Shenandoah, Schuylkill County. (Pennsylvania State Archives)

to limit the state's role in protecting workers, invalidated the enforcement plan. A child-labor activist estimated that some ten thousand boys below legal age still worked in and around the mines. On November 6, 1907, a boy named Patrick Kearney was killed when he fell into breaker machinery at the Greenwood washery in Lackawanna County. His father revealed that, although he had sworn that his son was fourteen so the boy could get a certificate, Patrick died before his tenth birthday.

In 1848, Pennsylvania had been the first state in the nation to try to prohibit child labor in factories by barring children under twelve from working in textile mills, but this law had lacked any practical means of enforcement. The state's first genuine effort to extend its protective reach beyond the mines was the factory inspection law of 1889, when Pennsylvania became the sixth state to enact such legislation. The statute prohibited any child under twelve from factory work and mandated a maximum work week of sixty hours for minors. Four years later the age limit was advanced to thirteen. To make workplaces safer, the law also mandated automatic doors for elevators, adequate ventilation, fire exits, and safeguards for belts, gears, and vats of molten metal and hot liquid. In succeeding years, so-called sweatshops, where clothing was manufactured in apartment buildings, were brought under the jurisdiction of the factory inspectors, as were bakeries and printing shops.

The factory inspection laws showed special concern for women workers. Employers were required to provide women with seats, separate wash rooms, and separate water closets. From 1897, adult women were also covered under the maximum work week of sixty hours. The enforcement process gave special attention to women. The governor appointed a state factory inspector who was required, in the original legislation, to appoint six deputy inspectors, half of whom were to be women. In subsequent acts the number of deputy inspectors was increased, until by 1903 it reached thirty-seven.

Just as child labor continued despite state regulation, safety legislation for the state's factories and mines by no means eliminated industrial accidents. A survey of Allegheny County conducted from July 1906 through June 1907 by sociologist Crystal Eastman compiled some 526 fatal accidents and many more disabling injuries. The two most dangerous industries in the county were steel, where almost 200 of the fatalities occurred, and the railroads, where 125 were killed. Across the state, the number of mine workers killed and injured continued to grow in the first decade of the century, although not quite as rapidly as the growth in employment and production. In the peak year of 1907, 708 Pennsylvania anthracite mine workers and 806 bituminous workers were killed on the job. A series of disastrous explosions which killed workers on an even greater scale than the Avondale catastrophe of 1869 caused the death toll to swell. Early in 1904, 177 mine workers met their death at the Allegheny Coal Company's Harwick mine near Cheswick in Allegheny County. Pennsylvania's worst mining disaster occurred on December 19, 1907 at the Darr mine of the Pittsburgh Coal Company in Westmoreland County, where 239 workers lost their lives. Less than a year later, an explosion at the newly opened Marianna mine of the Pittsburgh-Buffalo Coal Company in Washington County killed 154. A state mine inspector had pronounced that mine safe

Harwick mine disaster, January 25, 1904. (Alle-Kiski Historical Society)

only minutes before the blast occurred. In 1916, the state reported a total for all Pennsylvania industry of 2,670 fatalities and 71,293 "serious" injuries.

Companies would often, but not always, pay medical bills and/or funeral expenses, at least in part. They would also commonly offer workers some sort of continued employment, even if their injuries prevented them from doing their old job. However, little ongoing support was available for a worker who was maimed, or for the family when a breadwinner was killed, beyond insurance often obtained from membership in a beneficial society affiliated with their ethnic group. Part of the employer's motivation for offering aid was to avoid getting sued. A worker or his family could sue the employer for negligence, but such suits were difficult to win. First, the legal system viewed the worker as having assumed a job's customary risks. Second, no judgment could be obtained against an employer if negligence by the worker or a fellow employee contributed in any way to the accident. Workers sometimes won cases with the help of sympathetic juries, but then, as now, attorneys extracted a sizable percentage from any settlement.

Many boys worked in glass factories like this one on Pittsburgh's South Side. (Carnegie Library of Pittsburgh)

Thus the legal system provided little help to most workers. By the twentieth century, increasing numbers of companies, annoyed by negative jury verdicts, also looked for a more reliable way of disposing of claims. In perhaps its most important piece of Progressive legislation for workers, Pennsylvania enacted a program of workers' compensation in June 1915, after most of the nation's industrial states had already done so. Funded by employer contributions, the state's compensation fund provided 50 percent of an injured worker's wages for up to five hundred weeks of disability. A deceased worker's family received 40 percent of the worker's wages and an additional 5 percent for each child to a maximum of 60 percent for three hundred weeks. This measure surely helped workers and their families but fell short of providing real security. At the levels of assistance mandated, families who struggled to make ends meet would still face impoverishment if their breadwinner was killed or disabled.

Progressives also continued to push for more effective prohibition of child labor and greater protection for women and minors at the workplace. In 1909, the state raised the age limit for work in and

131

around bituminous mines to fourteen and mandated for all workers under sixteen a maximum ten-hour day and fifty-eight hour week. In 1911, the age limit for employment inside the bituminous mines was raised to sixteen to match the anthracite standard, and the state required school attendance to age fourteen. Four years later, the state further reduced the maximum workweek for those under sixteen to fifty-one hours with a maximum workday of nine hours. Fourteen- and fifteen-year-olds could still work legally in many industries, but they were required to have completed sixth grade and to attend "continuation school" for eight hours during the week.

As with the compensation law, child labor laws improved the lives of the state's working families, but only to a limited extent. One noteworthy trend, spurred in part by child labor laws, was an increase in the percentage of married women in the labor force and a delay by unmarried women in beginning work. But beyond its relatively ineffective efforts to enhance workplace safety, the Commonwealth of Pennsylvania did very little for adults unless they suffered a serious industrial accident. Workers would have to rely on their own collective action to achieve more substantive gains.

Bitter Battles, 1903-1916

At the turn of the century, eight of the nation's fourteen largest manufacturing plants in there were located in Pennsylvania. Five of these made steel, including Cambria Steel in Johnstown, Pennsylvania Steel in Steelton, and three in the Pittsburgh area. Two of the three other mammoth industrial facilities in the state were in Philadelphia—the Baldwin Locomotive plant and the William Cramp shipyard, while the Westinghouse Electric plant in East Pittsburgh completed the list. Each of these monuments to Pennsylvania's leading role in American industry employed more than six thousand workers.

Such large enterprises necessitated not only technological innovation but also changes in traditional management practice. Philadelphia was the birthplace of Frederick W. Taylor, who popularized the concept of "scientific management," flowing from his work in the 1880s and 1890s with such Pennsylvania firms as Midvale Steel and the Bethlehem Iron Company, which later became Bethlehem Steel. Theoretically, scientific management aimed to increase productivity by making managers more expert and giving workers new incentives. For workers, Taylor instituted "time-and-motion study" to analyze how effectively they performed their jobs. Many viewed his efforts as just another way to wring maximum production from workers. Furthermore, Taylor saw unions and the traditional ways in which workers had done their jobs as obstacles to efficiency. Whatever else scientific management advocated, its primary thrust was to give top management greater control.

The settlement of the anthracite coal strike brought hopes of a new era of industrial harmony. Instead, the growth of unions spurred businessmen's fears of losing control of their businesses and their workers. From 1903 until the entry of the United States into the First World War, Pennsylvania's industrial workers struggled with their bosses, not only for better wages and working conditions, but for the security of union representation. Some employers had been able to accept, however grudgingly, organization by skilled workers, who were largely native-born. But increasingly, industrial employers faced a work force composed of an ever-growing variety of ethnic groups in the era of the greatest immigration in the nation's history. They stubbornly resisted practically any organizing effort, leaving workers little choice but to strike. When employers responded by bringing in strikebreakers, workers took desperate measures to keep strikebreakers from taking their jobs.

Two institutions owed their existence to this escalation of industrial warfare, the Pennsylvania State Police and a new labor organization oriented toward revolutionary socialism, the Industrial Workers of the World (IWW), both born in 1905. Battles between the two in major strikes in McKees Rocks and New Castle in the summer of 1909 would capture the nation's attention. Use of the militia to maintain order during strikes had proved expensive to the state and difficult for the troops, who were private citizens rather than professional soldiers or police. Many corporations around the state had taken advantage of the unique provision in Pennsylvania's laws allowing them to hire Coal and Iron Police. The courts had interpreted the power of such police as extending beyond company property, but few public officials regarded their presence as an effective way to maintain order. A permanent, professional force of State Police offered to do so in a more flexible and efficient way, lessening reliance on both the militia and Coal and Iron Police. State Police would also monitor traffic on the state's expanding highway network and assist in the enforcement of forest, fish, and game regulations. Still, they would become best known for their actions during labor disputes. Intimidating figures on horseback, they received the nickname "Cossacks" from workers across the state, many of whom remembered the brutality of the Tsar's forces in eastern Europe.

At an unguarded moment in a 1912 interview, John C. Groome, superintendent of the State Police, stated his belief that each state trooper "must be equal to one hundred foreigners." The IWW held the burgeoning immigrant population in much higher esteem, viewing them as a revolutionary vanguard that could lead an assault on American capitalism. The IWW concentrated its organizing on workers often neglected by AFL unions—the unskilled, women, the foreign-born, and African Americans. Although in numbers its role in the labor movement was peripheral, it had much greater symbolic significance. In crafting its revolutionary appeal, the IWW could point quite accurately to numerous struggles in which moderate demands by moderate unions had nevertheless been defeated by the staunch resistance of employers.

Such a struggle occurred in Philadelphia's textile industry in 1903, where females constituted more than half the work force, with a substantial proportion in their teens. Older women earned from six to eight dollars for a sixty-hour week, while thousands of young women generally earned one-half that amount. In 1903, the regional union to which the organized portion of textile workers belonged, the Central Textile Workers Union, demanded a cut in the work week to fifty-five hours. But the union had made little effort to organize less skilled workers, in particular the thousands of women and girls who dominated work in the hosiery, silk, and cotton sectors of the industry. The union expressed its willingness to accept proportionately lower pay along with the decrease in hours. While a shorter week surely appealed to the women and girls, their wages were so low that they had misgivings over any reductions. When the strike began on June 1, female workers across the city responded, despite the lack of interest the union had shown in them. At the strike's peak, approximately 70 percent of Philadelphia's more than sixty thousand textile workers walked off the job. But the proprietors of the numerous establishments in that diverse industry adamantly refused to negotiate with the union. Workers began to return after a week, especially in the industry's lowest-paid sector, whose workers could least afford a lengthy strike. To galvanize support, Mary Harris "Mother" Jones, the famed seventy-three-year-old veteran organizer of many struggles in the mine fields, arrived on June 15, armed with a contribution of some $8000 from the UMWA.

Mother Jones called for a march from Philadelphia across New Jersey to New York to dramatize the workers' plight. On July 7, some 150 adults and fifty children left Philadelphia. Two days later the sixty marchers who remained camped in Morrisville while Mother Jones begged labor leaders in Trenton for money for food and for the toll to cross the Delaware. When the group reached Princeton, Mother Jones excoriated the students in a talk near the Princeton University campus: "What are your young men at Princeton but a lot of bums? They are wasting a lot of money on an education which will do them no good. The money ought to be given to organized labor." Conditions on the march only became more dreary as it proceeded north through New Brunswick and Elizabeth to New York. To recapture public attention, Mother Jones requested a meeting for her group with President Theodore Roosevelt, summering at his home on Long Island. But the president declined, and the remaining marchers returned to Philadelphia, where the strike had long since been lost.

Otherwise, 1903 appeared to be a good year for Philadelphia's workers. Some five thousand men's garment workers negotiated a contract giving them better wages and an eight-hour day, and the Allied Printing Trades Council obtained a three-year contract from employers. Even in 1904, the city's building trades forced leading contractors to increase wages and acknowledge labor's right to declare sympathy strikes. But the pathetic outcome of Mother Jones's march served as a harbinger more difficult times for labor. As early as 1902, employers affiliated with the National Association of Manufacturers began a nationwide antiunion campaign. Winning a series of strikes and lockouts, by 1907 Philadelphia employers curtailed bargaining with unions in printing, men's clothing, and the metal trades. Meanwhile, the strong turn-of-the-century expansion of the

135

economy slowed in 1903 and 1904, and financial markets experienced a severe panic in the fall of 1907. As it always had, economic weakness threatened labor organization and discouraged initiatives by unions. However, as the economy began to improve in 1908, militancy returned in a great many industries.

In April 1908, workers at the Chester Trolley Company were determined to resist plans to decrease wages by 10 percent. The company anticipated trouble, especially since Patrick Shea, vice-president of the Amalgamated Association of Street and Electric Railway Employees (AASERE), had been organizing their employees. It had already begun to bring in strikebreakers when the trolleymen met in the early hours of April 13 after learning of the wage cut. Hearing that strikebreakers were arriving, the workers adjourned to stone a trolley full of them, sending a dozen to the hospital. That morning, as a crowd of strikers and sympathizers surged around the company's trolley barn, the chief of police, who had only recently taken office, called for State Police to come from Reading. But when they arrived and began to make arrests, both the chief and the mayor told them they were not needed. The local police showed considerable sympathy to the strikers, but after two strikebreakers were shot, the local authorities agreed ask the State Police to return.

Their arrival restored order along the trolley lines, but the presence of the State Police in no way broke the strike. Most of the community supported the strikers by boycotting the trolley, adopting the slogan, "We'll walk to win!" After the troopers left at the end of May, some disorder resumed. Several local policemen resigned, refusing to protect the company's property. Those who stayed on the force did not give the company their full support. In a number of cases, police gave tickets to trolley motormen who exceeded the speed limit to avoid crowds chasing them with stones. Strikebreakers and their families were mercilessly boycotted by the rest of the community, and store owners were similarly threatened if they sold goods to the strikebreakers. The strike continued through the summer with the company refusing to recognize the union and very few people riding the trolleys. In September, a spy for the company who had masqueraded as a union sympathizer accused Vice-President Shea, along with the president of the local union and eleven others, of plotting to destroy company property. Although the jury deadlocked during the trial in October, the strike had been dealt a blow from which it could not recover.

No challenge proved to be so daunting for organized labor in the Progressive Era as keeping unionism alive in the steel industry. A walkout by workers at the South Bethlehem plant of the Bethlehem Steel Company showed the resources of the powerful corporations that dominated that industry could be brought to bear against strikers. Bethlehem's president, Charles M. Schwab, learned his hostility toward unions from Andrew Carnegie, who made Schwab superintendent of the Homestead works after the 1892 lockout. When several hundred of Bethlehem's workers left their jobs early in February 1910, Schwab informed them that he would consider their grievances only after they returned to work. Three weeks later, company officials persuaded local authorities to call in the State Police, despite the fact that little disorder had occurred. The troopers established their own brand of order, setting up their headquarters on company property and dispersing practically any gathering in the streets. As the strike approached two months, with more than five hundred workers still out, Schwab summoned seventy-five local businessmen. He accused them of helping the strikers and threatened to move his plant. Merchants obediently cut off credit to the strikers, who were also denied access to the hall where they had held meetings. They had little choice but to return to work—that is, those whom Bethlehem would take back.

Yet the power of Bethlehem Steel paled next to that of world's first billion-dollar corporation, United States Steel. In 1901, J.P. Morgan purchased Carnegie's interests and combined them with numerous other plants across the nation. The AAISW tried to revive its strength in steel by striking shortly after the corporation's birth, but the union's traditional reliance on skilled workers—in an industry increasingly dominated by the unskilled—made victory impossible. From that point, the AAISW did little more than try to hold on at the dwindling number of plants where it had contracts. Most of those were sheet steel and tin factories, and when U.S. Steel announced its abandonment of those contracts in June 1909, the AAISW had no choice but to strike. In contrast to the Iron and Steel Workers, the IWW saw unskilled immigrant workers as an opportunity, not a threat. It had established one of its first locals in the East at New Castle for workers of the American Sheet and Tin Plate Company, a subsidiary of U.S. Steel. Cooperation between the IWW and the AAISW made New Castle the only plant where workers held out in 1909 for several months, although that strike eventually failed too. Once again, the State Police banned picketing and vigorously dispersed workers' gatherings near company property.

Unskilled workers also showed their militancy and potential for unionization in the summer of 1909 at McKees Rocks, across the Ohio River from Pittsburgh's North Side. Workers at the Pressed Steel Car Company struck in July because management had refused to consider their grievances. Most were eastern European immigrants who worked on an early version of the assembly line. Cranes moved rail car frames along a track while the workers assembled the rest of the car onto the frame. Along with this system, company president Frank Hoffstot devised a plan to pool the wages of each gang of workers. The gang supposedly was to be paid according to its production, but the company did not post its rates. Not only did managers urge the men to work as fast as possible, but co-workers tended to pressure one another. Wages had been cut substantially in 1907, and workers charged that foremen demanded bribes to hire men and sometimes discharged workers just to collect additional bribes.

Unions played no role in initiating the dispute. Instead, several thousand men struck on July 13 after management refused to speak with the grievance committee. Only a few hundred skilled men, most of whom were native-born workers whose wages were not pooled, remained at work. In the next few days, immigrant strikers extended the walkout by pulling the native-born off trolleys headed for the plant. Immediately the company tried to bring in strikebreakers. On July 14, in an episode reminiscent of Homestead some seventeen years before, strikers repulsed a boatload of strikebreakers who tried to land near the plant, amidst a barrage of gunfire from both sides which miraculously injured no one. The company also moved, with the help of the State Police, to evict workers from the shabby homes rented from the company. But the strikers and their families did not hesitate to resist the "Cossacks," turning the immigrant community into a battlefield.

Despite growing violence, strikers had public sympathy because Hoffstot refused to consider negotiation or arbitration. Meanwhile, a group of skilled workers decided to join the strike with the immigrants, and formed a joint strike committee whose members represented various ethnic groups. Thus, skilled workers moved into a leading role, despite their relative lack of interest in the walkout. But suspicion characterized the alliance between skilled and unskilled, natives and immigrants. Management agreed to negotiate with the joint committee, and twice that committee proposed settlements which promised some concessions but would have allowed the company to decide whether or not to retain individual strikers. The mass of unskilled workers rejected this, since they were most likely not to be rehired. They continued to man the front lines of the struggle, resisting evictions and intensified efforts to bring in strikebreakers. In mid-August, IWW organizer William Trautmann arrived to lend his support.

On August 22, six strikers, two of their sympathizers, two strikebreakers, and one state policeman were killed in gun battles. More state troopers came to town and made a house-to-house search of immigrant homes for weapons. But just as their role in the violence began to turn public opinion against them, it was revealed that the company had dragooned immigrants from outside of the area into strikebreaking and held them against their will. This brought Charles P. Neill, federal commissioner of labor, to McKees Rocks. As negotiations resumed early in September, Neill met with both management and the leader of the strike committee, skilled worker C.A. Wise. The company declared its willingness to make concessions, but it would neither sign an agreement with the committee, nor promise to rehire all strikers. The strike committee persuaded most of the men to return to work, despite a second brief strike by immigrant workers who, encouraged by Trautmann, trusted neither the company nor the committee. Those suspicions proved justified when Wise had Trautmann arrested and identified the leaders of the second strike so the company could fire them. Wise then presided over the formation of a company union, the United Car Workers of the World, which resembled the IWW in name only.

Through this conflict and the one at New Castle, the IWW retained the loyalty of hundreds of immigrant workers. For the next several years, western Pennsylvania would remain one of the few IWW strongholds in the East. It could draw big crowds to its rallies, like the fifteen thousand who assembled at Kennywood Park in August 1912. It also presided over a successful strike of Pittsburgh's Jewish stogie workers the following year, as well as courageous but unsuccessful organizing efforts at various steel plants. In Philadelphia, the IWW achieved one of its few long-lasting triumphs by organizing four thousand longshoremen who worked on the docks along the Delaware, half of whom were African Americans. Prominent in this campaign was Benjamin Harrison Fletcher, an African American native of Philadelphia. Born in 1890, Fletcher organized dockworkers in Philadelphia and elsewhere along the east coast in the 1910s. One of the leading blacks in the IWW, he would be arrested in 1918 and sent to federal prison along with other IWW officials because of the organization's opposition to World War I. In a series of strikes from 1913 through 1916, the IWW presided over unprecedented solidarity between recent immigrants and African Americans. The IWW's Marine Transport Workers' Local #3 achieved raises, recognition, overtime pay, and control over hiring, thus meriting the praise offered by a Philadelphia minister of the African Methodist Episcopal Church: "The IWW at least protects the colored man, which is more than I can say for the laws of this country."

The IWW demonstrated the possibility of organizing the unskilled and building solidarity among workers of various ethnic groups. But the greatest demonstration of solidarity in this era occurred in Philadelphia in March 1910, when some one hundred thousand workers left their jobs in sympathy with a strike of six thousand trolleymen. The workers of the Philadelphia Rapid Transit Company had grievances just as strong as their counterparts in Chester, chief of which was the "split shift" for morning and evening rush hours which gave them an effective work day of fourteen to eighteen hours. When company officials refused even to meet with workers organized by the Amalgamated Association of Street and Electric Railway Employees at the end of May 1909, a brief strike occurred which quickly became violent when the company brought in strikebreakers. Most of the city's workers had no love for the company because of a recent fare hike, and the Philadelphia Central Labor Union threatened a general strike of the city's union men.

140

State Police on strike duty—Philadelphia, 1910. (Temple University Libaries Urban Archives)

But political leaders brokered a settlement that increased wages slightly, ended the split shift, and won the company's agreement to negotiate with the AASERE over future grievances. Yet while this looked like recognition to the union, the company thought otherwise. It set up its own company union, the "Keystone Carmen," along with an insurance and pension plan to wean workers away from the AASERE. In January 1910, the company fired several workers who criticized it, and more than five thousand voted to authorize a strike against the company's efforts to undermine the union. Talk of arbitration ended when the company fired 173 union men on February 19, immediately provoking a walkout. Mayor John E. Reyburn, who had pushed for a settlement the previous June, now backed the company, and city police guarded strikebreakers. Thousands of Philadelphians joined strikers in attacking them and the trolley cars that went out on the streets. Nonunion workers at the massive Baldwin Locomotive Works destroyed a street car and then

141

threw tools and bolts at police, who fired back at them. Losing control of the situation, the mayor requested Governor Edwin S. Stuart to send the State Police. The Central Labor Union responded with a call for a general strike to begin March 4 for all workers except those who handled daily necessities. The number who left their jobs would reach one hundred thousand.

Labor leaders summoned Philadelphians to show further support by gathering on March 5 at Independence Hall. Mayor Reyburn banned the meeting, but twenty thousand came anyway, only to be driven away by mounted State Police. The Pennsylvania Federation of Labor then threatened to extend the general strike to the whole state if the company continued to refuse arbitration. But that threat was an empty one, and most of the city's sympathy strikers returned to their jobs within three weeks. Still, the general strike increased momentum toward a settlement. The company offered a wage increase and promised not to discriminate against union men. The AASERE tried to obtain full recognition, but national union leaders urged them to drop the demand. The union accepted the company's offer, but the rank and file rejected the settlement by seven votes out of several thousand cast. Under intense pressure to end the strike, the union declared that since the vote was so close, it had decided to order its members back to work. The Philadelphia Rapid Transit Company had been pushed to the edge of bankruptcy. But ironically, new ownership so influenced workers by improved wages and benefits delivered through the once reviled Keystone Carmen that support for the AASERE dwindled over the next several years.

In the western part of the state, two of the longest disputes in Pennsylvania labor history showed the bitter depths of conflict over union recognition in the Progressive Era. Strong union support enabled both Westmoreland County mine workers and Erie iron molders to resist their bosses for sixteen months, but both lost their strikes. The thirteen thousand bituminous mine workers in the eastern part of Westmoreland County had never been able to win United Mine Workers representation and the benefits the union had brought workers in the Central Competitive Field. Miners' concerns over state-mandated changes in the explosives they could use mushroomed into UMWA organizing at the Keystone Coal and Coke Company in Greensburg. When the company fired those who signed up, workers declared a strike for the UMWA contract. By June 1910, some ten thousand mine workers had been organized and the walkout spread to other companies near Irwin and Latrobe. But the companies were determined to keep the competitive advantage of non-union operation. They evicted so many strikers from company homes that the union set up more than one hundred tent colonies. Overall, it would provide more than $1 million in aid for the strike, but even that level of support could not achieve victory. Court injunctions and favorable enforcement by sheriff's deputies and the State Police curtailed picketing and efforts by strikers to intimidate strikebreakers. In one case which shows the extent to which employers would go to keep workers in line, a pro-union priest named Father Yusek was arrested for trespassing because he visited parishioners who lived in a company house. The UMWA called an end to the strike in July 1911.

Iron molders were approximately 40 percent of Erie's industrial work force. Although their trade required considerable skill, workers faced low wages, especially during the lengthy apprenticeship period. Danger characterized their work as well, ranging from burns from molten metal to the occupational disease of silicosis. But the Erie Manufacturers Association, like other groups of employers in the metal trades, maintained an implacable hostility toward unions. The firing of the president and another member of the Erie iron molders' union local by the Erie Engine Works touched off a series of walkouts beginning late in November 1912, and by February 1913 some five hundred were on strike against ten different employers. The companies obtained injunctions to limit activity in support of the strike, and one striker was arrested merely for calling a strikebreaker a "scab." As the conflict dragged on into the summer, a few employers settled, recognizing the union. But most stayed with the Manufacturers Association and rejected the city council's efforts to arbitrate. Violence increased, resulting in one death and several shootings, and local authorities requested State Police assistance from the governor in August. Like others across the state, Erie's workers first tried to resist by refusing to clear the streets, but mounted troopers drove them away. A number of foundries went out of business as the walkout dragged on, but the strikers could not win recognition. The union's international headquarters ended

State Police on patrol in Erie during moulders strike, 1913. (Pennsylvania State Archives)

its financial support, and in February 1914, those molders who remained on strike voted to return. Disgruntled workers asserted themselves at the ballot box, where they turned out the mayor and a number of anti-labor city councilmen.

Industrial conflict across Pennsylvania only intensified after Europe went to war in the summer of 1914. At first the American economy was hurt by fears of war and the disruption of trade. In 1915 and 1916, however, factories across the nation and the state turned out war supplies for the combatants as coal mines, steel mills, and other industrial facilities functioned at capacity. The end of immigration from Europe further tightened the labor supply, offering new opportunities for African Americans to leave the South for industrial work, initiating the "Great Migration." As at other times of nearly full employment, workers moved to take advantage of their bargaining power, striking some 574 times in 1916 in Pennsylvania alone, approximately one-seventh of the nationwide total.

More than twenty thousand workers found employment among various plants established by inventor and industrialist George Westinghouse in the industrial suburbs of East Pittsburgh, Wilmerding, and Swissvale. Workers ranged from highly-skilled machinists to unskilled female light-bulb assemblers, and they made an incred-

144

Women winding transformer coils at Westinghouse Electric and Manufacturing Company—East Pittsburgh, early twentieth century. (Pennsylvania State Archives)

ible variety of products from circuit breakers, transformers, and electrical motors to railroad safety equipment and, increasingly, ammunition and other war materials for export to Europe. A great many workers at this state-of-the-art manufacturing complex experienced the pressure of incentive wage plans adapted from Taylor's "scientific management." Several brief walkouts occurred in 1914 and 1915. In October 1915, to forestall further agitation, the company gave a bonus of 6 percent and reduced the work week from fifty-four hours to fifty-two at no reduction in pay. The International Association of Machinists (IAM) organized some skilled machinists at Westinghouse, but other machinists believed that dividing workers into the IAM and a number of other AFL craft unions would never succeed at a firm as diverse as Westinghouse. Instead they formed an independent union open to all employees called the American Industrial Union. When one of its leaders, John Hall, was fired on April 20, 1916, some thirteen thousand workers, most of whom were unskilled, left their jobs on the next day. They demanded a wage increase and a further cut in hours. Officials from the IAM and AFL offered support, since the IAM was in the midst of a nationwide drive for the eight-hour day. But the strike's local leaders took their

145

own militant action. On May 1 and again on May 2, in an effort to expand the strike beyond plants owned by Westinghouse, several thousand workers marched the several miles from East Pittsburgh to the industrial towns of Braddock and Rankin on the Monongahela River. Among the many factories along the route was the area's foremost symbol of antiunionism, U.S. Steel's Edgar Thomson Works. On both days the crowd fought with guards and deputies to enter that plant, among others. On May 2, a battle occurred in and around the Thomson Works for about one hour, resulting in three dead and more than thirty wounded. This brought the state militia, which would be housed on Westinghouse property. Local authorities then proceeded to arrest a number of marchers and their leaders. These included a twenty-one-year-old worker named Anna K. Bell, who was charged with inciting a riot but later acquitted. Workers soon returned to their jobs, and it would be two decades before unionism would revive at Westinghouse.

A final walkout shows the limitations on the growing power that the union movement could bring to confrontations with management. In one of the state's strongest union towns, Wilkes-Barre, trolley workers struck for fourteen months in 1915 and 1916, but without success. This strike demonstrated that state and federal mediators could not guarantee a peaceful resolution. The UMWA had strengthened its presence in the anthracite region since 1902 and lent its considerable support to union organizing. For example, UMWA support had helped youthful silk workers in the Lackawanna Valley organized by the United Textile Workers win the right to join the union in a three-month dispute in 1907 in which they achieved a wage increase. In Wilkes-Barre, the same organizer who led Chester's strikers in 1908, P.J. Shea, came to organize the workers of the Wilkes-Barre Railway Company for the AASERE in 1914, and the union threatened to strike in January 1915. But pressure from Congressman John J. Casey and state and federal mediators led to a settlement that resulted in union recognition. This resolved all issues except the amount and scope of a wage increase, but the arbitrators took several months to reach an agreement on this issue. The settlement fell apart when one of the arbitrators, John Price Jackson, Pennsylvania's secretary of labor and industry, decided to change his vote on the issue of the differential between veteran employees

State Policeman on damaged trolley car—Wilkes-Barre, 1917.
(Pennsylvania State Archives)

and recent hires. After ten months of wrangling over the arbitration award, the company imposed a settlement and some three hundred employees walked out on October 14, 1915.

Victory seemed likely for the union, since perhaps three-quarters or more of the Wyoming Valley's workers were union members. They boycotted the trolleys so effectively that the number of passengers dropped by more than 70 percent on most routes. With aid from the UMWA and other unions, the strikers received relatively generous strike benefits as well. Yet the company quickly brought in strikebreakers and gradually restored service. As the strike dragged on, it became clear that the company could hold out longer than the workers. Workers voted to accept the company's terms by a narrow margin on December 16, 1916. The union could not even guarantee work for all of those who wanted to return to their jobs, only that those not hired would be taken back as vacancies occurred.

The entry of the United States into World War I in April 1917 would give labor unions an unprecedented opportunity. Mobilizing the world's most powerful industrial nation for war demanded a level of organization from American society that would shatter what remained of the myths of individualistic independence that characterized the world view of Abraham Lincoln. To win the war, both federal and state government expected labor and capital to work together, and labor disputes could no longer be viewed as essen-

147

tially private matters. To gain worker support for the war effort, government officials would solicit the cooperation of conservative, "respectable" labor leaders. When faced with disgruntled workers, managers could no longer merely refuse to bargain with unions. Meanwhile, the war induced the expansion of Pennsylvania's mines, mills, factories and the communities that surrounded them. Thousands of Pennsylvanians went overseas to fight the Germans, but many more stayed at home to fight battles of their own, where the identity of the enemy and the strategy for victory would be much less clear.

Perry K. Blatz is an associate professor in the department of history at Duquesne University and the author of *Democratic Miners* and *Work and Labor Relations in the Anthracite Coal Industry, 1875-1925.*

Keystone Vignette

Terence V. Powderly

Perry K. Blatz

Terence V. Powderly was born January 22, 1849 to Irish immigrants in Carbondale, Pennsylvania. At seventeen he went to work in a machine shop and, a few years later, joined the Machinists and Blacksmiths Union and became active in the Scranton local. In 1873, he joined the growing Knights of Labor, a union he would eventually lead as he became the most important labor leader in the United States during the 1880s. His association with the Knights in the 1870s led to blacklistings and firings, yet he maintained his commitment to the ideals of unionism and vigorously organized workers across the state.

In 1878, Powderly won election to the post of mayor of the City of Scranton as a candidate of the Greenback-Labor Party. One year later he was elected as the "Grand Master Workman" of the Knights of Labor. As head of the union, Powderly discouraged strikes and struggled to steer the union away from radicalism. He succeeded at eliminating some of the pomp and mystery surrounding the Knights by curtailing its quasi-religious rituals. During his tenure the union grew to more than 700,000 members nationwide by 1886. But internal problems, Powderly's lack of administrative skills, and other issues brought the union to virtual collapse by the early 1890s. Powderly was ousted as its leader in 1893.

Powderly had begun to study law in the 1870s. Following his ouster from the Knights of Labor, he returned to it and was admitted to the Pennsylvania Bar in 1894. He practiced mainly in Scranton. In 1897 President William McKinley appointed Powderly as commissioner of immigration. For most of the remainder of his life, Powderly worked in Washington on immigration issues. He passed away on June 24, 1924, and was interred in his native Scranton's Cathedral Cemetery, not far from the grave of John Mitchell, the president of the United Mine Workers of America who had led anthracite mine workers in their successful strikes of 1900 and 1902.

Keystone Vignett

The Lattimer Massacre

Kenneth C. Wolensky

Perhaps the most horrifying incident of violence in American labor history occurred at Lattimer Mines, near Hazleton, on September 10, 1897. Immigrants from eastern and southern Europe who dominated that area's mining work force had numerous grievances. For one, coal companies held paternalistic attitudes toward them and many experienced prejudice and bigotry (Slavic miners were frequently referred to as "Hunkies," for example). As relative newcomers to the region, they were often assigned the most difficult and dangerous jobs in the mines. In addition, their employers expected them to shop at company-owned stores where prices were inflated. Workers were also troubled by and "alien tax" enacted that year by the Pennsylvania General Assembly which required a three-cent per-day levy on all immigrant workers.

Adding to the list of grievances was a new policy implemented by Gomer Jones—the Welsh superintendent for the Lehigh and Wilkes-Barre Coal Company. Jones required mule drivers, most of whom were in their teens or even younger, to work longer days for no extra pay to pick up and return their mules to a new, more distant stable. On August 14, mule drivers at the Honey Brook Colliery in McAdoo left their jobs. The following day Jones approached picketers at the colliery and attacked John Bodan, a young boy, with a crowbar. In defense of Bodan, Jones was nearly killed by strikers. The strike spread rapidly in the next few weeks so that by early September, some five thousand workers had walked off the job.

As mine workers marched through the area to extend the strike, coal operators demanded that Luzerne County Sheriff James L. Martin quell the unrest. Martin declared a state of civil disorder and formed a posse of eighty volunteers consisting mainly of professional men with English, Irish, and German backgrounds—people whose livelihoods were, in one form or another, linked with the coal

Strikers marching on the day of the Lattimer Massacre. (Pennsylvania State Archives)

operators. Martin armed his deputies with Winchester rifles and metal-piercing bullets and buckshot.

On Thursday, September 9, a delegation of Lattimer workers met with members of the new United Mine Workers local at Harwood, requesting that they march to Lattimer the following day to close the colliery. On a warm and sunny Friday, September 10, three hundred men assembled at Harwood and set off for Lattimer. As the column neared Hazleton they encountered Martin who drew his pistol, pointed it at the head of a marcher, and ordered them to disperse. They refused and a fight broke out. Further violence was averted when the police chief said that the column could continue if they agreed to march around Hazleton. They agreed and proceeded peaceably.

Anxieties were running high. Martin and his deputies boarded trolleys to pursue the marchers at Lattimer. Trolley passengers reported that the talk was of shooting. One deputy was overheard saying "I bet I drop six of them when I get over there." A reporter relayed to the *Wilkes-Barre Times* that serious trouble was on the horizon. Word spread quickly. In Lattimer, children were hustled from the schoolhouse by apprehensive mothers. The colliery whistle sounded a shutdown. Company police met Martin's force, totaling over 150 men, and lined the forked entrance to the town.

At about 3:45 in the afternoon the marchers, who now numbered over four hundred arrayed behind an American flag, approached Lattimer. Martin walked to the head of the column and announced that they must disperse. Not all marchers, particularly those in the back, could hear or see him. Martin attempted to tear the flag from the hands of immigrant Steve Jurich.

Thwarted, he grabbed a marcher from the second row and a scuffle broke out. Martin drew his pistol and pulled the trigger, but the weapon did not fire. Then someone yelled "Fire!" and "Give two or three shots!" Several eyewitnesses claimed it was the sheriff, though he would later deny it. A barrage of shots rang out. The flag bearer appealed to God in Slovak, "O Joj! Joj! Joj!" as he fell mortally wounded.

Marchers scattered, some running toward the nearby schoolhouse. Teachers Charles Guscott and Grace Coyle watched events unfold and thought, at first, that the bullets were blanks until several men running toward them fell to the ground. Some deputies broke ranks to take better aim at fleeing marchers. Many were shot in the back as they ran. Trying to escape a bullet, miner John Terri threw himself on the ground. Another miner fell on top of him, dead. Andrew Jurecheck attempted to run toward the schoolhouse and was stopped by a bullet in his back. He cried out in vain that he wanted to see his wife before he died. Mathias Czaja was also hit in the back and fell. Clement Platek stumbled and clutched his side then fell. Some of the wounded cried out for help, to which one eyewitness heard a deputy respond, "We'll give you hell, not water, hunkies!"

The shooting continued for at least a minute and a half, though some eyewitnesses claimed it may have been three minutes or more. Perhaps as many as 150 shots were fired. The magazines in many of the Winchesters were fully discharged. Blood, smoke, road dust, and cries of anguish overwhelmed the scene. Nineteen marchers—Poles, Slovaks, and Lithuanians—lay dead while thirty-six were wounded. The force of the steel bullets tore many of the bodies to pieces. News of the carnage spread quickly. Wagons and trolleys moved the dead and dying to local hospitals and morgues. While

Sheriff Martin departed for Wilkes-Barre to meet with his attorney, families of marchers gathered in disbelief to learn the fate of the men. The deputies scattered, some to Atlantic City to seek refuge under assumed names in a seaside hotel.

The next day, Governor Daniel H. Hastings dispatched the Third Brigade of the State Militia to the area. Many feared reprisals against the deputies. However, except for one attack on the home of Gomer Jones, the immigrants remained peaceful and hoped that the legal system might bring the deputies to justice. Funerals continued for several days, some drawing crowds of as many as eight thousand. Within two weeks the strike had sputtered to an end, with the workers winning only limited concessions at a few mines. A trial began early the following year and lasted twenty-seven days at the Luzerne County Court House. To the amazement of immigrant communities, the jury, none of whom were mine workers or of eastern or southern European descent, acquitted Sheriff Martin and his deputies of complicity in the massacre. They could not fix responsibility for the shootings, and refused to assign collective blame.

Kenneth C. Wolensky is a historian with the Pennsylvania Historical and Museum Commission.

Keystone Vignette

Rinaldo Cappellini
The Knox Mine Disaster
and the Decline of the
Anthracite Coal Industry

Perry K. Blatz
Robert P. Wolensky

The life of Rinaldo Cappellini illustrates the opportunities within the labor movement for immigrants as well as the bitter struggles for power which often characterized unions, especially in a declining industry like anthracite coal, which reached its peak production in 1917. Cappellini was born in 1895, in Nocera Umbra in the central Italian province of Perugia. He emigrated to the United States with his mother and two older brothers in 1903. The family settled in Pittston, Luzerne County, and young Rinaldo and his brothers soon went to work in the mines. At the age of fifteen, Rinaldo lost his right arm and several fingers on this left hand when he was pinned beneath a set of runaway coal cars. He was one year less than the legal age for work in the mine, sixteen. Thereafter, Rinaldo worked on several occasions in the mines and as a waiter, earning a reputation for his restaurant singing charades.

In the summer of 1920, twenty-five-year-old Rinaldo Cappellini led a strike that had little to do with the United Mine Workers of America. Despite the union's fitful attempts at organizing anthracite miners, it had accomplished little in and around Pittston. By 1920, the mainly Italian work force at the Pennsylvania Coal Company's operations in Pittston grew increasingly distressed over the company's practice of giving control of ever-larger portions of its mining operations to independent contractors who hired their own men. Such contractors had long been charged with making labor conditions worse by brutally commanding workers and demanding bribes from them in order to keep their jobs. Cappellini galvanized the Pennsylvania Coal Company workers in a three-month strike to end contracting. The company refused to end the practice, but some contractors acquiesced after having their homes dynamited. Cappellini's actions catapulted him to the presidency of anthracite District One of the United Mine Workers with its nearly sixty thousand members in 1923. The strike temporarily curtailed contracting and reinvigorated the UMWA's organization among Pittston's Italians.

Cappellini was reelected in 1925 and 1927. But, by the late 1920s the anthracite industry had begun a decline which would accelerate in future decades. With fewer jobs available, contracting returned as companies attempted to cut costs. A 1928 wildcat strike at a Pittston mine of the Pennsylvania Coal Company initiated by Cappellini's own local led to the murder of union officials that many blamed on a few contractors and their allies in organized crime.

These episodes, combined with mine workers growing discontent over contracting, unemployment, and underemployment inspired an insurgent movement against Cappellini. Amidst growing chaos, UMWA President John L. Lewis persuaded Cappellini to resign the district presidency in July 1928.

Rinaldo Cappellini would never again exercise similar power in union affairs, although he devoted the remainder of his career to the labor movement. Apparently regretting his decision to resign, in 1933 he helped to form the United Anthracite Miners of Pennsylvania, a rival to the UMWA, to better represent the interests of hard coal labor. The alternative union—whose leader Thomas Maloney would later be murdered by a letter bomb—collapsed under tremendous pressure from the UMWA in 1935. Cappellini would in later years accept a position with the UMWA as an organizer in District 50, which focused attention on organizing workers in non-mining industries. He organized chemical workers in Niagara Falls, many of whom had come from Pittston in search of work because of the continuing decline in anthracite mining. Cappellini also organized for the UMWA in West Virginia, all the while maintaining a residence in northeastern Pennsylvania. He died at Harveys Lake, north of Wilkes-Barre, on July 5, 1966.

The contracting that Cappellini battled in the 1920s continued

Rinaldo Cappellini. (F. Charles Petrillo Collection, Wilkes-Barre)

to expand during the long decline of the anthracite industry over the next few decades. Some major contractors had questionable backgrounds and connections, like Pittston's Santo Volpe—alleged to be a founder of northeastern Pennsylvania's leading organized crime family. During the 1930s, the large anthracite producers expanded the contracting system by leasing entire mining operations to independent companies. Leasing and its associated corrupt practices eventually brought about the end of deep mining in the northern anthracite region with the Knox Mine Disaster of 1959.

On January 22, 1959, employees of the Knox Coal Company, a lessee of the Pennsylvania Coal Company, dug an illegal chamber under the Susquehanna River in Port Griffith near Pittston. The river broke through the mine, killing twelve, and eventually flooding several adjacent underground workings. The disaster exposed the extent of corruption which had emerged in the contract-leasing system. Officials of the Knox Coal Company—co-founded by John Sciandra, identified by the Pennsylvania Crime Commission as "top boss" of northeastern Pennsylvania's leading organized crime family—ignored safety rules and union wage scales as they mined perhaps the most pristine coal vein in the region. A subsequent investigation revealed that a silent partner in the Knox Coal Company was August J. Lippi, a president of UMWA District One as Cappellini had been. Lippi and UMWA Local 8005 official Dominick Alaimo—a reputed member of the Sciandra and, later, Bufalino crime syndicate—received payoffs to secure labor peace among Knox workers, blatantly violating the Taft-Hartley Act. Indictments and convictions resulted in prison terms and fines for Lippi, Alaimo, and other officials from the Knox and Pennsylvania Coal Companies.

Perry K. Blatz is an associate professor of history, Duquesne University, and Robert P. Wolensky is a professor of sociology, University of Wisconsin-Stevens Point.

Readings for Chapter Three

Aurand, Harold W. *From the Molly Maguires to the United Mine Workers*. Philadelphia: Temple University Press, 1971.

Blatz, Perry K. *Democratic Miners: Work and Labor Relations in the Anthracite Coal Industry, 1875-1925*. New York: State University of New York Press, 1994.

Bodnar, John; Simon, Roger; and Weber, Michael P. *Lives of Their Own: Blacks, Italians, and Poles in Pittsburgh, 1900-1960*. Urbana: University of Illinois Press, 1982.

Bodnar, John. *Workers' World: Kinship, Community, and Protest in an Industrial Society*. Baltimore: Johns Hopkins University Press, 1982.

Bomberger, Bruce and Sisson, William. *Made in Pennsylvania: An Overview of the Major Historical Industries of the Commonwealth*. Harrisburg: Pennsylvania Historical and Museum Commission, 1991.

Broehl, Wayne G. *The Molly Maguires*. Cambridge: Harvard University Press, 1964.

Bruce, Robert V. *1877: Year of Violence*. Indianapolis: Bobbs-Merrill, 1959.

Burgoyne, Arthur. *The Homestead Strike of 1892*. Pittsburgh: University of Pittsburgh Press, 1979.

Butler, Elizabeth B. *Women and the Trades: Pittsburgh, 1907-1908*. Pittsburgh: University of Pittsburgh Press, 1984.

Cox, Harold E. "The Wilkes-Barre Street Railway Strike of 1915," *Pennsylvania Magazine of History and Biography* 94 (January 1970): 75-94.

Foner, Philip S. *A History of the Labor Movement in the United States*. Volumes 3, 4, and 5. New York: International Publishers, 1947-1988.

Fones-Wolf, Ken. *Trade Union Gospel: Christianity and Labor in Industrial Philadelphia, 1865-1915*. Philadelphia: Temple University Press, 1989.

French, John D. "'Reaping the Whirlwind': The Origins of the Allegheny County Greenback Labor Party in 1877," *Western Pennsylvania Historical Magazine* 64 (April 1981): 97-120.

Golab, Caroline. *Immigrant Destinations*. Philadelphia: Temple

University Press, 1977.

Greene, Victor R. *Slavic Community on Strike: Immigrant Labor in Pennsylvania Anthracite.* Notre Dame: University of Notre Dame Press, 1968.

Gutman, Herbert G. *Work, Culture, and Society in Industrializing America.* New York: Knopf, 1976.

Ingham, John. "A Strike in the Progressive Era: McKees Rocks, 1909," *Pennsylvania Magazine of History and Biography* 90 (July 1966): 353-77.

Krause, Paul. *The Battle for Homestead, 1880-1892: Politics, Culture, and Steel.* Pittsburgh: University of Pittsburgh Press, 1992.

Kuritz, Hyman. "The Pennsylvania State Government and Labor Controls from 1865 to 1922," Ph.D. dissertation. Ann Arbor: University Microfilms, 1968.

Lane, Roger. *William Dorsey's Philadelphia and Ours.* New York: Oxford University Press, 1991.

McFarland, C.K. "Crusade for Child Laborers: 'Mother' Jones and the March of the Mill Children," *Pennsylvania History* 38 (July 1971): 283-296.

Montgomery, David. *The Fall of the House of Labor.* New York: Cambridge University Press, 1987.

Novak, Michael. *The Guns of Lattimer.* New Brunswick: Transaction Publishers, 1996.

Powderly, Terence V. *Thirty Years of Labor, 1859-1889.* New York: A.M. Kelley, 1967.

Rich, Judith and Kenneth C. Wolensky. *Child Labor in Pennsylvania.* Pennsylvania Historical and Museum Commission Historic Pennsylvania Leaflet No. 43. Harrisburg, 1998.

Roberts, Ellis. *The Breaker Whistle Blows.* Scranton: Anthracite Museum Press, 1984.

Salay, David (Ed.). *Hard Coal, Hard Times: Ethnicity and Labor in the Anthracite Region.* Scranton: Anthracite Museum Press, 1984.

Scranton, Philip. *Figured Tapestry: Production, Markets, and Power in Philadelphia Textiles, 1885-1941.* New York: Cambridge University Press, 1989.

Stepenoff, Bonnie. "Child Labor in Pennsylvania's Silk Mills: Protest and Change, 1900-1910." *Pennsylvania History* 59 (April 1992): 101-121.

Wall, Joseph F. *Andrew Carnegie*. New York: Oxford University Press, 1970.

Wallace, Anthony F.C. *St. Clair: A Nineteenth-Century Coal Town's Experience With A Disaster-Prone Industry*. New York: Knopf, 1987.

Ware, Norman A. *The Labor Movement in the United States 1860-1890: A Study in Democracy*. New York: Vintage, 1929.

Wolensky, Kenneth C. *The Lattimer Massacre*. Pennsylvania Historical and Museum Commission Historic Pennsylvania Leaflet No. 15. Harrisburg, 1997.

Whelan, Frank A. "'I Can Stand It': Charles M. Schwab and the Bethlehem Steel Strike of 1910." *Canal History and Technology Proceedings* XIII (March 1994): 63-80.

Chapter Four

Shaping a New
Labor Movement,
1917-1941

Peter Gottlieb

Swift currents of change converged upon Pennsylvania labor from the beginning of the First World War to the eve of the Second World War. Exigencies of war production, decline in foreign immigration, rural migrant recruits to the work force, corporations' open-shop offensives, new patterns of household consumption and family life, growing government involvement in industrial relations—all these combined to alter the environment in which workers lived and labored. Sharp reverses in labor unions' fortunes after World War I convinced some observers that employers in the Commonwealth had mastered workers' organizations. But challenged by their collective weakness and the bitter hardships of the collapsed economy of the 1930s, unionized and nonunionized employees in Pennsylvania reformed their institutions and confronted their adversaries on both the economic and political front.

Pennsylvania Labor During World War I

When the United States declared war on the European Central Powers in April, 1917, Pennsylvania workers had already been feeling the effects of hostilities for many months. Munitions contracts from Britain and France had increased the pace of industrial production in many manufacturing centers; the immigration of workers to the United States had been interrupted; and the fortunes of organized labor in the state had improved because of employers' need for workers. For the next two years, the war would exert a profound influence on organized labor in Pennsylvania, and its aftereffects determined many of the crucial developments in the years immediately following the armistice.

Most of Pennsylvania's political leaders enthusiastically supported the United States' entry into World War I. Yet many ordinary Pennsylvanians did not share their sentiment. Antiwar attitudes were widespread before 1917 among the large population of German descent and in some parts of the labor movement, particularly the socialists. Large antiwar rallies were staged in Philadelphia in 1915, and feelings against British imperialist policies ran high. Though support for the Allied war effort grew stronger through 1916 and early 1917, considerable antiwar sentiment lingered on the eve of America's declaration of war. In Reading, the local Socialist Party increased its voter registration and its share of the votes cast in the mayoral election of 1917. (For a profile of a Pennsylvania Socialist leader, see Keystone Vignette: "James Hudson Maurer," p. 203.) When military conscription began, it was resisted in industrial towns like Donora, where 40 percent of draft registrants gave their draft boards fictitious addresses. Both latent and active opposition to the war effort among Pennsylvania workers resulted in a patriotic drumbeat of pro-war propaganda by such vital armament producers as Midvale Steel and Ordnance, and Westinghouse Electric.

American participation in World War I military campaigns from 1917 to 1918 had varying effects on Pennsylvania's working population. The lives of young men who enlisted or were drafted changed most quickly and drastically, of course. Most soldiers and sailors came from working-class families, and the state units that saw combat took heavy casualties. Pennsylvania workers who stayed home

162

Shipbuilding during World War I—Hog Island, Philadelphia. (Pennsylvania State Archives)

did their fighting in other ways. Propaganda from federal and state governments and from employers encouraged men and women to work intensively for long hours, seven days a week to turn out clothing, fuel, food, ships, locomotives, and munitions. The war economy provided larger incomes for Pennsylvania workers due to increased full-time employment and enhanced hourly wages. In 1914, there had been considerable unemployment among Pennsylvania blue-collar employees, but joblessness gradually disappeared in 1915

163

and 1916. The huge requirement for industrial production in 1917 and 1918 afforded steady work to anyone in the state who sought it.

The need for labor throughout Pennsylvania drew workers who previously had not performed industrial labor to factories and mines. Women entered Pennsylvania's garment, textile, and cannery industries in large numbers from 1916 to 1918, while some took positions in traditionally male occupations like machinists, train yard laborers, and foundry workers. Bethlehem Steel Corporation's mill in Steelton employed women for manual labor in 1918 while General Electric hired an entirely female force for its new Philadelphia plant that opened in 1917, because it could not find "efficient" men to employ. A few fortunate women also had opportunities in skilled labor.

Hopeful jobseekers came to the state's industrial centers from other parts of the country as well. Some were encouraged to relocate by large employers whose established source of labor had been cut off by the war. Both black and white southerners, for example, were recruited to move north and take jobs in the state. Men and women from rural districts of Pennsylvania switched from housework or farming to manufacturing jobs during the war. While both they and their supervisors often viewed the war work as temporary, the new jobs usually paid these workers much higher incomes and allowed greater savings than had their previous employment. Black workers from the South who came to Pennsylvania cities and towns were especially conspicuous among the newcomers. Seldom welcomed by the residents of the towns they moved into, southern blacks found unfair treatment both at work and in the community, restrictions on opportunities for obtaining higher-paid jobs, and abominable housing. Many of them, particularly the young and single, responded by moving from one employer to another and from town to town in search of better opportunities. They could do this because there was high demand for their services. Some black men were provided free transportation from Florida and other southeastern states in 1916 to work on railroad track maintenance gangs, blast furnace crews, steel mill labor pools, and construction teams. While most black women continued in the cooking, cleaning, and laundering jobs to which they were almost completely restricted in normal periods, a few also entered factories and industrial workplaces in 1917 and 1918.

Living and working conditions for Pennsylvania wage earners grew worse during the war years. Increased production and long hours led to exhaustion and an increase in industrial accidents. The arrival of thousands of new workers to cities and towns created severe overcrowding in working-class houses and tenements. Even the comparatively high earnings of the war years were often just enough to cover the increased costs for shelter, food, clothing, and other necessities. War workers in Pittsburgh and other cities ate and slept in converted warehouses, railroad cars, and river barges. These crowded and unsanitary conditions contributed to the outbreak of an influenza epidemic in 1918.

During this period benefits and drawbacks were evident for organized labor in Pennsylvania. The drawbacks took two quite distinct forms. One was the forcible silencing of labor radicals by both the state and federal governments. Antiwar members of the Socialist Party, as well as other groups like the Industrial Workers of the World and the Socialist Labor Party, were put under official ban after 1917. Some were fired from their jobs and some were imprisoned. Office records, bank accounts, and newspapers of radical organizations were seized under federal anti-treason statutes, disrupting the groups' daily operations and communications. Despite the fact that these pro-labor, antiwar groups did not have large followings among workers in the state, they had been vital allies of trade unions. Their demobilization was actually welcomed by conservative unionists who did not foresee a time in the near future when organized workers would need the help of these militants.

Another drawback of the war economy for the labor movement was the immense turnover of wage earners in Pennsylvania workplaces. The rapid shifting of employees from job to job, the departure of thousands of workers for military service, and the arrival of many new employees in dozens of towns to take war jobs amounted to a significant reconstitution of the state's labor force. It would have taken a far stronger and more inclusive labor movement to prevent such labor force shifts from weakening union organization. Larger and better-organized unions absorbed men and women in union work places, but the labor movement as a whole had to struggle to maintain discipline and collective bargaining.

Federal government sponsorship of collective bargaining in the interest of continuous war production was one of the benefits of the war effort that partially offset such difficulties. Railroads and coal mines employing thousands of Pennsylvania workers were administered directly by federal officials during the war to insure sufficient support for the military. Government officials responsible for operating these industries attended to union demands favorably. Workers were freer to join unions without employer interference than ever before and enrolled in the labor movement in unprecedented numbers.

The National War Labor Board (NWLB) created local boards throughout Pennsylvania to mediate labor-management conflicts and adjust disputes between unions and employers. Often reluctantly, employers had to negotiate with labor organizations and sign wage, hour, and working conditions agreements. Where companies adamantly refused to recognize bona fide unions, federal policy forced them to recognize and bargain with employees. In 1918, union machinists at the Midvale Steel and Ordnance Company mill in Nicetown complained to local NWLB officials of management resistance to their requests for conferences. The board began an investigation, prompting the company to create its own employees' organization and begin collective bargaining. Some Pennsylvania companies responded by accepting alternative company unions to satisfy NWLB policy and to avoid dealing with real unions.

Virtually full employment increased unions' bargaining power, allowing workers to settle disputes, reach new agreements, and conclude strikes quickly—and often in their favor. Employers, who were competing fiercely with each other to attract employees, often had to meet unions' demands or suffer irretrievable losses. The record high demand for labor in 1917-18 provided workers with the luxury of choosing among several available jobs—of bargaining, in effect, for the best position available.

Coupled with favorable government policies and the propaganda over war goals, the advantageous labor market made Pennsylvania workers eager for a new order in industry and in the state's economy. Expressed in different ways according to their nationality, race, skill level, and gender, workers' rising expectations gave unions an opportunity to lead decades-old struggles for shorter hours of work and greater economic security. Iron mill workers in Washington, Pennsylvania claimed that, by establishing a local union in 1918, they had been "victorious in our first fight for democracy." Employees at Johnstown's Cambria Steel Works paraded on Labor Day, 1918, with signs proclaiming, "We Are for the Shorter Day and More Pay."

Such high expectations and growing militancy continued into the post-war years. Railroad workers and coal miners who had worked under government administration during the war proposed schemes for public ownership of their industries, including forms of workers representation in the management of enterprises. John Brophy, the head of the United Mine Workers' central Pennsylvania district, helped to formulate the plan for nationalization of the coal industry. Across the state, workers who toiled, rented, voted, and socialized under the close control of their employers were eager to unionize and lift employers' rule over their lives.

Labor's Defeat in the Postwar Crisis

After the war, the aspirations of Pennsylvania workers collided head-on with the equally firm determination of employers to return to the form of labor-management relations over which they had presided before World War I. Businessmen recognized that industrial democracy was a widespread idea among their employees begging for acknowledgement. Yet they resolved to defeat its progressive forms of public ownership and joint union-management control over terms of employment and working conditions. They were determined to roll back the gains in membership and the collective bargaining contracts that unions had made in 1917-18 and to bring back the open shop as a basis for industrial relations. Conflicting goals of workers and employers were highlighted in the 1919 steel strike, a national dispute in which Pennsylvania antagonists played a pivotal role.

In the summer of 1918, the American Federation of Labor formed the National Committee for the Organization of Iron and Steel Workers. Led by William Z. Foster and John Fitzpatrick, Chicago trade unionists who had succeeded in unionizing the stockyards and packing houses during World War I, the National Committee included representatives of twenty-four unions who claimed jurisdiction over

167

The shop floor at Pencoyd Iron Works, Montgomery County. (Pennsylvania State Archives)

workers in the steel industry. Many steelworkers joined the organizing campaign in the Chicago area and the National Committee, headed by Foster, soon concentrated its efforts in western Pennsylvania. Mill employees in this bastion of the open shop soon showed the same zeal for unionization as did their counterparts in the Midwest. But the steel companies in Pennsylvania, exemplified by the U.S. Steel Corporation and the Bethlehem Steel Company, claimed to protect their workers' interests by listening to any employee's complaints and by running a large number of welfare programs. The companies, nevertheless, took precautions against a strike by fortifying mills, deputizing sympathetic residents of the company towns, and advertising the virtues of the open shop in newspapers. Steel companies also refused to meet with union representatives, adhering strictly to a policy of talking only with groups of their own employees.

When the strike deadline of September 2, 1919 was reached without an agreement, several hundred thousand steelworkers left their jobs. In Pittsburgh, Johnstown, and Bethlehem the strike began with strength and determination especially among foreign-born workers. Additional workers joined the strike during its first two weeks. The National Committee, with the help of the American Federation of Labor, tried to persuade President Woodrow Wilson to intervene to bring about a settlement. Yet White House conferences failed to produce an agreement between steel industrialists and the unions on basic principles. The strike became a test of endurance.

The advantage, however, swung decisively to the employers' side. The Pennsylvania State Police—labeled "Cossacks" by strikers and sympathizers—controlled the streets and alleys around the mills, breaking up picket lines and groups of strikers. In Natrona, where workers at West Penn Steel and Allegheny Steel joined the strike, a resident recalled the police intimidation:

> My Dad, Mother, one brother, and two of my sisters were setting on a porch when one of the police on horseback passed by and my sister, about five years old, hollered that a Cossack was comming [sic] down the street. He must have heard and also understood her because he turned his horse and rode up the steps and pointed a big club at my Father and said, "If I ever hear her or anybody call us Cossacks, we will haul you away to jail."

The steel companies drew on all of their resources to defeat the strike. They assembled crews of strikebreakers to operate the mills. Pro-employer newspapers broadcast misinformation about the National Committee and kept the companies' law-and-order stance steadily in the minds of readers. The growing national scare over radical activities during 1919 offered steel employers another weapon with which to attack the strike. By claiming that the rank-and-file workers' real goal was to revolutionize America, employers heightened fear among the general population and gained strong supporters in veterans groups and patriotic citizens organizations, some of which joined police in attacking picketers.

The National Committee for the Organization of Iron and Steel Workers could not match employer propaganda. Despite courageous efforts by famous labor organizers like Fannie Sellins and Mother

Jones, committee efforts to sustain the strike were curtailed effectively by employer control over police and news sources. Many steelworkers stuck to the strike and supported the National Committee. This was especially true of immigrant employees and their families. "The strike went underground," a sympathetic observer reported from the Monongahela Valley. "It did not live in meetings, it could not live in the congregation of men, it had no expression, but underneath the silent terror flowed the current of the strike."

Fannie Sellins, who helped to organize thousands of steel and iron workers in western Pennsylvania's Alle-Kiski Valley was murdered just before the strike began. Born Fannie Mooney in New Orleans in 1872, she later moved with her family to St. Louis where she worked in a clothing factory and helped organize Local #67 of the United Garment Workers. Her union activities brought Sellins to the attention of Van Bittner, president of the United Mine Workers District 5. In 1913 she went to work for the UMWA in Colliers, West Virginia, aiding families who had been driven out of their homes by the Pennsylvania and West Virginia Coal Company. Sellins moved to the Alle-Kiski valley in 1916, where her work with the miners' wives proved to be an effective way to organize workers across ethnic barriers. She also recruited black workers, who originally came north as strikebreakers, into the UMWA. During a tense confrontation between townspeople and armed company guards outside the Allegheny Coal and Coke company mine in Brackenridge on August 26, 1919, Fannie Sellins and miner Joseph Starzelski were brutally gunned down. A coroner's jury and a trial in 1923 ended in the acquittal of two men accused of her murder.

Many strikers refused to ask for their old jobs while the walkout continued. However, many gradually returned to work as the situation grew hopelessness. The National Committee called off the strike in January, 1920. In the end, steelworkers lacked the unity and power to overcome employer resources, even though they had shown that unskilled workers in the country's strongest open-shop industry could be organized.

The employers' victory in this decisive episode was only one of several in the postwar years. Bituminous coal miners staged two great walkouts during this period. In November 1919, they joined a national strike for higher wages which was halted by federal court

170

injunctions and President Wilson's denunciation of the strikers. Though UMWA members subsequently gained their objectives through awards by federal commissions, seventy-five thousand Pennsylvania bituminous miners who wanted the protection of union contracts were less fortunate. After striking for several months in 1922 with UMWA members, these miners in central and southwestern Pennsylvania continued their own "strike for union" when the UMWA settled its dispute with coal operators without bringing the nonunion miners under their contracts. They formed delegations to visit the White House and to picket homes and offices of anti-union coal operators as far away as New York City. They found support from District 2 (central Pennsylvania) of the UMWA, whose officials insisted that the strike continue until all miners employed by each operator—union and nonunion—were given recognition. After carrying on the strike on dwindling benefits for months, nonunion miners capitulated.

The combination of federal, state, and employer anti-union policies also reversed the gains of railroad employees. Machinists, blacksmiths, molders, sheet metal workers, and members of other trades employed in railroad shops had joined unions in great numbers during the war. They had benefited from federal operation of the railroads and wanted wartime union recognition to continue. But railroads resumed management of their property in 1920 and soon began a policy of retrenchment under which employees faced wage reductions, loss of work, and reduced overtime pay. The United States Railroad Labor Board, established at the same time that railroad property was returned to private ownership, supported this retrenchment. A strike against these moves was voted overwhelmingly by shop craft workers in 1922 and sanctioned by the American Federation of Labor.

The strike began in July, 1922, when railroads refused to reverse their policies. In Pennsylvania, employees on the Pennsylvania Railroad, the Baltimore and Ohio, the Philadelphia and Reading, and many other lines quit work to join the nationwide walkout of 400,000 workers. Railroads hurried to replace sufficient numbers of strikers to maintain operations. Soon other unions of railway employees joined the strike. President Harding and the Railroad Labor Board could not bring the railroads and the unions together to rec-

171

Extractive industries remained important in the postwar era, South Springfield, Delaware County, 1921. (Pennsylvania State Archives)

oncile their differences. The attorney general secured a sweeping injunction from a federal district court against the strike on September 1, making it impossible for unions to support the walkout in any way without incurring heavy fines. Gradually, employers replaced strikers and the strike weakened. While some companies settled with their union employees, most railroads—including the powerful Pennsylvania Railroad—simply broke off relations. The strike against the Pennsylvania Railroad was not officially called off by the unions until many years after the walkout had actually ended.

Pennsylvania Labor at Bay

The defeat of Pennsylvania workers' hopes for a prosperous and democratic postwar ushered in a period of decline for the labor movement. Business interests were accommodated by the state General Assembly and by most township and municipal governments. Though unions in the building and printing trades and some other skilled occupations maintained their membership and economic power, the ranks of organized labor lost a substantial part of members gained during World War I. Moreover, racial and ethnic divisions among Pennsylvania workers were exacerbated by rising antagonisms among some native white Americans against immigrant Catholics, Jews, and African Americans. Women workers faced opposition to their attempts to gain better jobs from almost all male authority figures. Ironically, unskilled, immigrant, and minority workers who had fought hardest to gain the economic security of unionization from 1918 to 1922 suffered the most from the aftermath of labor's defeats in those years.

Foreign-born workers and their children in Pennsylvania—comprising between 40 and 50 percent of the state's population—struggled against a campaign to isolate and silence them in the 1920s. The Ku Klux Klan focused resentment among native whites against immigrants and their children. The Klan's stronghold in Pennsylvania was in the southwestern counties of Armstrong, Westmoreland, Washington, and bordering areas. But its members assembled in many parts of the state to rally, demonstrate, march, and intimidate their designated enemies. The Klan enlisted members from several groups including both blue- and white-collar workers, small businessmen, and professionals. Attacking "non-Americans" both physically and symbolically, it injected a racial and national meaning into the patriotic fervor of the war. By excluding Pennsylvania's non-Protestant, foreign-born, and black populations from its definition of the nation, the Klan implicitly undercut the labor movement.

Black workers in Pennsylvania, the majority of whom had been residents only since the war years, found white townsmen and city neighbors increasingly hostile as well. Tensions between black and white workers followed the arrival of southern black migrants and the entry of thousands of black worker into Pennsylvania industry from 1916 to 1919. But racial animosity rose to a new pitch in 1923. In the late summer, as the Klan rallied across the state, Mayor Joseph Cauffiel of Johnstown threatened to remove all blacks from the city who had arrived there since 1915 because of a shoot-out between a black resident and white policeman which had proved fatal for the black man and two white police officers. Hundreds of blacks fled after the erratic mayor took steps to fulfill his threat and local whites burned crosses and demonstrated. A similar episode took place in Stowe Township near Pittsburgh. A vigilance committee of whites demanded that all blacks evacuate after a black man allegedly committed a murder. Though white men and boys had paraded through a black residential area demanding that the inhabitants of a dozen houses leave the next day, blacks prepared to resist the vigilance. With support form local officials, blacks faced down angry whites.

The post-World War I years also brought trends in politics, labor-management relations, and working-class life that made necessary a new structure for the labor movement. Though the progressive Republican Gifford S. Pinchot was governor in the middle years of the 1920s, conservative business interests continued to dominate the state's policies. Pinchot tried to regulate utility companies and successfully mediated the 1923 anthracite miners' strike. But his successor, John Fisher, was inactive in the bitter 1927-28 conflict between bituminous miners and coal operators and disappointed unions by favoring the weaker of two legislative bills to control the Coal and Iron Police. Like the country as a whole, then, Pennsylvania government reflected some of the pre-World War I Progressive movement, but mostly in the form of businessmen's and public administrators' reforms.

Pennsylvania employers consolidated their gains over organized labor after 1922 by revamping their labor relations policies. They drew on the prewar practices of the open shop, company unionism, and employee welfare plans to form the basis of a new industrial relations scheme called the American Plan. Lending coherence to these formerly disparate elements was widespread application of scientific management and formalized personnel administration. Businessmen hoped that careful monitoring of employees would reduce turnover and develop a stable, pacified work force. It was toward this larger objective, rather than merely the goal of blunting union organizing, that the American Plan was directed.

The open shop was the key to the success of the American Plan, since real unions in the work force would have competed effectively with company unions and employee welfare plans.

The major steel corporations had always been the model open-shop employers, and their influence on Pennsylvania companies in

Pairing, folding, and packing stockings for shipment—Philadelphia, 1922. (Pennsylvania State Archives)

this regard was strengthened by their victory in the 1919 strike. The Pennsylvania Railroad, another major industrial employer in the state, declared an open-shop policy soon after the federal government returned operation of the railroads to their managers. Many other metal and machinery manufacturers, textile firms, electrical equipment makers, oil refiners, and apparel firms joined the swing to the open shop in the postwar years, particularly from 1919 to 1923. Even the Pittsburgh Coal Company, which had signed contracts with the UMWA for more than two decades, began enforcing the open shop in its mines beginning around 1925. Other bituminous coal producers in western and central regions of the state soon followed suit. Many Pennsylvania employers also established company unions through which their workers could engage in controlled collective bargaining.

The specific forms of employee representation plans (ERPs) varied from one company to another, but they had several charac-

Company sponsored baseball at U.S. Steel plant, New Castle, Lawrence County 1918. (Archives of Industrial Society, University of Pittsburgh)

teristics in common. Most important, they were created unilaterally by plant managers and higher officials of firms, often in response to union organizing drives or in the aftermath of a strike. Typically, representatives from the work force were elected by employees in each department of a firm and met with management in a plant-wide council several times a year. Company unions did not have the power to strike, and the fact that they only included employees in a single work place prevented them from representing all the employees of multi-plant firms. Their meetings often dwelled at length on working conditions of comparatively little importance, like upgrading of washrooms or scheduling of social events for employees. In some cases they allowed for grievances to be discussed and for work hazards to be corrected.

Several Pennsylvania corporations installed ERPs that received wide notice. When Bethlehem Steel acquired Midvale Steel and Ordnance Company, it inherited the shop committees that unions had established during the war at Midvale's Cambria Works in Johnstown. Bethlehem turned the committees into a conventional company union and extended it to cover all its employees. The Pennsylvania Railroad defied the federal Railroad Labor Board by establishing its ERP, despite solid evidence that its shop craft employees, clerks, and telegraphers wanted unions to bargain for them. In an industry where company unions were not as common as in heavy manufacturing and transportation, the men's clothing maker A.B. Kirschbaum of Philadelphia set up a parliamentary representation scheme, consisting of "upper" and "lower" assemblies where employee delegates could deliberate under the watchful eye of company supervisors.

Employee welfare plans also flourished between World War I and the Great Depression. They were adopted more widely after the war, partly because of the way they complemented the policies of the open shop and company unions. While denying workers the benefits of union representation, employers offered group insurance, death and burial benefits, stock ownership and profit-sharing, company-financed home mortgages, and similar programs. Such benefits were coupled with a host of other employer initiatives such as worker social and hobby clubs, singing groups, athletic teams, Americanization courses for immigrants, home economics classes for rural migrant women, garden competitions, home beautification awards, and summer picnics. Paid for by the employer, these types of programs established an economic and social network designed to connect employees and their families to their employers. Many times such programs were racially segregated.

During this era, Pennsylvania employers patterned their labor policies to the principles of Frederick W. Taylor's scientific management. This included close supervision of workers, time-and-motion studies, and incentive pay schemes to encourage productivity. Mills and factories consequently developed larger supervisory staffs and personnel administrators, labor relations specialists, and welfare officers played important roles in the growing field of supervision during the 1920s. It was the personnel administrators' responsibility to explain the company's labor policies to all employees and, in some cases, to supervise employer welfare programs. The manner in which workers performed their jobs within firms became more centrally controlled.

The American Plan in itself did not significantly alter Pennsylvania's union membership or the relative power of the labor

Women's softball team—Heilwood, Indiana County. (Historical Collections and Labor Archives, Penn State)

movement. Even unions who were least affected by the lost strikes of 1919-1922 made little progress in organizing workers in the mid- and late-1920s. Pennsylvania unions faced a seemingly insurmountable challenge in these years, particularly against the large, technologically advanced corporate employers. There is evidence that businesses where the American Plan was most deeply rooted succeeded to some degree in winning over former union members and in persuading nonunion workers that they could enjoy good earnings and job security without labor representation. Corporate progress and labor's failure in addressing worker concerns created a gap between the craft union movement of the past and Pennsylvania labor's future.

New currents in immigration, migration, and the family life of working people widened the gap between workers' circumstances in the postwar years and earlier conditions. Except for a brief expansion in Pennsylvania's economy during 1922-23, labor turnover

"Girls' Dining Room"—The Viscose Company, Marcus Hook, Delaware County. (Pennsylvania State Archives)

dropped from its World War I levels. Federal laws restricting the entry of Europeans into the country sharply reduced immigration to the state. The day of the immigrant laborer who secured his lodging and meals from a boarding house in the company town had by no means ended. Still, the dwindling streams of young single men and young families that flowed continually into dozens of Pennsylvania towns in earlier years altered the structure of immigrant family and community life. Without the large number of boarders seeking lodging in immigrant neighborhoods, eastern and southern European households after the war reduced themselves to the members of the nuclear or extended family—a transition that harmonized with the employer emphasis on family stability and employee welfare.

Though there was a decreased demand for labor during the postwar decade, the continuing movement of southern blacks and white rural families brought additional workers to Pennsylvania's growing industrial centers. Native-born Protestant migrants from the agricultural backcountry of the United States became the typical newcomers to Pennsylvania towns and cities in the 1920s. As a result, businesses were able to meet their labor requirements without European immigration and, in part, were aided by the growth in

179

productivity resulting from new labor-saving machinery and scientific management.

One part of the Pennsylvania workforce that experienced growth in the inter-war years was its female employees. The rate of increase for working women was almost twice as great as that of the total employees from 1920 to 1930. Traditional fields of work like domestic service and textile manufacturing remained among the leading female occupations after World War I. White-collar jobs were responsible for some of the growth in women's employment as well, especially in the fields of typing, stenography, and office clerking which became almost exclusively female by the 1920s.

Changes in working-class life after World War I could also be traced in the experiences of children and adolescents. There was some reduction in the number of Pennsylvanians under sixteen years old who worked during the 1920s, and an increase in the number of children attending high school. Though a majority of South Philadelphia Italian children went to work between the ages of fourteen and sixteen, for example, a growing proportion continued their education and graduated from high school. Many Pennsylvania school districts with large blue-collar populations proposed that vocational courses best suited the working-class students who wanted to complete public school, allowing some pupils to become skilled workers. During this era, the sons and daughters of European immigrants were also coming of age as Americans. Acute tensions were apparent between their attraction for American ways of life and their ethnic heritage. This conflict was only worsened by the prejudice against foreign-stock Americans that was prevalent during the 1920s. In *Out of This Furnace*, Thomas Bell's autobiographical story of a Slovak family in Braddock, Pennsylvania, John Dobrejcak vows to quit school. "I won't go back even if they arrest me. . . . They only make fun of me because I'm a Hunky anyway." Adolescents were especially susceptible to the attractions of an American lifestyle portrayed by the popular media of the age—radio, movies, and family magazines. Young married couples aspired to the consumption goals of American culture. Though many material possessions were beyond the incomes of all but a small minority of Pennsylvania workers, second-generation children adopted them as standards of mainstream American life.

Skilled Pennsylvania workers—mainly native-born, white male employees—had long before achieved higher status than foreign-born and black workers. In some places, this was reflected by better residential areas for skilled blue-collar workers. After the war, some skilled workers moved further from the old working-class neighborhoods of Pennsylvania cities, joining the shift of urban populations to suburban fringes like the South Hills of Pittsburgh and Frankford Avenue in Philadelphia. In these newer residential sections, the best-paid workers began to follow the American ideal of quiet domestic life far removed from the congested industrial districts.

Into the Great Depression

Though popularized images of the 1920s include general prosperity, optimism, and high-spirited fun, many Pennsylvania workers felt the chill of joblessness and declining incomes even in the midst of "good times." Employees in the state's steel, textile, garment, and agricultural sectors all suffered from rising unemployment and falling yearly incomes before 1929. After 1923, unemployment among black workers in the state became a persistent problem. The anthracite and bituminous coal industries in Pennsylvania best illustrated the ills prevalent in the economy.

Pennsylvania coal gradually lost its markets during the 1920s to competing fuels and less expensive coal from other states. World War I and postwar production peaks in tonnage were not to be attained again. Mine employment did not stabilize following the war. Operators attempted to stay competitive by mechanizing some phases of mining, which further reduced the demand for labor. Unemployed miners frequently left the coalfields in search of work as they could not easily find alternative industrial employment in their neighborhoods. The number of miners in Pennsylvania in 1930 was about 10 percent less than the number in 1920, and significantly less than that of 1910. Mining's decline coincided with the rise of John L. Lewis to the presidency of the United Mine Workers. Lewis hoped to heal industry problems by maintaining uniformly high wages to stabilize competition among companies and by exercising absolute control over union officers and members. Instead, such policies provoked a revolt against his leadership, led by John Brophy and

181

Snellenberg's Clothing cutting room, Philadelphia. (Pennsylvania State Archives)

other union dissidents, and a breakup of the bituminous bargaining structure.

Mineowners violated a new national contract in 1924 claiming that pressure from nonunion mines forced lower wages. The Pittsburgh Coal Company, owned by the Mellon family and connected by interlocking directorates with other large nonunion employers in Pennsylvania, temporarily closed its mines around Pittsburgh. In a few months, the company resumed operations at selected mines on a nonunion basis, paying wages that had last been in effect in 1917.

A deadly war spread over Westmoreland and Allegheny Counties from 1925 to 1927 as UMWA members struck. When negotiations between the union and all northern coal companies failed to produce an agreement in 1927, other central and western Pennsylvania mines went nonunion and followed Pittsburgh Coal's tactics of evicting union miners from company housing, placing armed guards at entrances to company towns, and hiring unemployed and inexperienced men to replace strikers.

Guerrilla war, involving miners and their families and law enforcement, replaced civic life in the coalfields. Companies cut off utilities and removed roofs from houses where strikers resisted eviction. Company guards and state police encouraged strikebreakers to attack union sympathizers and inflict vicious beatings on picketers. UMWA organizers worked to convert nonunion men by secretly infiltrating company towns and placing spies on payrolls of open-shop operators. Even school children were drawn into the fight, occasionally becoming victims, as when strikebreakers fired guns into a school at Bruceton attended by the children of union families. In another mining town, elementary students called a strike to demand that the children of strikebreakers be removed from class.

The coal strike of 1927 became the most publicized state conflict since the 1919 steel strike. Repression, violence, and suffering among miners' families resulted in a U.S. Senate investigation. Senators visited central and western Pennsylvania mining regions and were shocked at the local conditions. Newspapers from distant cities sent reporters to describe the dispute and the strikers' destitution. Yet, neither sympathetic reactions from public representatives and urban journalists, nor the UMWA's attempt to house, clothe, and feed strikers saved the union from calamity. By mid-1928, the UMWA, once the strongest labor organization in Pennsylvania and one of the oldest unions in the state, capitulated to the operators, instructing its members to seek the best wages they could.

Though anthracite miners had greater success than those in bituminous in maintaining a union wage scale despite the strikes in 1923 and 1925-26, they faced the same gloomy economic outlook as their soft-coal brothers. Anthracite consumers increasingly turned to heating oil and bituminous coal from nonunion districts when strikes shut off hard coal supplies. Thus the same pattern of mine closings, unemployment, and declining incomes that characterized the central and western Pennsylvania coal fields also developed in the anthracite region.

The men's clothing workers of Philadelphia faced a different challenge. Garment manufacturers had defeated nearly all union organizing drives in Philadelphia from World War I until the late 1920s. Beginning in 1920, the Amalgamated Clothing Workers of America (ACWA) brought its best organizers from around the country to the city and formed an organizing task force. Breaking with its earlier practice of holding large rallies and demonstrations, the union worked quietly to collect employee names and addresses. It then led small meetings in workers' homes. In mid-summer, 1929, the ACWA won its initial strikes against a few small clothing manufacturers. But the real test came in August and September when employees at large garment factories were asked to strike. Despite employer pleas for loyalty and a federal court injunction against the union, workers maintained the strike and forced nearly all of the city's garment manufacturers to enter into contracts by November, 1929. Many of the newly unionized men's garment workers soon lost their jobs in the wake of the stock market crash and ensuing economic crisis. But those who continued to work did so with union wages and a well-developed grievance and arbitration processes.

Economic Collapse and Union Revival

Pennsylvania's deteriorating economy was shattered by the Great Depression. With few exceptions, every occupational group bore the brunt of the crisis. Following a period of uncertainty and paralysis, Pennsylvania workers demanded and won relief from the hardships of joblessness and destitution. They also built new labor unions, revived old ones, gained political power, and brought about basic reforms in labor-management relations. Though earlier depressions had generally slowed the labor movement, the bleak 1930s became a period of fertile development.

The state's industrial concentration in mining, heavy manufacturing, and transportation exposed workers to the full force of the depression. Production of bituminous coal fell by 50 percent between 1929 and 1932. In the same period, pig iron production plummeted nearly 85 percent. The textile, clothing, electrical machinery, glass, and petroleum industries similarly sagged. Unemployment among Pennsylvania workers grew rapidly after 1929 and, by 1933, had reached 37 percent or 1,379,351 persons. The state's economy partially recovered between mid-1933 and 1937, but unemployment in the latter year still comprised one-fifth of the state's workers.

The impact of joblessness, reduced working hours, and pay losses was devastating. Per capita incomes in the state dropped from $775 in 1929 to $421 in 1933. As families used their life savings and fell behind on rent and mortgage payments, many lost their homes. The depression blasted standards for wages and hours that had been won in earlier years. Garment factories in northeastern Pennsylvania paid women and children under sixteen years old as little as $6.50 for fifty-four hours of work each week in 1933. As wives, sons, and daughters looked for employment to compensate for the loss of a husband or father's income, they took work into their homes. Older men with many years of employment in the same company found themselves out of work, deprived of the money they had contributed to pension funds. "Where are those millions that went into the pockets of some individual persons of the highest officials of your Company in forms of all kinds of bonuses and presents?" asked a minister on behalf of a group of elderly unemployed men who believed they deserved income from a pension fund. "Those millions properly used now would dry up rivers of tears of hungry thousands."

Economic decline in the early 1930s hurt nearly all working Pennsylvanians, but its effects were concentrated on some groups more than others. Men and women who worked in the service trades did not lose as many jobs as those employed in industry. Young wage earners, particularly women, were laid off before older workers because many employers favored heads of households over single men and women. In depression, just as in prosperity, black workers suffered from joblessness in large proportions. Unemployment among blacks was always several points above that for whites, and this difference lasted throughout the decade.

Under these conditions, Pennsylvania workers coped by seeking help from both charitable organizations and public programs. As poverty deepened throughout working-class communities, sheer survival dictated the activities of the homeless, jobless, and destitute. Scavenging, begging, selling produce and pencils on street corners, collecting discarded bottles and cans, and hunting and fishing became ways to stay alive. Often, self-reliance in the interest of survival took daring forms as well. In the coal regions, families tunneled into small veins of coal that companies had neglected in favor of richer deposits. Coal was brought out and sold to neighbors and townspeople. Sympathetic local authorities looked the other way and some police officers even aided coal "bootleggers" whenever mining companies tried to stop the illegal activity.

Accident at bootleg mine, Wiggans Patch, near Shenandoah, 1936.
(Pennsylvania State Archives)

Grassroots organizations emerged in 1932 and 1933 among homeowners threatened by foreclosures, taxpayers facing penalties for non-payment, and unemployed men and women demanding a better relief system. Veterans groups joined these organizations to protect the welfare of their members. Across Pennsylvania, these local groups cooperated with labor unions and branches of the Socialist Party to agitate for their goals. In 1933, many grassroots organizations joined the Pennsylvania Security League to press for legislation to establish old-age pensions, unemployment insurance, and minimum wages. For the next four years, the league mobilized voters to elect candidates favorable to its program. Following the creation of federal relief and public works programs, the league also worked to improve wages on and to increase welfare allotments.

Radicals worked within the local and statewide organizations of unemployed workers, homeowners, and taxpayers. They also created their own groups to agitate for related goals. The Communist Party built a network of Unemployed Councils throughout the state. In the anthracite region, fifteen to twenty thousand people joined or participated in the councils from 1931 to 1934, finding reassurance that an organization was voicing their concerns about housing, income, and clothing. As participation in Unemployed Councils broadened, jobless men and women demanded employment, relief payments, and allotments of food and clothing from local "poor boards." Though these demands were made on state and local officials, the councils also took their own actions to stop evictions of families of unemployed workers and sheriff's sales of mortgaged property. The councils became more ambitious and led a march of thousands of jobless men and women on Harrisburg in 1934 to demand public funds to relieve spreading economic distress.

The governor and General Assembly had not completely ignored the problem of unemployment and relief funds before 1934, though they had failed to allocate sufficient resources. Politicians gradually awakened to the seriousness of the crisis, but not before seeing thousands of hunger marchers and protesters from around the state gather in Harrisburg. An initial appropriation to supplement local relief funds was so badly managed by local organizations that the Commonwealth established the State Emergency Relief Board (SERB) in 1932 to distribute future payments. SERB improved the

Opportunities for skilled work grew for African Americans in the New Deal era—linotype operators, Philadelphia Tribune, 1938. (Pennsylvania State Archives)

administration of relief in Pennsylvania, though it had little power to reduce the number requiring assistance. Nearly two million Pennsylvanians were in need of some form of assistance. The partial economic recovery in the middle of the decade cut the figure to about 1.3 million.

The state also provided public employment in the winter of 1931-32, although there were many more applicants than available positions. Nearly thirty thousand jobless men sought work in six emergency labor camps in central and western Pennsylvania when there were only ten thousand positions to fill. When the jobs were announced, the extent of unemployment throughout the state became painfully clear in the crowds of men who poured into the camps to register for work. "Many of the men walked from ten to fifty miles from remote parts of the country, leaving home the afternoon before so that they could be one of the first men to apply. Others came in autos and they would be parked for blocks along the highway . . . and in the mountain counties a few came by horseback from way back in the hills." The physical and psychological condition of these jobseekers was a revealing as their num-

Racial segregation persisted on state work relief projects, Rothrock State Forest, Mifflin County, 1933. (Pennsylvania State Archives)

bers. "It was often necessary for them to stay in the camp three or four days to do light work before they were physically strong enough to do the heavy work required," one labor camp director reported. "It is hard to see men break down, this has often happened when they try to tell their story. They bring their children with them to show how badly they need shoes and clothing."

Organized labor increasingly looked to the state and federal governments to relieve the depression. Though most conservative trade unions of the American Federation of Labor traditionally opposed help from the government, preferring to sustain their own members in hard times, the overwhelming magnitude of the times moved most unions to seek help beyond their own ranks. Hopes for both unionization and government assistance soared in 1933 when Franklin Delano Roosevelt became president. Optimism sprang from new federal relief and public works programs of Roosevelt's New Deal and from the guarantee of the right to organize labor unions without interference from employers—a right granted in section 7A of the National Industrial Recovery Act (NIRA) which was signed by Roosevelt in June, 1933. Though this guarantee was initially intended as a minor element in the Roosevelt administration's

189

recovery program, it held out the promise to Pennsylvania workers that the federal government would at long last favor their goals.

Success or failure in forming lasting labor organizations during Roosevelt's first three years in office depended on the extent to which workers would unite behind a union. Speed was essential to give employees a role in the formulation of the codes for fair business competition that were the main feature of the president's recovery policy. Unity among the employees of an industry would give their labor organization greater strength in bargaining.

Coal miners in Pennsylvania and throughout the country, despite factionalism and severely depressed business conditions, rapidly revived the United Mine Workers as soon as the right to organize became law in 1933. The resurgence of the UMWA in Pennsylvania was especially remarkable in the central and western parts of the state where defeat in the 1927-28 strike had practically led to its annihilation. The terrible conditions in these bituminous fields from 1929 to 1933 and the companies' inability to set the industry on its feet made miners welcome the return of UMWA organizers to the coal "patches." There was little need for the union representatives to lecture Pennsylvania miners about the need for collective action. As long as the supply of membership cards and local union charters held out, the organizing campaign continued.

Garment workers' unions stormed back into Philadelphia in 1933, regaining thousands of members lost after 1929. Like the UMWA, the Amalgamated Clothing Workers of America and the International Ladies' Garment Workers' Union (ILGWU) succeeded in capturing the enthusiasm among workers that Roosevelt's administration and the NIRA had generated. Later needle trades unions' victories extended outside of Philadelphia to clothing manufacturing centers in northeastern Pennsylvania where some producers had relocated from New York City in earlier years in order to evade union contracts.

The upsurge of organizing swept through many other groups of workers as well. Workers from twelve to fifteen years old staged the "Baby Strike" of shirtmakers in the clothing shops of Allentown and its surrounding industrial district. Journalists in Scranton and Philadelphia affiliated with the American Newspaper Guild; petroleum workers in northwestern Pennsylvania's oil region signed up with

190

the Oil Field, Gas Well, and Refinery Workers; and steel and aluminum workers in the valleys around Pittsburgh established new lodges of the Amalgamated Association of Iron and Steel Workers.

Workers' progress toward unionization was far from easy, however. In Pennsylvania conservative Republicans controlled the General Assembly, blocking even mildly progressive measures proposed by Gifford Pinchot who served a second term as governor from 1931 to 1935. Employers fought unions with their proven weapons of firing activists, blacklisting, infiltration, and instigating violence against organizers. Conservative leaders of well-established unions did not always welcome enthusiastic newcomers to their organizations. Hopes for steel unionism dwindled when the rank and file's demands for militant action to win recognition from steel companies were sidetracked by the leaders of the Amalgamated Association and the AFL. When the United States Supreme Court declared the NIRA unconstitutional in 1935, many workers and unionists had already concluded that this federal program—despite its sanction for labor organizing—did not necessarily make collective action easier.

Adding to the unsettled conditions created by contending forces was the tendency for local organizing drives to diverge from the paths cleared by older unions and open new ways to unionize. This was partly a reflection of the very novelty of creating unions for some workers. A mediator for the Pennsylvania Department of Labor and Industry assisted two hundred steel workers in Latrobe who had tried to win recognition for their local in 1934 by showing their employer the charter granted to them by an AFL union. When this tactic failed, the workers asked for a large wage increase and mailed telegrams seeking support for their position to public officials they believed were sympathetic—Governor Pinchot, President Roosevelt, and the director of the National Recovery Administration. "They frankly told me," the mediator wrote, "they did not know how to function as a union and when I began to outline how they might act, they immediately proposed that they make me a member of their union so I could be their representative." Lack of experience did not necessarily spell disaster for organizing workers. At the Philadelphia Electric Battery Storage Company, a small group of testers and assemblers organized in 1933. They quickly called a strike which most of the employees joined and won a complete victory including union recognition.

Work relief for the unemployed, Centre County, 1933. (Pennsylvania State Archives)

The CIO, AFL, and Pennsylvania's "Little New Deal"

Many of the new union members of the 1930s departed from the forms of organization represented by most AFL unions. Especially in the mass production industries—where distinctions between skilled and unskilled workers had been altered by new technologies, scientific management, and other elements of the American Plan—recruits to the labor movement saw no reason to join unions corresponding to the particular job they performed. They preferred to form unions of all employees in a plant or company. They had learned that plantwide organizations could give workers greater strength than they would have if they divided themselves into separate organizations based on occupations.

Thus, industrial unionism was a prominent feature of the 1933-1935 wave of organizing in Pennsylvania. Coal miners and garment workers, who had long before adopted the industrial form of organization, were joined by aluminum, rubber, iron, steel, and electrical workers in forming unions. With UMWA leader John L. Lewis as their spokesperson, these groups requested that the American Federation of Labor issue industrial union charters for mass-production workers. Though pressed at the 1934 and 1935 AFL conventions, the industrial union issue was turned down by the delegates. Following the 1935 convention, Lewis called a meeting of supporters of industrial unionism and formed the Committee for Industrial Organization to assist mass production workers in forming unions.

The impetus of industrial unionism, opposition to the idea by the AFL, and the formation of the CIO led to deep divisions in the labor movement at the state and national level. The Pennsylvania Federation of Labor—dominated by the UMWA and the Amalgamated Clothing Workers and on record favoring industrial unionism since 1913—sympathized with Lewis and the CIO's campaign. As the conflict between the AFL and the CIO deepened in 1936-37, the state federation was pressured by the AFL to conform to its policies. When it refused to do so, William Green, national AFL president, instructed state federation officers to turn over all records and property to his representative. Green also expelled all local unions in the state that had affiliated with the CIO. At the same time, the CIO founded statewide and local affiliates of its own—called Industrial Union Councils—and held its constitutional convention in Pittsburgh in November, 1938. Organized labor in Pennsylvania was split into separate and often competing federations.

If interunion battles weakened the labor movement, electoral activity more than made up for the damage. Pennsylvania Democrats, fully supporting the New Deal and creating a coalition of organized labor, family farmers, and urban ethnic and black voters, emerged from their second-class status as a political party. Overcoming the long-entrenched Republican machines in Philadelphia and Pittsburgh, Pennsylvania Democrats won the statehouse in 1935, when George H. Earle, III was elected governor and Thomas Kennedy, secretary-treasurer of the UMWA, lieutenant governor (see Keystone Vignette: "Thomas Kennedy: The Little Giant of the Anthracite," p. 205). From 1935 to 1937, Earle-Kennedy reform legislation suffered at the hands of the Republican-controlled state senate, just as some of Pinchot's proposals had. But the landslide re-election of Roosevelt in 1936, with the overwhelming support or working people, completed the realignment of Pennsylvania politics that had already begun. Roosevelt's victory carried Democratic candidates for the Pennsylvania legislature into office, creating solid majorities for the party in both the Pennsylvania Senate and House of Representatives.

Democratic success was due in large part to the active campaign waged by organized labor for Roosevelt's re-election and for the election of pro-New Deal candidates for state and local offices. John L. Lewis and his allies formed Labor's Non-Partisan League (NPL) in 1936 to mobilize voters. A chapter of the league was soon working hard in more than half of the counties in the state, chaired by Patrick Fagan, a former western Pennsylvania UMWA official and president of the Pittsburgh CIO council. Following Roosevelt's landslide, the Pennsylvania league worked to produce Democratic majorities in both houses of the General Assembly. It made anti-New Deal legislators' records known to voters and called for a mandate for the Earle-Kennedy program. The league helped sweep conservative Democrats and Republicans out of office to be replaced, in most cases, with friends of organized labor.

What followed was a "Little New Deal" for Pennsylvania that lowered the bars to labor union activity, provided more assistance to the impoverished, and cemented the alliance between organized workers and the state Democratic Party. Laws passed between 1937 and 1939 improved worker's compensation, outlawed privately paid deputy sheriffs, and prevented employers from shipping strikebreakers into a plant where workers had walked out. A state Labor Relations Board was created with three members appointed by the governor to settle disputes and enforce provisions of the state's revised labor laws. Among important changes in state labor laws were provisions of the federal National Labor Relations Act that had been passed in 1935 which disbanded employee representation plans, protected workers' right to organize, and prohibited unfair practices toward labor. The Earle-Kennedy administration's legislative record benefiting working people also extended to more progressive tax laws, environmental programs to protect soil and water, and minimum wage/maximum hour laws aimed at sweatshops.

The Pennsylvania Democratic Party utilized patronage available through large federal programs like the Works Progress Administration to build strong local and statewide organizations. Filling appointive offices with New Deal Democrats and supporters—many of whom were found in the labor movement—developed a political organization that would defend labor unions and challenge the Republicans' deep-rooted strength in Pennsylvania.

Changes flowing from the power of pro-labor administrations in Harrisburg and Washington seemed nearly revolutionary when viewed from the perspective of Pennsylvania's employer-dominated towns. Workers who had seen mounted police and deputized anti-union citizens attack picket lines now listened to Lieutenant Governor Tom Kennedy promise state protection and relief payments for strikers during industrial disputes. Union organizers who had met clandestinely with small bands of die-hard members now opened storefronts with large painted signs announcing the beginning of organizing campaigns. And boroughs whose populations consisted overwhelmingly of wage workers threw the incumbent burgesses out of office and elected Democrats, often the first of that party ever to win borough elections.

The labor movement used its alliance with the Democratic Party most effectively in accomplishing the historic goal of organizing mass-production workers. Fully aware of the lessons of the 1919 organizing drive and of the failure to organize steelworkers in 1933-35, the CIO took a different approach when it formed the Steel Workers Organizing Committee (SWOC) in June, 1936. Unlike the loose-knit groups of unions that conducted the 1919 campaign, SWOC was a highly centralized body. It was officially composed of CIO union officials and administered by its chairman, Philip Murray of the UMWA, who was assisted by a staff of organizers. SWOC received a large amount of money from the UMWA and the CIO to conduct its campaign. In contrast to the Amalgamated Association, SWOC set out to mold all steelworkers into a single organization without occupational distinctions. Lewis, Murray, and the SWOC staff also understood the necessity of overcoming racial and ethnic divisions in the work force.

Organizing steelworkers in 1936, however, involved the same basic difficulties faced by earlier efforts. To create the impression that workers enjoyed the right to collective bargaining, steel companies had hastily resurrected employee representation plans after the National Industrial Recovery Act passed Congress. Though company-controlled unions were prohibited by later legislation, orga-

Strikers at the Hershey Chocolate Company were expelled from the plant by local farmers for whom the walkout prevented sales of milk to the company, April 1937. (Carnegie Library of Pittsburgh)

nizers had to spend time and money using the courts and the National Labor Relations Board to dislodge ERPs. Employers in 1936 also resorted to the old tactics of industrial warfare: firing union activists, planting spies in the SWOC, and simply refusing to deal with union representatives.

The Steel Workers Organizing Committee set out to instill confidence in the minds of steel workers. Lewis, Murray, and their

Close supervision of women workers at Artcraft Silk Hosiery Factory, Philadelphia. (Pennsylvania State Archives)

lieutenants were partially successful during the opening months of the drive in winning over ERP delegates and convincing them to adopt union wage demands as their own. But recruiting dedicated unionists was difficult. Though employees eagerly attended organizing rallies in McKeesport, Homestead, Johnstown, and other steel towns around the state, they were reluctant to openly declare themselves union members. This was especially true for most black workers, who wondered if this union would do anything to improve their status in the industry.

Two developments helped overcome steel workers' reticence. One was the 1936 election which placed Roosevelt back in office and resulted in victories for many candidates supportive of the New Deal. The Democratic landslide was understood by many workers as a national affirmation of the labor movement's organizing efforts and, in particular, CIO campaigns in auto, rubber, steel, and electrical industries. The election results may have been important in another development favoring SWOC's campaign—the surprise agreement in March, 1937, between U.S. Steel Corporation and CIO to recognize SWOC as the bargaining agent for its members in the company's mills. The giant steelmaker probably realized that elected officials would no longer tolerate its refusal to deal with unions. The announcement of this pact shocked the industry as well as many steelworkers, since U.S. Steel had lead the open-shop forces for so long. The agreement gave a great psychological lift to the entire organizing effort and began to quicken the tempo of unionization around the state. This was soon evident in several ways, including the strikes of 1937 that accompanied organizing efforts in steel, textiles, and other Pennsylvania industries.

Momentum from the U.S. Steel agreement and a successful strike against Jones and Laughlin Steel Company in May, 1937, drove SWOC into calling a strike against "Little Steel" companies which included Republic Steel, Youngstown Sheet and Tube, and Inland Steel. Bethlehem Steel also became a target in the 1937 drive when its opposition to union organizing provoked its Johnstown mill employees to join the strike. The company refused to surrender and conducted its own organizing drive among anti-union workers, townsfolk, and elected officials. These groups, helped by effective company propaganda, isolated the strikers from their communities. A back-to-work movement gathered strength after the initial week of the strike and by late June snuffed out the fragile SWOC units at Bethlehem Steel. The walkout also failed to bring other "Little Steel" companies to the bargaining table.

The loss of the "Little Steel" strike was one of the stumbling blocks that drastically slowed the CIO's progress in Pennsylvania. It also encountered increasingly adverse economic conditions. After a period of slowly improving business and rising levels of employment in the mid-1930s, industrial production slowed in late 1937. Unemployment spread throughout 1938 and remained high until 1940-41. SWOC continued to gain new members and to sign contracts with smaller steelmakers, yet workers—who again had to worry how long they would have their jobs—lost some of their interest in the labor movement. At Bethlehem Steel, SWOC reverted to its earlier strategy of worker-by-worker organizing and of challenging the legality of the company's open-shop policies.

The worsening of business conditions also upset organizing drives among Pennsylvania textile workers in 1937 and 1938. The CIO's Textile Workers Organizing Committee (TWOC) was established to bring as many as one million employees throughout the country into a single industrial union. Silk, hosiery, carpet, and cotton goods mills in eastern Pennsylvania, run largely with female workers, were included in the organizing plans. Hosiery employees, who had been battling their employers in Pennsylvania since 1931, were the best organized at TWOC's inception and experienced considerable success in the summer of 1937, especially in Philadelphia, where they used sit-down strikes to win contracts. Other textile workers also organized, such as silk workers in Scranton, who resorted to occasional strikes to win demands.

When the mills began laying off large numbers of employees in September, 1937, the organizing drive abruptly halted. Sidney Hillman, who served as the chairman of TWOC, became seriously ill at the same time and disputes among other members of the committee further drained its energy and cohesiveness. Despite these problems, the union persevered. It merged with the United Textile Workers-CIO in 1939 to form the Textile Workers Union of America, and by 1941 had 230,000 workers covered by contracts, mostly in the northeastern states and with a substantial part of the membership in Pennsylvania.

While mass-production workers responded to the CIO's call for industrial unionism, other workers joined AFL unions and the two labor federations competed with each other resulting in acrimonious relations from 1937 through the end of the decade. The AFL's chartering of a rival coal miners union and the CIO's attempt to organize building trades workers provoked particularly heated debates. The two federations also suspected each other of seeking political clout. This mutual suspicion diluted labor's strength in the gubernatorial election of 1938 which was won by Republicans who proceeded to weaken some of the Earle-Kennedy administration's prolabor enactments.

Though CIO unions had larger memberships, there were a greater number of AFL unions in the state, with some enjoying rapid growth in the late 1930s such as the Brotherhood of Railway Clerks, building trades unions, International Association of Machinists, and Teamsters. Many other AFL affiliates were spurred to vigorous organizing campaigns by 1936-37 CIO successes. AFL membership gains could be seen in the Pennsylvania Federation of Labor. Between 1938 and 1940, 151 local unions and central bodies affiliated with the federation, more than making up for the membership of industrial unions that had been expelled.

Preparations for war in Europe and growth in defense contracts for American businesses began to lift the pall of depression in Pennsylvania in 1939. As factories and mines throughout the state gradually resumed production and rehired furloughed workers, the labor movement took aim at some of its unfinished business from its earlier organizing campaigns. Most important was SWOC's efforts to unionize Bethlehem Steel. After defeating SWOC in the 1937 strike, Bethlehem maintained its employee representation plan, the oldest company union among the large steel producers. It claimed that its employees had the benefits of collective bargaining and did not want to unionize, but also moved quickly to dismiss any worker who became a union member.

SWOC adopted a two-prong attack on Bethlehem. It streamlined its organizing team by appointing Van Bittner (see Keystone Vignette: "Van Amberg Bittner, 1885-1949," p. 208), a veteran UMWA organizer and SWOC regional director, to lead the campaign and placed generous resources at his disposal for a long term effort. On the other hand, SWOC challenged Bethlehem's company union and anti-union tactics in the courts. It won these decisions and ensuing appeals. Bethlehem's intimidation of its employees made the building of local unions in Johnstown and Bethlehem difficult, but rank-and-file workers began to grow restless at the company's resistance to the union. Minor strikes broke out at several mills in 1940 and early 1941. When the National Labor Relations Board finally ordered an election at Bethlehem's Lackawanna, New York plant for February 1941, SWOC pressed for a maximum turnout of workers. It won that vote by a large margin, opening the way for successive representation victories at Bethlehem, Johnstown, and other Pennsylvania facilities of the company. These election triumphs not only allowed SWOC to begin planning for contract negotiations with Bethlehem, but also redeemed the bitter defeat in the "Little Steel" strike in 1937. Other steel companies that had fought the union in that strike did not resort to the formality of NLRB elections, but simply verified SWOC's membership claims among their employees by cross-checking their payrolls. SWOC had organized the basic steel industry in Pennsylvania by 1941, probably the most important stride the state's labor movement made during the depression era.

When compared to the smaller movement of the World War I years and the diminished ranks of the 1920s, Pennsylvania labor at the brink of World War II looked large and robust. The ability of labor unions to enroll previously unorganized workers, overcome historically antagonistic corporations, and sign contracts with employers where such agreements had been historically absent (such as Westinghouse Electric and Machine Company) marked their new role in industrial relations. AFL and CIO representatives from Pennsylvania held positions in national defense agencies and demanded that business receiving government contracts comply with the National Labor Relations Act as well as National Labor Relations Board order and rulings. The United States again turned to unions for assistance in mobilizing national resources as a world crisis appeared on the horizon. In 1941, however, labor was much larger and more strategically placed than it had been in 1917. This strength made it possible for the labor movement to further expand during World War II and to defend its interests against future adversaries.

Peter Gottlieb is director of the Archives Division at the State Historical Society of Wisconsin. He earned an M.A. and Ph.D. in labor history at the University of Pittsburgh, studying with Professor David Montgomery. He was formerly head of the Historical Collections and Labor Archives at the Pennsylvania State University.

Keystone Vignette

James Hudson Maurer

John C. Brennan

"Dutch" Jim Maurer was born in Reading in 1864, the son of a Pennsylvania German working-class family. His father's death, the depression of the 1870s, and his mother and step-father's low incomes forced him to live with relatives and to enter the work force when he was only ten years old. As a teenager, Maurer began a machinist's apprenticeship and almost simultaneously joined the Knights of Labor. He quickly assumed local leadership of the Knights and became an active supporter of the People's Party and, later, the Socialist Labor Party. His tireless campaigns for various labor and radical organizations made Maurer unpopular with employers in Reading and the surrounding area where he worked as a machinist and steamfitter. Finally, his enemies succeeded in blacklisting him from the machinist trade. He writes about these hardships in his autobiography—"my experiences were typical of the life of working men as a class, so long as most of them were unorganized and uneducated. It was 'hold your tongue or lose your job.'"

Maurer threw his energies into building the labor movement and labor's political power. He was elected to the Pennsylvania legislature in 1910 as a Socialist. Abolishing the Pennsylvania State Constabulary became Maurer's chief legislative aim, and he published his indictment of this anti-labor police agency in a popular book, *The American Cossack*. Though elected to the state legislature again in 1914, Maurer also assumed leadership of the Pennsylvania Federation of Labor and boosted the organization's membership until it was the largest and most progressive state labor body in the country, representing 400,000 unionized workers. Maurer served sixteen consecutive terms as the president of the federation.

As World War I threatened to draw the United States into international conflict, Maurer led the resistance in Pennsylvania to U.S.

involvement. The Pennsylvania Federation of Labor went on record in opposition, and, after the U.S. declaration of war, Maurer toured the country to speak for an immediate end to hostilities and a just peace. Reviled by conservatives and pro-war publicists as a notorious radical, Maurer good-humoredly accepted his opponents' characterization of him—"when I became active in the labor movement, they called me an agitator. Next, I was called a 'bone-headed Populist.' After that, they said I was an Anarchist. Then they called me a Socialist, and during the war, when I fought against repeal of labor standards and labor laws, they said I was 'pro-German.' Six months ago, they said I was a 'Bolshevist,' and now they say I am 'un-American.' Outside of that, I guess I am all right."

In the anti-labor climate which followed the armistice, Maurer defended unions and fought to win one of the labor movement's longest-sought goals—old age pensions. He kept up his public speaking and campaigning, winning election as a Reading councilman in 1927. Maurer's contributions to economic and social justice continued right into the depressed 1930s, when he joined the movements of the unemployed and unorganized workers. A strong believer to the end in labor's cause, he left a legacy of courage and will power, captured in the title of his autobiography, *It Can Be Done.*

The late John C. Brennan was employed by the United Food and Commercial Workers.

Keystone Vignette

Thomas Kennedy:
"The Little Giant of
the Anthracite"

Maier B. Fox

Tom Kennedy's roots were sunk firmly in the anthracite coal fields of Pennsylvania, and his early life mirrored that of the thousands of others, mostly immigrants, who composed the population of the region. The oldest son of a miner—in a day when miners were notoriously underpaid—Kennedy was forced to leave school to help support his family at the age of twelve. He became a slate picker at a mine near Lansford. Soon, however, Kennedy's career took a drastic turn away from that of the average miner, a testimonial to his outstanding ability.

After years of suffering from exploitation by the railroad companies that dominated mining in northeastern Pennsylvania, anthracite workers began flocking into the United Mine Workers of America (UMWA) around the turn of the century. Tom Kennedy became a member in 1900. As soon as he began to emerge from childhood, Kennedy became a significant figure in his union. In 1905 he was elected to office in his local union and in the following year was elected as a delegate to the district, anthracite tri-district and international conventions. He was still in his teens.

By 1909, Kennedy had been elected to the District 7 executive board. The following year he became the district president, a position he held until 1925. At that time, international Secretary-Treasurer William Green resigned his position to become president of the American Federation of Labor. Kennedy was chosen to succeed him and retained that office until 1947. He thus became the first representative of anthracite miners to fill one of the top three positions in the UMWA. From 1947 to 1960 Kennedy served as the union's vice president. Then, in his sixtieth year of union membership, John

L. Lewis retired and Tom Kennedy became the tenth international president of the UMWA. He held that position until his death in 1963.

But Tom Kennedy was much more than a union officer—he was a leader. His strength of character and commitment to principle won widespread respect—and a great variety of additional duties. He served on the Anthracite Board of Conciliation while district president and, thirty years later, as chairman of the board of trustees of the Anthracite Health and Welfare Fund, both for extended periods. He represented the anthracite workers before the U.S. Fuel Administration during World War I and at the coal code hearings of the National Recovery Administration in 1933. He was elected Pennsylvania's lieutenant governor in 1934. From 1941 to 1943 he was a member, first, of the National Defense Mediation Board and, afterwards, the National War Labor Board. In addition, Kennedy was regularly entrusted with contract negotiations, not only in anthracite but as far away as Canada's mining districts, and represented the UMWA at congressional hearings on such disparate issues as foreign trade, the St. Lawrence Seaway and unemployment compensation.

Closest to Kennedy's heart were the issues he saw as matters of social justice. In 1914 he began his long crusade—ultimately successful—to eliminate Pennsylvania's notorious Coal and Iron Police, who terrorized miners who insisted on their rights under law. He fought conservatives within the American Federation of Labor until he persuaded them to accept the concept of social security—and then helped to get it enacted into law. And he consistently fought for stronger unemployment compensation, workers' compensation, pensions and similar laws, with considerable success.

Meanwhile, Kennedy never lost touch with his roots. He moved the few miles from Lansford to Hazleton when he became president of District 7, and maintained a home there for the rest of his life. Kennedy took his responsibility to his community seriously and took an active role in church, charitable, and civic affairs throughout his life.

From humble beginnings, Tom Kennedy rose to prominence. But he never forgot the principles with which he began. Therefore, he enriched his union, his state and the lives of all workers—and all Americans.

Maier B. Fox is associate director for analysis at the Wilson Center for Public Research. He is also the author of *United We Stand: The United Mine Workers of America 1890-1990.*

Keystone Vignette

Van Amberg Bittner,
1885 – 1949

Russell Gibbons

Van Bittner was born in Bridgeport, Pennsylvania in 1885 and devoted most of his life in the labor movement to Pennsylvania's industrial workers. Despite his patrician-sounding name, he came with impeccable credentials for rank-and-file leadership among the hardened and oppressed miners and mill workers: going into the soft coal fields near Pittsburgh as a breaker boy of eleven, he was elected president of his mine workers local at the age of sixteen, and for half a century would be at the cutting edge of the industrial union movement.

A USWA (United Steelworkers of America) publicist would later write that Bittner was a "hard-working, determined young man [who] during his early years in the mines acquired a broad education by going to night school and by taking correspondence courses." In his mid-twenties, Bittner was president of UMWA District 5, a powerful union jurisdiction embracing ten counties that had 40,000 members during World War I.

When Bittner assumed direction of District 5, internecine warfare was rife among the miners and, according to one historian, "his locals were in a chronic state of revolt." The new UMWA leader had to contend with union defectors, company spies, and hostile operators as well as legitimate dissent. The national union sent in another young leader—a statistician and *UMW Journal* editor by the name of John L. Lewis—to resolve the District's problems. Soon a third rising star in the union, Philip Murray, was named to bring order out of the district chaos. Their careers would be entwined with that of Bittner for the rest of his union work.

Taking a trouble-shooting role with the union, Bittner led a drive to organize miners in Kentucky and Tennessee and later played key roles in Alabama and West Virginia. When Lewis and his rebel Committee for Industrial Organization launched the ambitious campaign to organize steel workers in the summer of 1936, Murray was named chairman and he in turn brought Van Bittner—then provisional director of UMWA District 17 in West Virginia—to coordinate the Steel Workers Organizing Committee activities in the Chicago area.

According to an early USWA history, "he was first to swing an entire company union into the new steel union when the South Chicago plant of Carnegie-Illinois, 3,000 in number, voted to affiliate in a body. . . following this up by another at Inland Steel." During the "Little Steel" strike, Bittner was a key strategist, who still found time to play an important role in organizing packinghouse workers into the CIO.

In the fall of 1940, Bittner assumed direction of the organizing drive at Bethlehem Steel, enabling the union to file National Labor Relations Board petitions at every Bethlehem facility in the nation. According to David J. McDonald, who later succeeded Murray as the union's second president, the Bethlehem victory "was a tribute to the negotiating genius of Van Bittner."

As a self-educated leader, Bittner rose with and shared power at the discretion of Lewis and Murray, and later McDonald. He did not follow the path of another contemporary, John Brophy, whose opposition to Lewis led to a period of exile from the labor movement before his re-entry through the ClO. By all accounts, he was respected and admired for his organizing and administrative abilities, which included an effort to obtain intercession from President Calvin Coolidge for a coal conference ("Silent Cal," true to form, dismissed Bittner without a comment).

Named an assistant to Murray at the first constitutional convention of the USWA in 1942, Bittner would later become a union vice president. He would serve three years on the War Labor Board with Brophy, participating in decisions that laid much of the groundwork for the extensive postwar benefit gains of the industrial unions. Bittner, whom McDonald lauded as "a giant in the labor movement . . . who could have been either a governor or senator" related to others in different ways. An early USWA intellectual, Harold J. Ruttenberg, wrote that he was "an intimate" of McDonald and "worked closely"

209

with other top USWA leaders but "was tolerated by Van Bittner."

Russell Gibbons is director of the Philip Murray Center for Labor Relations at the Community College of Allegheny County and formerly communications director of the USWA.

Readings For Chapter Four

Bernstein, Irving. *The Lean Years: A History of the American Worker,
1920-1933.* Boston: Houghton Mifflin, 1960
_____. *Turbulent Years: A History of the American Worker,
1933-1941.* Boston: Houghton Mifflin, 1970.
Blakenhorn, Herbert. *The Strike for Union.* New York: Arno, 1969.
Brody, David. *Labor in Crisis: The Steel Strike of 1919.* Philadelphia:
Lippincott, 1965.
_____. *Workers in Industrial America: Essays on the Twentieth
Century Struggle.* New York: Oxford University Press, 1980.
Brophy, John. *A Miner's Life: An Autobiography.* Madison: University of Wisconsin Press, 1964.
Clark, Paul F., Peter Gottlieb, and Donald Kennedy, eds. *Forging a
Union of Steel: Philip Murray, SWOC, and the United Steelworkers.* Ithaca: ILR Press, 1987.
Dubofsky, Melvyn, and Warren Van Tine. *John L. Lewis: A Biography.* Urbana: University of Illinois Press, 1985.
Foster, William Z. *The Great Steel Strike and Its Lessons.* New York:
B.W. Huebsch, Inc., 1920.
Fox, Maier. *United We Stand: The United Mine Workers of America,
1890-1990.* Washington D.C.: United Mine Workers of America,
1990.
Gottlieb, Peter. *Making Their Own Way: Southern Blacks' Migration
to Pittsburgh, 1916-1930.* Urbana: University of Illinois Press, 1987.
Greenwald, Maurine W. *Women, War, and Work: The Impact of World
War I on Women Workers in the United States.* Ithaca: Cornell
University Press, 1990.
Jenkins, Philip. "The Ku Klux Klan in Pennsylvania, 1920-1940,"
Western Pennsylvania Historical Magazine 69 (1986): 121-38.
Maurer, James H. *It Can Be Done: The Autobiography of James Hudson
Maurer.* New York: The Rand School Press, 1938.
McDonald, David. *Union Man.* New York: Dutton, 1969.
McPherson, Donald. "The 'Little Steel' Strike of 1937 in Johnstown,
Pennsylvania," *Pennsylvania History* 39 (April, 1972): 219-38.
Meyerhuber, Carl I. Jr. *Less Than Forever: The Rise and Decline of
Union Solidarity in Western Pennsylvania, 1914-1918.*
Selinsgrove: Susquehanna University Press, 1987.

Montgomery, David. *The Fall of the House of Labor*. New York: Cambridge University Press, 1987.

Schatz, Ronald W. *The Electrical Workers: A History of Labor at General Electric and Westinghouse*. Urbana: University of Illinois Press, 1983.

Sherman, Richard B. "Johnstown versus the Negro: Southern Migrants and the Exodus of 1923," *Pennsylvania History* 30 (October, 1963): 454-64.

Sweeney, Vincent. *The United Steelworkers of America: Twenty Years Later, 1936-1956*. Pittsburgh: United Steel Workers of America, 1956.

Zieger, Robert. *Republicans and Labor, 1919-1929*. Lexington: University Press of Kentucky, 1983.

Chapter Five

Glory Days: 1941-1969

Mark McColloch

The decades from 1940 to 1970 were the high-water mark for Pennsylvania's labor movement as union membership reached its greatest number and its highest percentage of the work force. During these years of unprecedented prosperity, labor played a significant role in industrial relations in the Commonwealth. While parity with the power and influence of the corporate world was rarely achieved, labor did succeed in obtaining substantial influence in employer relations. It might be said that, from 1940 to 1970, Pennsylvania workers won for themselves, if not "industrial democracy," at least "industrial citizenship." To some extent, this expanded power carried over into the community, particularly on the political level. At no other time in the twentieth century have workers and unions been so regularly consulted or incorporated into civic life. At no time, before or since, have so many union activists held political office.

World War II

The Second World War transformed the state's labor movement. Because of the very low unemployment rate during the war, workers and their unions enjoyed an unprecedented bargaining position. To a considerable extent, workers were able to capitalize on this opportunity and take major steps towards industrial citizenship. By the end of the war, Pennsylvania unions had achieved record size, strength, influence, and prestige.

As America rapidly transformed itself into a vast arsenal and workshop for the Allies, unemployment in Pennsylvania swiftly declined. The 1940s began with a Depression-level jobless rate of 20.2 percent in the Commonwealth, but fell rapidly even before Pearl Harbor. After a few months of dislocation in 1942, caused by the jolt of the sudden switch to a war-oriented economy, joblessness further dwindled in the state and virtually disappeared by mid-war. With an unemployment rate of only 1 percent in 1944, workers did not have to live with the constant fear of being out of work. One result was that workers were freer to choose unionization than ever before. Labor's ability to take full advantage of the tight labor market was, however, substantially limited by other factors. Immediately following Pearl Harbor, the leaders of almost every union issued a no-strike pledge. This action was prompted by the desire of most union leaders to support the war against the Axis and by the fear that the right to strike might be legislatively eliminated if it were not voluntarily foregone. With its major weapon in mothballs, Pennsylvania labor would have to fight the bargaining war with new methods.

The war brought dramatic changes in the role of the government, particularly federal agencies, in the collective bargaining process. Perhaps the most important of the new agencies was the War Labor Board (WLB). President Roosevelt established the board on January 12, 1942, to oversee labor relations in war industries. It was composed of twelve members, a third each from labor, industry, and "the public." Regional offices were established in Philadelphia and Pittsburgh. One of the first cases on which the WLB ruled was a pattern-setting approval of a night shift bonus in the Pennsylvania plants of the Aluminum Company of America. The most famous and

214

important of all decisions, the "Little Steel Formula," also involved thousands of Keystone State unionists. Reviewing a dispute between the Steel Workers Organizing Committee and firms such as Bethlehem and Republic Steel, the board ruled that negotiated wage increases should be limited to 15 percent above their level of January 1, 1941. An additional 2.3 cents per hour was allowed to compensate workers for the particularly swift price increases in the steel towns, which were experiencing rapid population gains. Although some important exceptions would be allowed, the Little Steel Formula fell well short of equaling the increased cost of living, which rose by about 45 percent in Pennsylvania over the course of the war. A *Fortune* reporter visiting Pittsburgh in 1943 wrote, "To the workers it's a Tantalus situation: the luscious fruits of prosperity above their heads— receding as they try to pick them."

Nevertheless, there were some important concessions granted to the labor movement. In June 1942 the WLB allowed maintenance of membership provisions in the contracts reached between major companies and those unions that complied with the no-strike pledge. Such provisions, which kept workers as union members for a year once they had joined, boosted union rolls. By 1944, most Pennsylvania unions in the manufacturing sector had won such a clause. These agreements, however, put a powerful stick in the hands of the WLB, a stick that could be wielded against any union that violated the no-strike pledge.

The War Labor Board also encouraged the implementation of incentive payment plans. Many militant trade unionists temporarily dropped their traditional hostility to piecework. They hoped that the new payment systems would hike the output of war materials, and they utilized the willingness of the WLB to approve the incentive plans as a way to boost otherwise capped wages. In steel, for example, 65 percent of the state's work force was on incentive by 1945, versus 50 percent in 1940. The widespread adoption of the plans meant higher wages but led to some internal divisions among the work force.

The real gross wages of Pennsylvania blue-collar workers did rise during the war. In steel, for example, wages increased by 26 percent and in coal 36 percent. Overtime at premium pay was the major source of the increase in wages. In steel, workers' real earn-

215

ings fell until May 1, 1943, when the War Manpower Commission ordered corporations to institute a forty-eight-hour-week schedule (with the last eight hours at time and a half). There was also a substantial increase in the taxation of the earnings of workers, both from an increased federal income tax and from a new state sales tax. On the other hand, about one-third of all Pennsylvania workers moved to better-paying jobs during the war as new positions increased and existing jobs were vacated by the one million Pennsylvanians who entered the military. Most Pennsylvania wage earners had never lived so well.

Some Pennsylvania workers still took home shockingly low amounts. At a time when journeymen in the building trades in Pittsburgh and Philadelphia were averaging around $1.65 per hour, female dime store clerks there were making just thirty-three cents an hour. Workers in major Pennsylvania department stores made only sixty-five cents an hour on average, while the wages of janitors fell somewhere between the two figures.

One of the most important steps towards "industrial citizenship" was the substantial expansion of the size of the Pennsylvania labor movement during the war. The 50 percent growth during 1941-1945 meant that hundreds of thousands of workers joined unions. Some of the new members came "automatically," as industries with maintenance of membership clauses swelled their employment rosters. There was also a wave of organizational victories for labor. For example, Bethlehem Steel, with major plants in Johnstown and Bethlehem, signed its first union contract with the United Steelworkers of America in August, 1942. Sylvania factories in Emporium, Mill Hall, and Warren were organized by the United Electrical Workers during the war. Overall, Steelworkers' membership in the state doubled during the war years, while that of the Electrical Workers tripled. The International Ladies Garment Workers Union (ILGWU) had organized 90 percent of Philadelphia's women's and children's garment factories by 1944 and continued to organize in the anthracite region. Laundry workers in Philadelphia achieved a 100 percent closed shop. By 1945, fully 85 percent of manufacturing workers in Allegheny County held union cards, one of the highest percentages in the nation.

Organizational victories were not limited to the blue-collar sec-

War production at the United Engineering and Foundry Company, New Castle. (Archives of Industrial Society, University of Pittsburgh Libraries)

tor. The United Office and Professional Workers won representation for the Prudential industrial insurance agents in the state in 1942. They added the Metropolitan agents two years later. Clerical and technical workers in mass-production industries began to form locals in the late war years, usually joining the AFL or CIO union that organized the blue-collar group in their plant, but sometimes choosing unaffiliated groups.

As over one million Pennsylvania men and women joined the

217

military, hundreds of thousands of new workers entered the work force. By 1945, 340,000 more women were employed in the state than in 1940 and women's share of the total work force rose markedly, from 25 to 34 percent. Women were encouraged to enter the work force as a patriotic duty. This encouragement was extended to mothers of young children, the group with the sharpest percentage rise in female employment rates. Pennsylvania was one of only six states to appropriate money to provide day care for such young women, many of whom, while their husbands received a private's pay, were the major support of their families. In greater numbers, women over thirty-five years old joined the work force. From the Delaware River shipyards to the steel mills and auto parts plants, many of these new workers found blue-collar jobs. In the anthracite region's garment factories, women provided a large pool of labor to factory owners. Among Pennsylvania's major employers, only coal mining and commercial construction remained exclusively male. Nevertheless, despite all the attention given to the new "Rosie the Riveters," the typical new female employee in Pennsylvania, as in the nation, was a clerical or service worker.

Despite the large increase in the numbers employed, women were not a majority of the new entrants into the work force. Teenagers (the high school dropout rate in Pennsylvania grew by 50 percent during the war), older men, (often unemployed for many years as a result of the Depression), and Southern migrants swelled the labor force. Black migration to Pennsylvania increased substantially during the war, and black males made unprecedented gains in employment status, often facilitated by pressure from civil rights groups and the federal government. In 1940 only 3.6 percent of Pennsylvania steelworkers were black, a figure that almost doubled during the war. By 1943, 15,000 of the 35,000 workers at the Sun Shipbuilding Company yard in Chester were black. Perhaps the best measure of the progress of blacks in Pennsylvania, as well as the depth and persistence of discrimination, was the fact that their average annual earnings rose from 63 percent that of whites to 70 percent by the end of the war.

With most Pennsylvania industrial unions opening their doors to all employees in their plants, the number of black unionists in the state more than doubled. Yet, many trouble spots remained. African

"Colored Workers' Shacks Near Midland" (M. Bernstein Collection, Historical Collections and Labor Archives, Penn State)

Americans at Sun Ship initially worked in a black-only shipyard, which the company union condoned. The CIO union, the Industrial Union of Marine and Shipbuilding Workers, had to fight a sharp battle against the corporation and a company union to overturn this practice. Many construction craft and white-collar jobs in the state remained closed to blacks. In the summer of 1944, after the Transit Workers Union pressured Philadelphia streetcar companies to begin hiring black operators for the first time, a strike erupted among white drivers, abetted by a company union. More generally, the wage ratio between women workers actually fell for African Americans during the war to 57 percent that of their white sisters, since few black women could participate in the expanded female employment opportunities in the white-collar sector.

The influx of new workers had a mixed impact. On the one hand, tens of thousands of new workers had jobs, and often, for the first time, union jobs. On the other hand, their position was far from equal and since they had not experienced the union struggles of the 1930s, their union consciousness differed from the veterans of those battles.

The number of strikes in Pennsylvania decreased following Pearl Harbor and the majority of unionized workers did not partici-

219

Increasing numbers of African Americans found work in the steel industry during World War II. (William Gaughen collection, Archives of Industrial Society, University of Pittsburgh Libraries)

pate in a strike during the war years. The most important exceptions to this pattern were a series of major walkouts by the state's coal miners. Faced with unique problems, such as the rapidly escalating cost of living in coal towns—a 1943 UMWA survey found that in eighty Pennsylvania mining towns, food costs had risen by 125 percent since 1939—organized miners sought relief from the coal companies and the WLB. Sparked by walkouts in the anthracite fields, a series of four strikes occurred in 1943. The result was that the miners won payment for all the hours spent underground. The price was public hostility to the strike in the midst of war, a hostility inflamed by the anti-union press, by the government, and even by some labor leaders.

A brief wildcat strike during Christmas, 1943, by most Pittsburgh-area steelworkers was the state's next largest strike in the war years, and in late 1943 a threatened strike by railroad workers led to a three-week government seizure of the railroads and brought parity with the wage hikes of factory workers. By 1945, some unions, most notably the Textile Workers, began to drop the no-strike pledge. Yet strike rates remained minimal in the state until the surrender of Japan. (For one of the first postwar strikes, see Keystone Vignette: "The Postwar Strike Wave: The Case of the Plate Glass Workers," p. 257.)

Pennsylvanians contributed mightily to the war effort. Over one million residents joined the Armed Forces and about thirty thousand died in the war. Fully one-tenth of all the Army/Navy awards for excellence went to workers in Pennsylvania plants. Thirty percent of the nation's coal, much of its lubricating oil, and its Portland cement came from the Commonwealth. The Philadelphia Navy Yard produced hundreds of ships for the Navy and the Dravo yards in Pittsburgh launched scores of amphibious landing craft. Most of the Army "D" Rations were made in Hershey. Perhaps most important of all, by 1944 Pennsylvania workers produced more steel than the entire Axis combined.

By the end of the war, the labor movement in Pennsylvania was larger than ever before. For the first time, tens of thousands of Pennsylvania workers were actually bargaining with their employers. The standard of living, while still quite low, was the highest it had ever been. Pennsylvania workers had moved forward during the war. By the end of the war they faced the challenge of utilizing their wartime gains in order to achieve permanent industrial citizenship.

The Postwar Labor World

From 1945 to 1949, Pennsylvania labor would consolidate its wartime gains in a series of significant victories on the picket line. These triumphs would stabilize and systematize industrial citizenship for most Pennsylvania workers. At the same time, there would be important setbacks on the political front that would limit the possibility of moving towards industrial equality.

With the surrender of Japan in September 1945, the question of the nature of labor relations in the postwar period rapidly came to the fore. Unemployment reappeared as military contracts ended. By early 1946, the Pennsylvania jobless rate was about one-quarter higher than the national average. Overtime, the main component of the higher wartime standard of living, had disappeared. The average Pennsylvania steelworker lost $52 a month in overtime earnings in the last six months of 1945. Workers faced the fact that their wage rates had lagged far behind inflation. With the war well behind the nation, price hikes accelerated as price controls were rapidly lifted.

Most workers and employers expected a return to the depressed economic conditions that had prevailed before the war. Both sides remembered the labor battles that had followed World War I. Labor's defeats on the picket line had reversed a decade of union growth and had resulted in the exclusion of the movement from most sectors of the economy in the 1920s.

As the war ended, major industrial unions formulated demands for a 25 percent wage increase and for the standardization of the forty-hour week. Behind these specific proposals was their effort to insure that workers would not have to return to Depression conditions and that unions would have an important voice in the postwar economy. Most major corporations responded with proposals for smaller wage increases or for no gains at all, arguing that the standard work week should be set at between forty-four and forty-eight hours. Lurking behind these demands was a determination to test the strength of the labor movement and to discover if management would be able to return to its pre-Depression position of unquestioned dominance in labor relations.

In early 1946 the greatest strike wave in Pennsylvania history emerged. Among strikers were tens of thousands of steelworkers as well as employees of Westinghouse, General Electric (GE), and General Motors. (The leaders of the United Steelworkers of America is profiled in Keystone Vignette: "Philip Murray: Pennsylvania's Mid-Century Labor Giant," p. 259.) Workers at smaller firms struck as well. The walkouts were very powerful. In a few state locations companies and police attempted to break the picket lines; the police beat marching GE strikers in Philadelphia and assaulted striking AFL bus drivers in Lancaster. In these cases, mobilization by the United Electrical Workers and others in the Philadelphia labor movement and a successful two-day general strike in Lancaster resulted in the continuance of the picket lines. In the settlement of these contests a pattern emerged endorsing the forty-hour week and raises of about eighteen cents per hour.

Pennsylvania coal miners also joined the picket lines in April and May, 1946, for a fifty-nine-day strike. The miners won modest health and welfare funds, financed by a ten cent royalty on each ton of coal they mined. From this fund, the United Mine Workers financed a network of group practice clinics and hospitals, a dozen of which were located in Pennsylvania. Railroad workers also struck for two days, forcing government intervention and a partial victory.

Corporations were stunned by the effective mobilization of support for the strikers. Veterans rallied behind the unions; they marched on Harrisburg ten thousand strong to back their unions, demanding unemployment compensation while on strike. Local politicians passed resolutions favoring the strikes and did not encourage police to interfere with picket lines. At Homestead, the scene of historically bloody repression of unionists, both the burgess and the state senator joined the picket lines. It became clear to most major employers that, for the time being, the labor movement had to be tolerated and that a new era of industrial citizenship was in the making for most workers. The corporate approach changed from the attempted immediate destruction of unionism to a policy of containment, trying to hold labor to a position of limited influence and strength.

An important aspect of the corporate containment policy was a serious modification of state and national labor law in 1947 that had its roots in significant political shifts resulting from elections in 1946. Republicans gained control of Congress (Pennsylvania Democratic Senator Joe Guffey lost to Republican Edward Martin), a Republican

Striking steelworkers received considerable community support during their 1946 walkout. (Carnegie Library of Pittsburgh)

governor was elected, and the GOP won a majority of both houses of the General Assembly.

Soon a series of drastic changes to the National Labor Relations Act (NLRA) were approved by Congress. Among the modifications included in the Taft-Hartley Act were a halt to direct union contributions to candidates in federal elections, a ban on the closed shop, state option to outlaw the union shop, and restricted use of secondary boycotts. In addition, union officers were required to sign affidavits stating that they were not Communists, or lose the protections of the NLRA. The president was given the power to impose eighty-day back-to-work orders in what he deemed to be national emergency strikes. Federal employees were denied the right to strike, and companies were given greater latitude to intervene in union representation elections including the right to file decertification petitions.

Despite active union mobilization to defeat what was referred to as the "slave labor bill"—that included a strike by 17,000 Pennsylvania coal miners that lasted several days, and a vote by one-third of the delegates to the state CIO convention for a one-day general strike—a majority of congressional Democrats joined Republicans to override President Truman's veto of the bill. Truman would soon utilize the eighty day no-strike provisions of the new law against Pennsylvania coal miners and railroad workers. Despite election pledges to the contrary, there was no repeal of the bill following the Democratic victory in the 1948 elections. After twelve years of progress under the Wagner Act, labor's legislative progress had been seriously eroded.

A similar development occurred in Pennsylvania. Although the 1937 Pennsylvania Labor Relations Act had suffered minor conservative amendments in 1939, it had remained essentially intact. In 1947, despite protests that included a Harrisburg rally of four thousand workers, the legislature enacted a "Little Taft-Hartley" law, Act 492. The new measure banned all strikes by state and local government employees, and forbade almost all secondary boycotts. Strikes by public utility workers were also outlawed and arbitration was mandated to settle bargaining disputes. (This action followed on the heels of a bitter twenty-seven day strike by an independent union at Pittsburgh's Duquesne Light in Fall, 1946, in which two Republican judges sentenced union president George Mueller to one year in prison. Only a march by seven thousand workers on city hall forced his release. Nonetheless the workers were forced to accept arbitration.) Perhaps prodded by the 106-day "Beer War" in Pittsburgh between the Teamsters and the Brewery Workers, all jurisdictional strikes were also banned. At the same time the legislature rejected the establishment of a Fair Employment Practices Commission and tightened eligibility for unemployment compensation. The Taft-Hartley Act and Act 492 provided formidable new legal weapons for employers to use in the postwar period. Powerful barriers had been placed in the way of the further empowerment of workers.

As the Cold War intensified in the late 1940s and the nation moved politically to the right, a split developed within the CIO. Fundamentally, the division involved a bitter dispute between a right wing, intent on support for U.S. foreign policy and a close alliance with the Democratic Party, and a left wing, critical of the

George L. Mueller welcomed by his supporters following his release from jail in September 1946. (Carnegie Library of Pittsburgh)

U.S. role abroad and willing to stake labor's political fate on a third party to the left of the Democrats.

As early as August 1946, the Philadelphia CIO Council voted to bar Communist Party members from holding office. Although most Pennsylvania labor leaders vowed not to sign the non-Communist affidavits of the Taft-Hartley Act, many leaders of the right wing soon complied. This gave them a free hand to raid locals of the unions controlled by leftist elements. The House Un-American Activities Committee (HUAC) and other governmental bodies began investigations of the left wing. In one case a HUAC hearing was held in East Pittsburgh in August 1949, immediately preceding a crucial internal union election at the gigantic Westinghouse plant. Companies jumped into the fray by firing many left-wing activists, who had long been thorns in their sides. In October 1949 the split in the CIO was formalized, as eleven left-wing unions withdrew and were expelled from the federation. The CIO chartered rival unions, and soon most of the left-wing unions were destroyed. At the same

*Vigorous unions were also a result of World War II—Amalgamated
Clothing Workers on the march. (Pennsylvania AFL-CIO)*

time, left-wing activists were purged from other unions. In Pennsylvania, only the leftist United Electrical Workers retained significant
strength in the 1950s, holding on to about half of the major electrical plants in the state. With this exception, the triumph of the right
wing and the purge of the left was complete.

This coordinated campaign by an anti-radical government-
corporate-union coalition resulted in a labor movement that could
more easily fit into the emerging postwar world of industrial citizenship. Labor was now less likely to pose an alternative to overall
corporate dominance.

The Fruits of Industrial Citizenship

Despite such problems, the Pennsylvania labor movement was
at its greatest relative size in history during the late 1940s. In 1946,
for example, nearly 40 percent of the Commonwealth's work force
carried union cards. Most workers in manufacturing, construction,

227

and transportation were union members in Pennsylvania. Furthermore, the unionized sectors of the economy were not experiencing joblessness. There were, in fact, more coal miners in the state in 1948 than there had been for decades even though, statewide, the percentage of mechanically processed coal had risen from 7 to 37 percent during the previous decade. Moreover, by 1947, the United States produced 57 percent of the world's steel, with the Commonwealth setting the national employment pace.

A considerable amount of new organizing took place. In 1946 hundreds of waitresses, cooks, and hotel workers joined the Hotel and Restaurant Employees and the union described its growth in Philadelphia as "sensational." By the end of the decade the meat counters in most supermarket chains across the state were staffed by union butchers. The Amalgamated Clothing Workers organized most of the dozens of hat shops in Reading and locals of the Office Employees were established in places like Warren and Hazleton. The International Ladies' Garment Workers' Union (ILGWU) was leading the struggle to organize workers in newly emerging garment factories in the anthracite coal region. Five thousand workers joined the Pennsylvania Federation of Telephone Workers. (For the career of an organizer in this era, see Keystone Vignette: "Gaston Le Blanc: Union Activist," p. 261.)

Strikes remained prevalent at the end of the decade. A major walkout took place in 1949 in steel (where production workers in the industry won pensions for the first time). There was a major telephone strike and several important disputes involving the UMWA. Aggressiveness, a large labor movement, and low unemployment pushed up wages in the state. Yet, due to spiraling inflation, the standard of living did not rise until 1950. The average male worker in the Commonwealth earned $1,970 in 1946, while the Labor Department estimated that about $2,400 was needed to support a family of four on a modest budget. Important regional wage variations were apparent, even in the same industries. Highly skilled tool and die men in Philadelphia outearned their counterparts in Scranton by over 30 percent. Skilled production workers in Erie earned about 70 percent more than common labor, a differential only slightly higher than that which prevailed across the state.

Yet workers had made modest strides in non-wage areas as

Consolidation Coal Company miners ride to work in safety, 1947.
(Carnegie Library of Pittsburgh)

well. Pennsylvania's industrial safety code, while far from adequate, was one of the best in the nation. For those out of work, the duration of unemployment compensation eligibility was increased in 1945 by a Democratic-controlled state government, and payments were hiked by the newly elected Democratic majority in the legislature in 1949. By that year the average payment to the jobless had reached $19.43 per week, a figure comparable to that of a decade earlier in real terms. By 1950, 40 percent of workers had some form of healthcare coverage, as compared to just 24 percent nationally.

Powerful contradictory forces framed the position of Pennsylvania labor by 1950. On the one hand, an unprecedented number of workers had won collective bargaining and successfully defended it on the picket line. They had formed the basis for a major improvement in their standard of living. On the other hand, the labor movement had suffered important political defeats and most of its radical component had been purged.

Reaping the harvest of industrial citizenship in the shadow of the steel mill—Homestead, 1940s. (William Gaughan Collection, Archives of Industrial Society, University of Pittsburgh Libraries)

The 1950s and 1960s: Structural Stability and Change

The 1950s and 1960s were, in one sense, years of great stability for the Pennsylvania labor movement. The decisive struggles of earlier decades established patterns of labor relations that would endure for a generation. Changes were also underway in the labor world: changes that would transform many areas of work, the workplace and the workers themselves.

Among the most significant of these changes was a substantial increase in the number and percentage of women workers in the state's labor force. The female proportion of Pennsylvania labor had fallen from its World War II temporary high. By 1950, however, it had begun a renewed rise that persists to the present. By 1963 female employment had topped the World War II high and by 1970 had reached 37 percent. While the work force participation rate for all women increased, growth was most marked for middle-aged

230

Switchboard operators for Bell Telephone. (Pennsylvania Historical and Museum Commission)

women. Despite this trend, Pennsylvania lagged well behind the national average for female work-force participation, trailing by about 10 to 15 percent into the 1970s, mainly because of the state's dominant heavy industries.

The Life of Riley and *Leave it to Beaver* were two popular family sitcoms of the 1950s and 1960s. In both shows, the father earned a living while the mother stayed at home tending to housework and children. Silly as such television programs may have been, each reflected, in part, the real world. During the 1940s, 1950s, and into the 1960s, most Pennsylvania women over twenty-five were full-time homemakers. For most working-class families, the higher wages brought by the "industrial citizenship" status of males meant that their wives—more than ever before or since—could stay at home and assume a role, at least superficially, more akin to that of traditional middle-class women.

Still, an important minority of women were employed. A majority of the textile workers in the state were women, as were almost 80 percent of the garment workers. Food processing employed about

33,000 women and electrical manufacturing about 47,500, but the increase in the number and percentage of women workers in the 1950s and 1960s did not occur in manufacturing. In fact, precipitated by job terminations after World War II, not only did the percentage of women workers who were employed in manufacturing in the state decline, so did their absolute number. The number of Pennsylvania women employed as domestics also fell—even so, these workers comprised 7 percent of the female work force as late as 1950. It was substantial expansion of clerical, retail sales, restaurant and hotel jobs, and professions such as teaching and nursing, that drew the greatest number of women into the labor force. By 1970, 31 percent of all women workers in the state were clericals, versus 27 percent just a decade earlier. Since these were sectors with very low rates of unionization in the 1950s, there was little growth in the number of female unionists in the Commonwealth. Only in the late 1960s, with a new wave of feminism, did this picture begin to change. At the leadership level the state AFL and CIO usually had one woman each on their executive boards. The merged federation had two female executive board members in the 1960s. Still, at a time when more women were working for wages, many of them were excluded from industrial citizenship. (For a profile of a pioneer female labor leader, see Keystone Vignette: "Amy Ballinger: Pittsburgh's First Lady of Labor," p. 263.)

In 1963 the federal Equal Pay Act amended the Fair Labor Standards Act to require equal pay for "equal effort and responsibility under similar conditions, for workers, regardless of gender." The next year, the Equal Employment Opportunity Act included women as a category protected against discrimination in hiring, pay, and promotion. On the other hand, the Pennsylvania discrimination statutes did not include gender in their provisions.

The role of African Americans in the state labor force also changed in the postwar period. The non-white component of the labor force rose from less than 5 percent in 1940 to over 9 percent in 1970. Heavy migration from the South to Pittsburgh and Philadelphia was the key to this growth, most of which occurred before 1960. There were few dramatic changes in the access African Americans had to production jobs in manufacturing. For example, African Americans made up 6 percent of the Commonwealth's steelworkers

in 1950 and 7 percent in 1969 and remained disproportionately concentrated at lower levels of the occupational ladder in manufacturing as a whole. Within the steel industry of the late 1960s they
comprised 15 percent of the unskilled, 3 percent of the skilled and
only 1 percent of the white-collar workers. Some white-collar jobs
were completely closed to blacks. In 1946, Pittsburgh's Urban League
picketed department stores to convince them to begin hiring blacks
as sales personnel. Before its organization by the United Electrical
Workers in 1965, the Union Switch and Signal plant in Swissvale did
not employ any salaried black workers. By the next year the union
had won a no-discrimination clause and blacks were 10 percent of
those hired for white-collar positions.

In 1955, Pennsylvania enacted a Human Relations Act banning
racial discrimination by the majority of employers in most cases.
Harry Boyer, president of the Pennsylvania CIO, was made the chairman of the Fair Employment Practices Commission (FEPC) created
by the new law. Unfortunately, the legislation was full of loopholes—proving that an act of discrimination had taken place was
difficult.

In 1961, the Pennsylvania Equal Rights Council, in which the
state's labor movement played a crucial role, spearheaded the passage of additional civil rights legislation. The new law transformed
the FEPC into the Pennsylvania Human Relations Commission. Boyer,
by now the head of the Pennsylvania AFL-CIO, continued to head
the civil rights agency that began to move somewhat more aggres-
sively over the decade. Philadelphia and Pittsburgh had enacted
their own FEPC laws in the 1950s.

Other demographic changes took place in Pennsylvania's work
force. Growth in teenage part-time employment, mostly in the
minimum-wage service sector, was more apparent. In 1950, only
15.6 percent of boys ages fourteen to seventeen held regular part-time
jobs. By 1970, that figure had grown to 23 percent. There was,
however, a noticeable drop in the work force participation rates of
men over sixty-five, falling from 40 percent in 1950 to 23 percent in
1970. This drop was largely due to the increase in the availability of
pension plans, enabling older workers to retire.

In terms of the composition of the work force, the main internal
division of the past—the split between "old" and "new" immigrants

Construction workers faced a multitude of dangers—downtown Pittsburgh in the 1950s. (Carnegie Library of Pittsburgh)

to America—had weakened during this era. The strict quotas of the 1920s had choked off the flood of immigrants from abroad, and the Depression and World War II had solidified the trend. Despite some increase in immigration from Latin America and East Asia, the percentage of Pennsylvania workers who were foreign born and those with one or both parents foreign born fell sharply from 1940 to 1970.

The enormous drop in the number of first- or second-generation immigrants meant that the vast majority of the workers spoke fluent English, and the "old" and "new" intermarried with growing frequency. While ethnicity still influenced behavior and employment patterns, it is clear that its diverse impact was substantially less in 1970 than in 1940.

The dimensions of change in the occupational structure of the

234

Pennsylvania labor force were surprisingly small in these years. From 1950 to 1960 manufacturing's share of total employment only fell from 35 to 34 percent. Even in the 1960s, when change became somewhat more rapid, the percentage dropped slightly, to 32 percent. The change that did occur was mostly accomplished by a marked growth in the service sector rather than by an absolute decline in manufacturing. For example, primary metals employed only about 10 percent fewer workers in 1970 than twenty years earlier, and the number of metal-fabricating workers statewide actually increased over the same period. Clothing and electrical manufacturing were the next biggest manufacturing employers. The number of clothing workers fell somewhat during this period, while the ranks of electrical manufacturing workers grew, boosting it to the number two position by 1970. Coal mining was one exception to this pattern of stability. As a result of the mechanization of coal cutting, employment in the state's mines fell to thirty-nine thousand by 1969, less than one-third of the number of miners in the state in 1950. The anthracite region was the hardest hit. On the other hand, commercial construction employment in the state grew by about 25 percent, although it was liable to severe cyclical fluctuations.

Among the biggest employment gains in the service sector were in some areas of retail sales and the low-wage, nonunion, food and drink establishments. The number of insurance and banking workers in the state also more than doubled in the two postwar decades.

A New Standard of Living

Overall, the standard of living of the average worker in Pennsylvania rose markedly in the postwar period. Among factors determining the standard of living was the fluctuating unemployment rate of the boom years. Pennsylvania's jobless rate fell during the Korean War boom. The rate then remained stubbornly high for the rest of the 1950s, topping off at 10.1 percent in 1958, well above the national average. The early 1960s reflected the same trend. However, as the Vietnam War escalated, joblessness fell sharply in mid-decade, bottoming out at just 2.9 percent by 1969.

Within this statewide picture, regional variations were apparent. The Harrisburg and Lancaster areas had low unemployment

Steelworkers on Pittsburgh's South Side in the 1940s. (Pennsylvania Historical and Museum Commission)

rates through the 1960s. Altoona, Clearfield-Dubois, and Johnstown were quite the opposite. The Uniontown-Connellsville area was the hardest hit. Fully 23 percent of its work force was unemployed in 1961, consistently over double the state average. In the mid-1950s, the cities of Scranton and Wilkes-Barre in northeastern Pennsylvania were designated as the only two urban areas in the United States

236

with unemployment rates in excess of 15 percent. Significant reindustrialization efforts in the 1960s would reduce unemployment in the anthracite region well into the single digits.

Growth in the average hourly wage in Pennsylvania outstripped price hikes over this period. From 1960 to 1968, for example, weekly wages of production workers rose by one-third. By 1969 the typical factory worker earned $3.18 per hour, with workers in primary metals weighing in as the wage leaders at $3.76. Not all workers in the state shared equally in wage gains. Since the mid-1940s the International Ladies' Garment Workers' Union had been organizing garment factories in northeastern Pennsylvania that had "run away" from the union and higher wages in Manhattan. Wages in the "runaway" factories were typically lower than those paid to workers elsewhere in Pennsylvania and New York. Through the coming decades, union president David Dubinsky and Wyoming Valley ILGWU District leader Min L. Matheson and her successors would continually take action to hike the wages of unionized workers. (For more information see Keystone Vignette: "Min Matheson and the Wyoming Valley District of the ILGWU," p. 265.) Moreover, salaries of thousands of federal government workers based in Pennsylvania, dependent as they were upon action by Congress, also lagged in the 1950s. For example, as late as 1960, the average letter carrier in the state earned only $4,640 per year.

Home ownership among the non-farm population increased during this period. By 1970, 66 percent of urban families owned their own home, versus 56 percent in 1940. Working-class suburbs arose such as Penn Hills or West Mifflin near Pittsburgh, and Levittown and Willingboro near Philadelphia (almost 75 percent of whose home owners were skilled blue-collar workers, technicians, teachers, clerical, and sales workers). In Willingboro, twelve thousand houses priced at $11,500 to $14,500 with $100 downpayments were purchased, mostly by those employed in Philadelphia or its industrial environs, especially the Fairless steel mill. Important in-city "suburbs" also developed, such as Pittsburgh's Stanton Heights and Northeast Philadelphia. According to one description of growing suburban neighborhoods, workers sought "a way of life that brought the life's savings out of South Philadelphia and West Philadelphia and Kensington and set them down in a little corner of heaven in Ox-

*Technological change in the work place demanded new skills from
Pennsylvania workers—Port Allegany, McKean County, 1953. (Carnegie
Library of Pittsburgh)*

ford Circle or Mayfair or Frankford."

Not only did people move from the inner city, industry did as
well. Most new residents of Willingboro enjoyed shortened com-
muting time by moving, as had 252 factories, which left Philadelphia for its adjacent counties from 1962 to 1971. In fact, only 20
percent of all of Philadelphia-area suburban workers were employed
in the city itself by 1970. Even in Northeast Philadelphia the new
in-city "suburbs" developed near such factories as Budd, Yale &
Towne, Nabisco, and the huge new Internal Revenue Service
Mid-Atlantic headquarters. The automobile went hand in hand with
growing suburbanization as the primary mode of transportation. In
1940 most workers in Pennsylvania did not own an automobile. By
1960, 59 percent of households owned a car, and by 1970 the figure
had risen to 77 percent.

The educational levels of working-class children also rose sharply.
In 1970 the average adult over twenty-four had 12.0 years of schooling versus 10.2 in 1960 and 8.0 in 1940. By 1970 a working-class
child was very likely to graduate from high school and had a roughly

*Strip mining contributed to the decline in employment in the coal
industry. (Carnegie Library of Pittsburgh)*

fifty-fifty chance of attending college. By 1954 Pennsylvania had
almost three times the number of college students as in 1940. The
number tripled again from 1954 to 1970. The high school dropout
rate, meanwhile, fell from 35 percent in 1940 to 15 percent in 1967.

Before improvements in living standards are exaggerated, however, it should be remembered that as late as 1963, half of all Pennsylvania families earned less than $5,000 a year. This was at a time
when the Labor Department estimated that over $6,000 was needed
for a family to achieve a "modest" standard of living. Worse, a half-
million residents earned less than $3,000 in annual income, a
sub-poverty condition. In 1961, one-seventh of all housing in the
state was listed as dilapidated or badly deteriorated. There were
also sharp inter-industry wage differentials. In 1960 the average coal
miner in the state was earning $122 per week, double that of a
textile or bank worker. Even in manufacturing, Pennsylvania's ten

239

thousand cigar makers, mostly based in Philadelphia and York, averaged just $1.54 per hour as late as 1964.

The rate of strikes and lockouts in the state declined in the 1960s as compared to the 1950s, when the total of such events was always well above the national average. A peak was reached in 1959, when a steel strike propelled the total strike days to 1.83 percent of scheduled workdays. By the 1960s, however, the strike rate declined sharply and the tiny 0.35 percent of 1969 was actually the highest of the decade.

On-the-job accidents decreased by the 1960s as well. In 1968, for example, 626 Pennsylvania workers were killed. As shockingly high as this figure is, it was less than half the annual toll during World War II and only about 60 percent that of an average year in the 1950s. The change, however, was attributable primarily to a shift to less dangerous occupations and the decline in the number of mining and railroad workers, rather than to improvements in the safety of a given job. New safety rules governing construction sites, for which the building trades unions lobbied, did bring improvements. The death toll in construction dropped by almost 21 percent from 1957 to 1962.

Two problems plaguing labor during these decades were automation and increased overseas competition. The mechanization of industry had been increasing since the Industrial Revolution. Overall, such trends did not significantly accelerate during the 1950s and 1960s yet several phenomena did heighten the impact and visibility of mechanization in the postwar period. The first of these was the fact that in some sectors such as coal mining, mechanization brought massive regional unemployment. Secondly, the declining availability of adequately paid unskilled or semiskilled positions made transfer to another occupation difficult for the displaced, particularly for older workers. Finally, the dramatic presence of automatic control devices that, for the first time, posed the possibility of "workerless factories," caught the public eye. Indeed, in 1965 there were fewer than a dozen automatic control devices operating in Pennsylvania steel mills. By the end of the decade, two-thirds of all manufacturing firms of more than one hundred employees used at least some automatic control devices or data systems. By 1965 there were a few handworkers left in the Pennsylvania cigar industry where the introduction of homogenized bindings now permitted simplified, one-position, automatic feeding machines, greatly reducing the need for skilled cigar workers. Application of such technology was greatest in communications, transportation, and electrical manufacturing.

The thirty-five hundred members of Philadelphia's Locals 1116 and 1291 of the International Longshoreman Association felt the impact of automation, despite the rising tonnage shipped through their sprawling ten miles of docks. For example, grain elevators, which had used twenty-eight-man loading crews, had been reduced to six-person crews by 1966.

The biggest productivity increases in the 1950s came in textiles, chemicals, coal mining, and railroads, partly as a result of automation. The number of brewery workers in the state fell by about 25 percent despite rising production. Almost 60 percent more telephone calls were placed in 1960 than in 1946. Yet, due to automatic switching, employment in the industry fell by about 5 percent. Some service occupations, such as elevator operator or pinsetter, virtually disappeared as a result of mechanization. Despite the fact that primary metals did not set the pace in automation, productivity per worker rose substantially. By 1963, 12.1 worker hours were needed to produce a ton of steel, compared to 18.4 in 1945. Key factors in this productivity growth were the introduction of oxygen roof jets in open hearths from 1958 to 1963 and the erection, in the late 1960s, of basic oxygen furnaces with capacities about 250 percent greater than those of the open hearths.

Competition from imports varied from sector to sector. Statistics from the steel industry illustrate the growing problem. In 1947, with Europe, Japan, and the Soviet Union still devastated from the war, the United States produced nearly 57 percent of the world's steel. By 1969, the figure had fallen to 22.5 percent. The ratio of steel exports to imports, that had been 3:1 in 1952, fell to 1:1 in 1959, although the impact of the strike that year distorted the figures to some extent. In some sectors, such as specialty steel or synthetic fibers, where imports increased by 400 percent from 1963 to 1968, the impact was severe. Overall, however, the actual level of imports remained small in most sectors of the economy at least by comparison with the period following 1970. In 1968, Pennsylvania still produced more steel than any foreign country except the Soviet Union.

241

Furthermore, Pennsylvania manufacturers exported close to $1 billion worth of products per year in the late 1960s, and 50 percent more than that was exported through the state's Delaware River ports.

Organized Labor at Its Peak

Pennsylvania labor began the 1950s in an aggressive mood, spurred by the inflation and low unemployment of the Korean War period. The early years of the decade saw a series of major strikes in Pennsylvania, and most of them resulted in settlements generally favorable to the labor movement.

After a long strike, the United Mine Workers achieved a landmark industry-wide pact in 1950. In return for a free hand for employers in the mechanization of the industry, major additions were made to the miners' health and welfare fund. This was especially important at a time when the average age of Pennsylvania miners was rising, with two-thirds being over thirty-five in 1950. Miners struck again in 1952; the settlement added more funding to their benefit plan. The United Steelworkers were on the picket line, too. A late 1949 strike brought the first pension plan for most blue-collar steelworkers. Two strikes in 1952 resulted in gains including the union shop.

Among major strikes was the 156-day Westinghouse conflict in 1955-56. Several unions, including the United Electrical Workers (UE), International Union of Electrical Workers (IUE), and International Brotherhood of Electrical Workers (IBEW) led walkouts in East Pittsburgh, Beaver, Essington, Sharon, and Sunbury. The strike was fought over the corporation's attempt to increase production and reduce incentive rates. A settlement was reached with mixed results. This strike/lockout reflected a general post-Korean War attempt by business to regain control of incentive rates and work rules.

The biggest strike of the decade occurred in basic steel in 1959. Steel corporations hoped to significantly tighten their control over work rules and incentive rates. Over one hundred thousand Pennsylvania steelworkers struck for 116 days before President Eisenhower obtained a Taft-Hartley injunction, ordering an eighty-day end to the strike. A settlement was reached following the union's return to work.

Striking ILGWU members, Pittston, 1958. (ILGWU UNITE!)

During the Korean War the federal government created, as it had during World War II, a government agency to review wage increases. This agency, known as the Wage Stabilization Board, set a ceiling of about 10 percent on wage hikes. In early 1951 labor members walked off the board, protesting the fact that the ceiling was not equal to the soaring inflation rate, though they later returned following a compromise agreement. Nonetheless, in sharp contrast to World War II, a no-strike pledge was not issued by unions during the Korean War era and strikes in Pennsylvania and the nation remained among the highest ever.

The early 1950s saw a record number of union cardholders. By 1953, there were 1.54 million unionists in the Commonwealth, more than double the total before World War II. The majority of the growth had come from within the ranks of the AFL, but the largest union in the state was a CIO affiliate, the USWA. Fully 18 percent of union members in the state belonged to the steel union. Half of all the unionists in the state belonged to the five largest unions: the USWA, United Mine Workers, International Brotherhood of Teamsters, Amalgamated Clothing and Textile Workers (ACTWA), and the International Ladies' Garment Workers. The Teamsters were particularly active in organizing in the state during the 1950s and carried out successful unionization drives in Erie, and in Sears warehouses during 1959. By the end of the year they had 110,000 members in Pennsylvania, of which 77 percent worked in the Philadelphia area.

Pennsylvania's labor movement possessed substantial political clout in the mid-1950s. The election of Governor George Leader in 1954 broke a sixteen-year GOP reign. Democrat Joseph Clark was elected to the U.S. Senate in 1956. Labor played a very strong role in the election of another Democrat, Governor David Lawrence, in 1958. The pattern of labor-endorsed Democratic victories also prevailed in the General Assembly where Democrats held a majority in the House after 1954. Significant labor-related legislative changes included a hike in the minimum wage to $1 an hour in Pittsburgh and Philadelphia and 75 to 85 cents per hour elsewhere. This law protected about 150,000 workers in the state who were not covered by the federal Fair Labor Standards Act. In 1958 the state government also issued a revision of the rules governing the hours and working conditions of the Commonwealth's eight thousand migratory farm workers.

Labor's political influence at the local level was significant as well. In Pittsburgh, for example, John Feigel, president of the AFL Central Labor Union, was a member of the city's board of education and served on the board of the Greater Pittsburgh Airport Committee, Regional Industrial Development Corporation, Red Cross, and Community Chest. John Kane, chairman of the Allegheny County Commissioners since 1935, was the head of Local 9 of the Printing Pressmen, while Thomas Gallagher of the Flint Glass Workers was president of the city council.

A labor-sparked political upheaval took place in Philadelphia in the early 1950s. It was not until the election in 1951 of labor-backed Democratic mayoral candidate Joseph Clark that the Republicans relinquished their seventy-year domination, the largest major city in the country in which they had continued their control. By 1954 the city was firmly Democratic. The CIO-PAC and the ACTWA and ILGWU political action arms were the major labor contributors in the city, each raising about $50,000 per year from their members.

By 1952 average unemployment benefit payments had risen slowly to $24 weekly. Yet, Republican-controlled legislators had enacted significant cutbacks in unemployment compensation taxes for corporations in 1949 and 1951, some of which were made retroac-

244

tive. Westinghouse, the biggest beneficiary of the new rules, obtained twelve free quarters of compensation liability. As a result, during the long economic slump of 1958-61 the state's unemployment compensation fund ran persistent deficits.

In 1959, Congress passed the Labor Management Disclosure and Reporting Act, better known as the Landrum-Griffin Act. Less significant in its amendment of labor law than the Taft-Hartley Act of a decade earlier, enactment of the bill was preceded by a well-publicized set of congressional hearings that highlighted corruption among a relatively small number of union leaders. One subject of these hearings was a series of dynamitings carried out in a few labor disputes in the Scranton area. Revelations about the Teamsters and several smaller unions led to their expulsion from the AFL-CIO. In Pennsylvania this led to a series of jurisdictional battles between unions. The most important of these pitted the Teamsters against the Brewery Workers and the Seafarers, as well as the expelled International Laundry Workers Union versus a new, AFL-CIO-chartered, Laundry and Dry Cleaning Union, much of whose strength and leadership came from Pennsylvania.

By the 1960s, labor faced a more difficult political position than it had in the 1950s. The GOP regained the governorship in 1962 with the election of William W. Scranton, and retained control of the office for the remainder of the decade. For most of the 1960s Republicans also dominated the legislature. In the 1964 Democratic landslide, however, the party regained the state House of Representatives but lost control again in 1966. Paradoxically, John F. Kennedy carried the Commonwealth in 1960, the first Democrat since 1940. Labor's support for Lyndon Johnson in 1964 and Hubert Humphrey in 1968 helped them to carry the state as well. One indication of the level of political involvement at the grassroots came from Allegheny County, where about 25 percent of unionists contributed to Labor's Committee on Political Education (COPE) during the 1960s.

In 1961 the state's minimum wage was increased to $1 per hour for most workers. This brought wage increases to about 47,500 employees who were not covered by federal law. However, an important setback was suffered in 1964 in the area of unemployment compensation. Although a protest rally of twenty thousand unionists in Harrisburg on March 19, 1964 almost blocked the bill (it passed the House by one vote), drastic cutbacks in coverage were enacted by the legislature. Employer taxes were cut almost in half, and the harsher eligibility rules of the legislation resulted in 34 percent fewer applicants receiving benefits in 1964 than in 1963. A package of labor bills in 1968 made only modest improvements in unemployment compensation, but substantially improved the outdated workers compensation payment schedule.

After twenty years of often bitter dispute, the AFL and the CIO merged in 1955. The declining intensity of the debate over industrial versus craft unionism, the political homogeneity of the two federations, the growing sense of common goals, and the passing of old leadership played a role in the merger. The agreement was generally hailed by the labor movement. At the final CIO convention, the Wilkes-Barre Industrial Union Council delegate cast one of only two votes against the step. Nevertheless, in Pennsylvania, twenty years of hostility between the two groups was difficult to overcome. Disputes emerged regarding who would serve as officers of the merged statewide group.

It was not until June 1960 that the Pennsylvania amalgamation was carried out, at a joint convention held in Pittsburgh. The merger agreement gave two officer positions each to the AFL and CIO. Harry Boyer, a former Hosiery Workers and USWA staff member and president of the Pennsylvania CIO was one co-president. As his partner, the convention selected Joseph F. Burke, a Sheet Metal Worker officer and president of the Philadelphia Building Trades Council. Harry Block, of the CIO's IUE, was chosen secretary and Earl Bohr, from the AFL, was selected as treasurer. In 1962 Burke retired, leaving Boyer as the sole president. A new position of executive vice president was created and went to Michael Johnson, another former Pennsylvania AFL leader and activist for the ILGWU.

Most local labor councils merged soon thereafter. Philadelphia's amalgamation on November 30, 1960, united 250,000 workers in that labor council, led initially by Norman Blumberg of the Painters and Joseph T. Kelly of the IUE. In September 1961, facing an October deadline imposed by the national AFL-CIO, the last major holdout, Allegheny County, achieved amalgamation of its four rival federations (two each from the AFL and CIO). John Feigel of the AFL's Typographers was chosen as president and Paul Stackhouse of the

Tarentum CIO was chosen executive vice president.

About 40 percent of the Commonwealth's labor force was already organized in 1961, well above the national average. Many more medium-size and small groups of workers turned towards unionization during the decade. A few examples illustrate this trend. In May 1965, the Steelworkers brought one thousand workers at Superior Tube in Collegeville into their ranks. One of that union's biggest victories of the decade was achieved in March 1966 with the ousting of a company union by the three thousand workers at Textile Machinery Works in Reading. In 1967, the USWA organized a group of three hundred technicians at U.S. Steel's Ambridge works, and six hundred workers at Kennedy Van Saun in Danville.

The Amalgamated Clothing and Textile Workers climaxed a twenty-five year effort at Weldon Pajama in Williamsport, when employees voted to unionize in 1963. The union also won two large victories in the state in 1967 with the organization of over eight hundred workers at Masland Carpet in Carlisle and twelve hundred at Magee Carpet in Bloomsburg. In 1966, employees of Curtis Publishing in Philadelphia and Sharon Hill chose the Bookbinders as their union. The union-label conscious worker could now be imagined lounging in union-made pajamas, walking on union-made carpets and reading union-printed publications. Such a Pennsylvanian could also eat the union-made snacks produced by the one thousand Wise Potato Chip workers in Berwick, who joined the Amalgamated Meatcutters in 1967. If they spilled while snacking, they could wipe it up with the union-made towels produced by Scott Paper in Chester, whose seventeen hundred workers organized into the Brotherhood of Pulp and Paper Workers in 1967, after two unsuccessful drives.

If they were in a mood to dine they could patronize the Horn and Hardart restaurant chain in Philadelphia, organized by the Bakery Workers and the Retail Clerks and the Hotel and Restaurant Employees (HERE) in 1967. If union business took them to Harrisburg they could stay at the HERE's newly-organized Penn Harris and could drive there on tires produced by the five hundred new members of the United Rubber Workers (URW) at Carlisle Tire, who organized in 1968.

While it is true that the overall strike rate in the state dropped off in the 1960s, there were many picket line clashes. A bitter strike by machinists at Yale & Towne in Philadelphia lasted twenty weeks in 1961 before the threat of AFL-CIO mass picketing stopped the hiring of scabs and helped win the strike. Teamster taxicab drivers in the same city struck for thirty-six days the same year protesting the use of part-time drivers. In 1963 in Erie, members of the United Rubber Workers Local 61 at Continental Rubber were forced on strike when the company was sold to new owners who demanded concessions. Mounted deputies attacked and beat pickets, but three thousand union workers rallied to protest and the strike was won. The IUE waged a seven-week strike at Philco in 1964 that brought an improved contract. Bakery Workers at Nabisco in Pittsburgh and Philadelphia struck in 1969 and, after a seventy-day strike, the newly unionized USWA members at Coleman Stove in Somerset won their first contract. Few who were active in the Pennsylvania labor movement in the 1960s can forget the grape boycott. By the end of 1969, boycott centers in support of the United Farm Workers had been set up in twenty towns and sales had fallen off considerably.

The biggest battle in the state in the 1960s, in terms of workdays lost, was the 1969-70 General Electric strike. For the first time since 1950, all of the unions at GE united on the picket line. In Pennsylvania, striking plants included Erie, Philadelphia, and Allentown. Important support was received from the entire labor movement as well as student and consumer groups. The result was what UE Secretary Treasurer James Matles referred to as "the first negotiated settlement with GE in twenty years."

Slowly, African Americans began to reap some of the benefits of prosperity enjoyed by the labor movement. The passage of federal Equal Employment Opportunity portions of the 1964 Civil Rights Act created a major tool for African Americans to use in their quest for equal hiring in the state. Perhaps the most dramatic battles in Pennsylvania were fought over their efforts to penetrate the construction trades. Until the mid-1960s almost no progress was made. For example, while blacks made up 16.4 percent of the construction workers in the Philadelphia area, this figure masked the fact that almost all were laborers or plasterers. Many craft locals had no black members at all. Similarly, in 1963, only 4.7 percent of Pittsburgh construction workers were black, in a 20 percent Afro-American city. Almost two-thirds of these were laborers, plasterers, or cement masons, among the lowest in pay and status of the crafts. In that same year, the Pennsylvania Human Relations Commission ordered seven Pittsburgh building trades locals to begin admitting black apprentices. Despite some progress, in 1964 there were two black plumbers, one iron-worker and no electricians admitted to apprenticeship in the entire state, out of hundreds of apprentices accepted. It was not until a 1969 order by the U.S. Department of Labor imposing quotas on Philadel-phia apprenticeships, that blacks began to enter many crafts in the state in substantial numbers.

In August 1969, a Pittsburgh confrontation transpired over this issue. Hundreds of African Americans demanded of contractors and the building trades unions that they be hired in numbers proportional to their share of the Pittsburgh population. Picketing major construc-tion sites—including Three Rivers Stadium—hundreds were arrested and the city's mayor shut down ten important construction sites in the city for several days. A few days later, three thousand white con-struction workers marched on city hall to demand that they be paid for the canceled work days. Negotiations followed and black hiring was increased, defusing the explosive period of the crisis.

Public Employee Upsurge

The 1960s brought a large and unexpected increase in the union-ization of government employees in Pennsylvania. Until 1960, most public workers in the state had not been union members and only a few of them had been able to engage in collective bargaining. The NLRA had never covered government workers and the 1947 Penn-sylvania Labor Relations Act banned all strikes by state and munici-pal workers. A partial breakthrough came in 1957. After meetings with representatives of the American Federation of State, County and Municipal Employees (AFSCME), Democratic Governor George Leader signed an executive order allowing state workers to join unions and to present grievances through union channels. Unions could be recognized and would be "consulted" when work rules were changed. AFSCME District Council #33 had bargained with the city government in Philadelphia since at least 1952. By 1961 the union, led by William McEntee, won a limited union shop contract

249

in the city.

Many factors spurred public employees in the Commonwealth to turn to collective action in the 1960s. Low wages were one crucial factor. In 1961 the average government worker in Pennsylvania earned only $384 per month, about 5 percent below the national average. When eighty thousand state employees received a raise in 1965, it was their first in five years. Declining status, rapidly increasing numbers—Pennsylvania state and local government employees tripled to about 450,000 from 1947 to 1969—and the example of the gains being won by organized workers in the private sector all spurred the drive.

Teachers were in the forefront of this campaign in Pennsylvania. In 1965 the insurgent Philadelphia Federation of Teachers (PFT), buoyed by the endorsement of Dr. Martin Luther King Jr. and other civil rights leaders, compelled the school board to agree to a representation election. On February 1, 1965, with 95 percent of the teachers in the district voting, the PFT won, by a margin of 5,403 to 4,671. The PFT subsequently achieved substantial contract gains. By 1967, a Philadelphia teacher outearned nonunion suburban counterparts by about 20 percent: the reverse of the situation of five years earlier. Later in 1965 lay teachers in the Philadelphia Catholic archdiocese struck, marking the first time such an occurrence had taken place in the nation. These teachers had earned only $4,400 per year, and $100 less if they were women. In 1966 the Hotel and Restaurant Workers Local 434 was chosen by over a thousand cafeteria workers in city schools, and in 1967 thirty-five hundred custodial workers in the Philadelphia school system voted for union representation. (Organizing by teachers in Pittsburgh is profiled in Keystone Vignette: "Pittsburgh Teachers and Collective Bargaining," p. 270.)

Such militancy spread across the state. In 1967, eighteen hundred technical and service workers at Penn State chose Teamster Local 764 as their representative and won university recognition. By March 1968 the Pennsylvania Education Association, moving rapidly toward the full acceptance of collective bargaining, led a successful march of twenty thousand of its members on Harrisburg to demand a raise in the starting salary for teachers, then pegged at a lowly $4,500. In 1968 there were thirteen public employee strikes in the state and double that number in 1969. By the end of the decade, sanitation workers, highway maintenance personnel, firefighters, and others had walked off the job. Collective bargaining had begun for public employees. Technically, however, their militant actions remained illegal.

Responding to the growing unrest, in 1968 Republican Governor Raymond Shafer appointed a twelve-member commission, led by Leon Hickman, a former vice-president of ALCOA. The commission was to review and make recommendations concerning the "whole area of public employees and public employers." In 1969 the commission recommended that the law be modified to legalize some strikes by public employees and to require that state and local government agencies negotiate in good faith with the duly certified collective bargaining representatives. The bill, passed by the House, was defeated in the Senate and languished until the next year. Another piece of legislation, Act 111, providing for binding arbitration and banning strikes, was enacted for police and firefighters.

For the 463,000 federal government workers who lived in Pennsylvania, the decade also brought important changes in their patterns of labor relations. Spurred by the militant example of local government workers, hundreds in the state joined unions. John F. Kennedy's issuance of an executive order in January 1962, giving approval to the unionization of federal workers and authorizing collective bargaining to be carried out by most federal agencies, was an important step forward. Strikes, however, remained forbidden by the Taft-Hartley Act.

Membership in federal unions grew rapidly. In 1962, the National Association of Letter Carriers won representation rights for the carriers in Pittsburgh and Philadelphia and the Postal Clerks won the rights for the mail handlers in the Steel City. The next year, workers at the large Social Security Center in Philadelphia voted for the American Federation of Government Employees as their representative, by a three-to-one margin. By the end of the decade, expanded membership meant that bargaining was being carried out for the first time by large numbers of federal government workers, although the strike ban still limited their bargaining clout.

Hospital and nursing home workers constituted another sector to which unionization spread in the 1960s. Such workers were not covered by the protection of the NLRA in the 1960s. Local 1199C of

251

the Drug, Hospital and Nursing Home Workers won bargaining rights at a number of Philadelphia health institutions. Their sister local, 1199P, did the same in central and and western portions of the state. A major strike in 1969 at Pittsburgh's Presbyterian Hospital was, however, broken by management's use of a full range of anti-union tactics. Hospital workers remained unprotected by collective bargaining legislation as the decade ended.

The Movement toward "Union Democracy"

In the late 1960s, an important revitalizing battle began to develop within the ranks of the United Mine Workers against the dictatorial leadership of W.A. "Tony" Boyle, who had headed the union since 1963. A number of factors contributed to this unrest. In Pennsylvania most UMWA districts were in receivership and corrupt leadership no longer met the needs of the rank-and-file who were shocked at revelations regarding once-trusted officials. Perhaps the best illustration is the early 1960s conviction and imprisonment of long-time District 1 (anthracite) president August J. Lippi for his involvement in the Knox Mine Disaster near Wilkes-Barre.

On January 22, 1959, the Susquehanna River whirlpooled into a mine of the Knox Coal Company, killing twelve miners and flooding adjacent workings, bringing underground operations to a halt in the most productive hard coal fields in the state. Thousands were immediately unemployed as underground mine workings were permanently sealed off by billions of gallons of river water. Subsequent federal and state investigations revealed that Knox employees had illegally dug a chamber under the river—on company orders—to extract coal from a large vein. Safety rules and union wage scales were flagrantly violated by owners of the Knox Coal Company in the quest to increase production.

It was soon revealed that ownership of the company was directly linked to the area's leading organized crime family. To the shock of many, it was also revealed that District 1 leader August Lippi was a "silent partner" in the company's ownership, in flagrant violation of the Taft-Hartley Act. Local 8005 officials were also indicted for involvement in the affair, including Dominick Alaimo, a reputed member of organized crime, who had received nearly $30,000 in illegal payoffs from Knox officials to secure labor peace.

Despite this significant setback in the already dying anthracite industry, statewide coal production began to increase in the mid-1960s. Pennsylvania remained a leading producer of coal, particularly in the bituminous fields. With this increase came substantial hiring for the first time in two decades and a lowering of the average age of miners, ushering in younger, more militant union members. In addition to the move against union corruption, the drive for enhanced mine health and safety was one of the most crucial spurs to the battle for democracy in the coal fields. Black lung, an ailment in which the lungs were scarred by coal dust, took a heavy toll among miners. In 1965 Pennsylvania enacted a black lung bill providing some modest payments to victims of the disease. Coal companies denied the very existence of the ailment and found collusive doctors to back their arguments that smoking and heredity could account for the high rate of lung illness among miners.

An explosion at a mine in Farmington, West Virginia on November 20, 1968, that claimed 128 miners—about twenty of whom lived in nearby Pennsylvania—highlighted lax mine safety. The mine had been cited sixteen times in the previous five years for excessive methane gas, but small fines had given the coal operators little incentive for improving these conditions. The attitude expressed by the coal operators and by President Boyle—that the disaster was a tragic but inevitable fact of mining life—further inflamed the rank and file.

Pressure began to build in the coal fields for the payment of black lung benefits and for improved health and safety conditions. Mass marches and wildcat strikes, although centered in West Virginia, spilled over into Pennsylvania. In October 1969, under the spur of this unrest, the federal government enacted a new Coal Mine Health and Safety Act, incorporating black lung benefit payments.

Such issues encouraged reform candidates to run in the upcoming 1969 UMWA presidential election. Joseph "Jock" Yablonski, president of UMWA District 5, based in Pittsburgh, broke from the Boyle administration and announced his candidacy. He was quickly supported by most reform-minded unionists. Following a bitter and violent campaign, it was announced that Boyle had won the December election. Yablonski refused to concede defeat and charged fraud. On December 31, 1969, Yablonski, his wife and daughter were shot to death as they slept in their southwestern Pennsylvania home. Three weeks later the assassins were arrested and, in time, the conspiracy to murder Yablonski traced back to Boyle himself, who would be found guilty and sentenced to prison for the remainder of his life. Meanwhile the reform movement, Miners for Democracy (MFD), was born at Yablonski's funeral in Washington, Pennsylvania. The movement was led by Pennsylvanian Mike Trbovich. In the early 1970s the MFD ousted Boyle and elected reform candidate Arnold Miller, who promised democracy within the union .

Two more of Pennsylvania's largest unions experienced internal battles in the 1960s that brought new leadership to the fore. Dissatisfaction had grown within the USWA over the autocratic and sometimes ineffective leadership of David J. McDonald, who moved into the presidency of the steel union upon the death of Philip Murray. As early as 1956, a loosely organized Dues Protest Committee, headquartered in McKeesport and primarily based in western Pennsylvania and eastern Ohio, garnered one-third of the votes for their presidential candidate, the little-known Donald Rarick. Following an unsatisfactory 1963 contract settlement, unhappiness crystallized among the USWA leadership. USWA Secretary Treasurer I.W. Abel broke with McDonald and ran a victorious campaign against him in 1965.

In the early 1960s, the increasingly erratic and dictatorial leadership of IUE President James Carey sparked growing opposition. He was challenged for the presidency of the union in 1964 by Paul Jennings. Carey announced a narrow victory in the subsequent election. An investigation by the U.S. Department of Labor, however, revealed massive voter fraud by the Carey forces (thousands of votes were altered in his favor at the East Pittsburgh and Sharon Westinghouse plants alone). Carey was forced to resign and Jennings became the union's new president.

An Era Draws to a Close

As the 1960s drew to a close, Pennsylvania's labor movement enjoyed the benefits of the most significant era in its growth and

Workers on picket duty in Homestead during the 1959 steel strike.
(Carnegie Library of Pittsburgh)

power. Public and private employees drew ever closer to collective representation offered by labor unions to address longstanding problems and grievances. The state, indeed, reflected the pinnacle of the American labor movement with its diversity of unions and union members. Important symbols of labor's progress were deeply embedded in the consciousness of the Keystone State, such as Unity House, the ILGWU's thousand-acre vacation and education resort in the Pocono Mountains which, by the end of the decade, attracted ten thousand unionists from throughout the nation during the summer season.

Yet, ominous threats, such as the Vietnam War, divided the movement. With a handful of exceptions, unionists in the state did not oppose deepening American involvement in that war in its early days. By the end of the decade, as the war dragged on and casualty lists (especially high among the sons of workers) mounted, and as the domestic costs of the war became more clear, opposition grew. Most labor leaders, however, remained silent until the issue drove their political ally, President Lyndon Johnson, out of office. As late as April 1968, at the Pennsylvania AFL-CIO convention, the delegates voted to describe the war as a "tragic, though necessary military involvement." Only two delegates spoke out against this view, Henry Dropkin and George Nejmah of the Amalgamated Clothing and Textile Workers, and only a handful dared oppose it in a voice vote. From that point on, more of the leadership in the state began to raise objections to the continuation of the increasingly bloody conflict, and official or unofficial union delegations were present at the major antiwar rallies in the state held during the Fall of 1969.

By the end of the 1960s, organized labor had come through thirty years of unparalleled gains. Workers were far better paid and treated than they had been thirty years before and labor had won for itself an enhanced position in society. Storm clouds were, however, appearing on the distant horizon, harbingers of the tempests that would threaten to topple many of labor's hard-earned gains and cause many Pennsylvania workers and unionists to longingly recall the "Glory Days."

Mark McColloch received a Ph.D. from the University of Pittsburgh. He is the author of *White Collar Labor in Transition, Cold War in the Working Class,* and *The Rise and Decline of the United Electrical Workers* with Ronald Filippelli. He is professor of history and assistant academic dean at the University of Pittsburgh, Greensburg.

Keystone Vignette

The Postwar Strike Wave: The Case of the Plate Glass Workers

Richard O'Connor

Industrial citizenship was rarely achieved without major struggles, many of which boiled to the surface near the end of World War II. The five thousand members of the Flat Glass, Ceramic, and Silica Sand Workers of America (FGCSSWA) at Pittsburgh Plate Glass (PPG) plants in Creighton and Ford City looked forward to winning tangible economic gains, without a crippling strike, in the 1945 contract negotiations. PPG and Libbey-Owens-Ford enjoyed near-monopoly status as glass suppliers to the auto industry, and government reconversion plans had sparked a three-year high in monthly plate glass output. Stocks were known to be insufficient to withstand a shutdown of any duration. After two solid weeks of meetings, industry and union negotiators had settled all but four issues, none of which seemed insurmountable. Nonetheless, when plate glass workers at Libbey-Owens struck in mid-October over local issues, bargaining between PPG and the FGCSSWA came to a halt; the company refused to negotiate with the union while a strike was in progress. The union then made the strike industry-wide. For over three months plate glass workers and company officials faced each other from opposite sides of the company fence.

What lay behind this clash? During the late war years tensions between PPG and the union had increased. As production of B-29 and B-32 bomber glass intensified, wages and working conditions had deteriorated. Moreover, the company took advantage of the wartime no-strike pledge to stall settlement of the 1944 contract, insisting instead on daily extensions of the old agreement. In June 1945 the FGCSSWA initiated a strike vote to attempt to force a settlement. Before the results could be tabulated, Creighton workers struck over local grievances, sparking an industry-wide walkout. Joseph

Froesch, FGCSSWA president and a brother of an officer of the Ford City local, sought War Labor Board intervention to force a resolution of the dispute, but succeeded only in obtaining an airing of the union's grievances. Finally succumbing to the WLB's threat of retribution against the union on its incentive pay demands, workers returned to the plants at the request of the union leadership.

Given the intensity of local grievances, and the history of wartime national negotiations, the strike that began in October 1945 took on added significance. Without war-related pressures to return to work, local union officers sought resolution of long-standing local and national issues. Creighton and Ford City workers proved remarkably resilient in the three-month conflict, not only organizing regular strike-support activities, but helping to establish the Armstrong County Industrial Union Council and fighting to secure state unemployment benefits for returning veterans.

When negotiations resumed after the first of the year, however, intense pressures on the company and on the union resulted in a settlement. Union members were dissatisfied with the size of the wage increase and with the lack of resolution of many local issues. Over the next few decades these feelings gave rise to the most contentious environment in the American plate glass industry.

Dr. Richard O'Connor is an industrial historic preservation expert for the federal government.

Keystone Vignette

Philip Murray: Pennsylvania's
Mid-Century Labor Giant

Louis Pappalardo

Philip Murray was born in the village of Blantyre, Scotland in 1886. His deeply religious Irish parents were both wage workers—his father was a coal miner and his mother, who died when Murray was two, was a weaver. Philip began to work in the coal mines of Scotland at the age of ten. In 1902 he and his father emigrated to the United States, settling in the Westmoreland County village of Madison. Father and son soon found work in the nearby collieries and joined the United Mine Workers of America.

Two years later, the eighteen-year-old Murray quarreled with a company weigh boss who attempted to cheat him. Philip remembered that "the weigh boss took a shot at me with a balance weight from the scale. I hit him with a stool over the head." Murray was fired and his family was evicted from company housing. Sympathetic miners took the Murray family in. By 1905 Philip was elected president of UMWA Local 1197 in Cokesburg. He rose rapidly in the union, joining the UMWA executive board in 1912 and becoming president of District 5 in 1915. In 1920 he was chosen vice president of the UMWA, serving as a key lieutenant to UMWA president John L. Lewis.

In 1936, when the CIO decided to launch a drive to organize the steel industry, Lewis placed Murray in charge. From 1936 to 1941, despite difficult obstacles and some setbacks, Murray led the organization of basic steel. In 1942, the Steel Workers Organizing Committee became the United Steelworkers of America (USWA) and Murray was elected as its first president. By 1940, Murray had labored in Lewis's shadow for two decades. Now the former subordinate was destined to rise still higher, but at the cost of a break with his mentor. The two leaders clashed over the 1940 U.S. presidential election, with Murray endorsing Roosevelt's third-term bid. Still, when the UMWA chieftain decided to step down as CIO president following FDR's electoral triumph, he endorsed Murray as his successor. Murray was reluctant to take the post, styling it a "Crown of Thorns in the Garden of Gethsemane." Nonetheless, Murray assumed the office.

The war years were busy for Murray. Dividing his time between Washington and Pittsburgh, he became a prominent voice for America's factory workers, strongly backing the war effort, yet attempting to see that some of the vast profits created by the war were shared with the workers in steel and other industries. Following the war, Murray led the USWA through the 1946 strike, its biggest ever, and presided over a CIO engaged in huge and successful picket line struggles. As the political climate in the country moved rapidly to the right, he fought to stop the tide of anti-labor attacks which culminated with the Taft-Hartley Act. Influenced by his Catholicism, Murray supported the expulsion of eleven left-wing unions in 1949, believing that they had become a political liability and a threat to his position. His final years were spent in attempts to secure improved contracts for the USWA and in efforts to defeat the open enemies of labor at the polls.

Throughout his career Murray maintained a warm personal style in his dealings with most workers. He remembered his own roots and lived in a modest home in Pittsburgh's Brookline neighborhood, despite his increased wealth and power. He remained comfortable in his western Pennsylvania mill towns and coal patches and enjoyed socializing with his family and old friends. His death on November 9, 1952 was seen by many workers as a personal loss.

The late Professor Louis Pappalardo was director of the Murray Labor Studies Center at the Community College of Allegheny County.

Keystone Vignette

Gaston Le Blanc: Union Activist

Paul Le Blanc

Asked in 1950 why the United Stone and Allied Workers would be organizing the workers at the Clearfield Cheese Company in Curwensville, organizer Gaston "Gus" Le Blanc quipped, "Because they make brick cheese." The real reason was because there was no other union able to help them at the time. The willingness of Le Blanc and the Stone Workers to take on the task was indicative of its commitment to the old slogan "organize the unorganized." The Stone Workers later assisted in the successful campaign of the Amalgamated Meatcutters at Clearfield Cheese. Their own major base in Pennsylvania was among firebrick workers, primarily those employed by Harbison-Walker Refractories, which specialized in making bricks used in the furnaces of the steel industry.

Established with the aid of the AFL in 1903 as the Quarry Workers International Union, the union supported the CIO in the 1930s, adopting its new name to reflect an expanded organizing jurisdiction. Its membership rose from 2,000 in the depths of the Depression to more than 12,000 by the mid-1950s. Stone Worker locals existed in the Clearfield, York, Johnstown, and Pittsburgh areas. About 1,200 union members lived and worked in Pennsylvania, which comprised part of the union's District 2.

The Stone Workers had a reputation as a dynamic and democratic union and District Director Gus Le Blanc was an effective organizer, strike leader, and negotiator. His beginnings in the labor movement can be traced to the radical Unemployed Councils in New England during the 1930s. He also worked for a number of unions before securing a staff position with the Stone Workers in 1946. Adhering to a socially-conscious brand of unionism, Le Blanc pushed for broadened unemployment and workers compensation, and national health care. He was a vocal supporter of the civil rights movement and publicly opposed the war in Vietnam. A self-taught expert on the firebrick industry, he recognized that the growth of corporate conglomerates necessitated broader labor unity. Consequently, he helped to engineer industry-wide coordinated bargaining efforts involving the various unions which had organized firebrick workers throughout the country.

In the 1960s, Harbison-Walker and the Stone Workers battled over grievances and throughout contract negotiations. On a few occasions, the union struck. By the second half of the decade, the union was finally able to make substantial gains. The key was a combination of tough contract language backed up by the militancy of the members and by the decisive new factor of inter-union cooperation.

Convinced that his small union could not survive in the face of corporate mergers and technological change, Le Blanc became a partisan of merger with larger unions. In 1969 he was elected president of the Stone Workers. By 1971 he secured the union's merger with United Steelworkers. Several months later, at the age of sixty, Le Blanc died in a hotel fire in Cleveland, while directing a labor conference.

Paul Le Blanc received a Ph.D. in labor history from the University of Pittsburgh in 1989. He is the son of Gaston Le Blanc.

Keystone Vignette

Amy Ballinger: Pittsburgh's
First Lady of Labor

Dale Newman

One manifestation of industrial citizenship was that many Pennsylvania labor leaders held political office in the years 1940-1970, usually as part of the Democratic Party. They did not control the Democrats, nor were they elected governor or mayors of the largest cities, but they held many important secondary posts. Amy Ballinger was one such figure.

Ballinger was Pittsburgh's most visible and vocal female labor leader for more than three decades. Amelia was born in 1902, the daughter of German immigrants. She was the youngest of eight children and left school after the seventh grade to contribute to the family's income, subsequently acquiring two years of business school training. She was married to Carl Beatty.

After losing her job as a secretary in 1929 she began work at the Fort Pitt Laundry—"doing a little bit of everything—working in the office, ironing handkerchiefs, pressing clothes." She was paid twelve cents an hour and worked seven days a week for at least eleven hours a day.

During the wave of sit-down strikes that swept the country in 1936-37, Ballinger and several coworkers decided to protest their deplorable conditions. On one occasion about seventy workers, most of whom were women, shut down their machines and walked off the job. The company responded by increasing their wages by fifteen cents an hour, but fired Ballinger as the instigator of the dispute. She spent the next two years as an unpaid organizer for the laundry workers of the city. Her efforts culminated in the chartering of Local 141 of the Laundry Workers International Union. Ballinger was elected secretary-treasurer and retained that office until her retirement in 1976.

During the 1940s and 1950s, the three thousand-member Local

141 and its leadership were an important force in the city's economic and political life. Ballinger's organizing skills and the deplorable conditions in Pennsylvania's laundries resulted in her appointment to the state's first Minimum Wage Board in 1938. Her election to the executive board of the Pittsburgh Central Union in 1939 and her re-election for the next twenty years reflects the high regard in which she was held by labor's top echelon in the area. She frequently led the ticket in the elections to that body.

In 1939 Ballinger became the first woman to be elected a vice president of the International Laundry Workers Union, an office she held until 1957 when she refused to run again because other officers of the union had been charged with corrupt practices. Ballinger played an aggressive role in the ouster of the old International and in the chartering of its replacement, the Laundry and Dry Cleaners International Union. In 1958 she was elected vice president of the new group, an office she held until her retirement.

According to Ballinger, she "had to delve into politics" for the well-being of the labor movement. She worked for precinct, state, and national candidates. Her extraordinary speaking skills and sense of humor made her a frequent and popular speaker who captivated audiences. Ballinger urged women to take active leadership roles in unions and politics. She was appointed to Pittsburgh's City Council in 1970, and elected to two subsequent terms, retiring in 1976.

Dale Newman received a Ph.D. in labor history from the University of Pittsburgh.

Keystone Vignette

Min Matheson and the Wyoming Valley District of the ILGWU

Kenneth C. Wolensky and
Robert P. Wolensky

From 1944 to 1963, in northeastern Pennsylvania's Wyoming Valley, Min Lurye Matheson led the International Ladies' Garment Workers' Union (ILGWU). She was born in 1909, the second of eight children, to immigrant Russian Jews in Chicago. As a youngster Min observed the intensity with which her father, Max, approached his life's work to organize cigar makers. She listened as immigrants came to their apartment and talked about their daily struggles and toil in this new land of great promise. She heard her father's efforts to stimulate their interest in the idea of collective representation. She witnessed the fiery speakers who would gather at Riverview Park on Sundays and talk of economic and social justice. Such memories guided Min as she set out to organize the growing number of garment workers in the northern anthracite region: "You assimilate a lot of that stuff. And it always stayed with me. It stayed with the whole family. But with me, more so."

In 1928, at the age of nineteen, Min fell in love with Bill Matheson, an activist twelve years her senior whom she met at the Sunday meetings of the Chicago Federation of Labor. With Bill's encouragement she left Chicago in 1932 to assist striking textile workers in Paterson, New Jersey. When that strike was crushed, Min relocated to New York and began working as a dressmaker in the garment district, befriending leaders of the ILGWU who were impressed with her knowledge, sensitivity to issues of social justice, and ability to speak publicly. Gaining the respect of coworkers, in 1937 she was elected chairlady of ILGWU Local 22 with 32,000 members. Bill soon joined her and they both embarked on organizing careers.

In the early 1940s, Bill accepted an assignment in rural Sayre, Pennsylvania. Soon a daughter, Marianne, came along. And not long after, Betty was born to the Mathesons. In the near term Min chose a line of work that had great meaning to her: motherhood. In 1944 she got a call from ILGWU president David Dubinsky who explained that garment factories were "running away" from Manhattan to the anthracite coal fields of Pennsylvania in search of cheap labor and an escape from union contracts. The anthracite region had become an attractive locale as men, the traditional breadwinners, were jobless as the bottom fell out of the coal industry. Families were desperate and the wives and daughters of miners were eager to sit down at a sewing machine to earn what they could. Women worked long hours for very low piece rates.

Complicating matters was the underworld. It was no secret that criminal elements were a problem in the garment industry. Gangsters had been a concern in Manhattan for years and such elements had made inroads in northeastern Pennsylvania. So when the "runaways" came to Wyoming Valley towns like Pittston, Kingston, and Edwardsville, criminals were among the shop owners. Dubinsky asked Min and Bill to "clean up the mess down there." They accepted. Min was appointed Wyoming Valley District manager and Bill educational director. When they arrived in the valley, conditions were worse than they had expected. According to Min:

> All the mines were down. Men weren't working. We had organized in New York and surrounding areas. Wages were getting higher. The employers were looking for lower wages. And, things were happening with organized crime. The big shots in New York, the Genoveses and Anastasia were having legal problems and wanted a legal front for their illicit activities which included everything. The dress industry is easy. You need very little capital, a handful of machines, and you're in business. So they were running. And they ran to coal fields of Pennsylvania.
>
> They told the women, "We'll teach you to sew." They worked for weeks for nothing. And the hours! There were laws in the land but they weren't obeying any of the laws. They did what they wished and made it easy for the women to come in any time of the day or night. Double, triple shifts. At the Pittston end of the valley it was as if every empty space was occupied by dress shops.

266

Min Matheson speaks to striking ILGWU members from the back of a pickup truck, 1958. (ILGWU Unite!)

The ILGWU had a local presence since 1937. However, the relatively underdeveloped union was no match to the growth of the runaways. The Mathesons found about 650 union members in six organized shops in 1944. Remarkably, by the time they departed in 1963, the Wyoming Valley District consisted of 11,000 members in 168 organized factories. With the help of many, including the keen intellect of her husband, Min led the charge to transform women garment workers into a politically active and community conscious organization.

She recruited local people and developed indigenous resources who might be helpful to the cause. Since legal problems might result, Min turned to former stage actor and up-and-coming lawyer Dan Flood: "Dan helped us all the time. With his mustache and mannerisms and all, he fitted just perfectly into what we were doing." Members of other local unions, like the United Mine Workers, helped as well. Min recruited people like Angelo "Rusty" DePasquale, a UMWA member and Pittston resident who knew the local terrain well; "I was introduced to Minnie and she asked me about Pittston. We went to Pittston and she showed me the shops. The way she talked. The way she spoke to people. She treated me well. I said,

'Look Minnie, you want me to go along? I'll help you. Whatever I could do for you.'" John Justin, an ILGWU organizer and educator, joined in as well: "In organizing Min used the pressure of getting as many people in the union as possible. Of getting the Teamsters not to deliver products. We would use everything possible—not violence—but everything possible."

Workers began to pay attention to Min's soapbox speeches. According to Dorothy Ney, "They used to just pack the union hall because they loved to hear Min talk. She could convince anyone to join the union." Her actions weren't limited to speeches, however. Ney explains, "Min was right on the picket line with us. She went at six o'clock in the morning like we did and she was on the picket line most every morning."

She turned attention to the mob-controlled shops as well. Min engaged the local media, often broadcasting live on the radio, to bring attention to the situation and to rally workers to the union cause with fiery orations penned with the assistance of her husband. As one garment workers put it, "Bill made the snowballs and Min threw them!"

Known to initiate spur-of-the-moment tactics to counter the opposition, on one occasion, while leading a picket, Pittston mobsters verbally attacked her as a harlot, unfit to lead the women. Furious at the accusation, she phoned the union hall and ordered an associate to dress her two pre-school daughters in starched pinafores and bring them to the picket line. Once there, she handed them picket signs and placed them with her at the head of the column. How could the toughs call her such things now? The local press prominently featured the "Children on the Picket Line" story. By the mid-1940s momentum began to build. The area's garment workers were becoming increasingly aware of Min Matheson and the ILGWU. Additional factories were organized. Contracts were negotiated and workers joined the ranks.

In 1948, the union opened a district health care center in Wilkes-Barre, the only one of its kind designed to serve the entire anthracite region. For no cost garment workers and their families from Pottsville to Scranton received a variety of medical services. At nearly the same time Min formed a chorus to perform for community and charitable causes, at political events, and in holiday festivities. She recognized, too, that routine factory work provided few avenues for intellectual stimulation and, in response, developed a curriculum for workers ranging from courses on factory safety and personal health to day-long symposia on federal, state and local politics. Workers were regularly bused to the union's Unity House conference center in the Poconos to hear prominent speakers discuss topics of relevance to working people, or to Harrisburg and Washington, D.C. to tour, meet with policymakers, and attend legislative hearings, or to New York to visit and tour the United Nations. One of Min's proudest accomplishments was a partnership with local Wilkes College which gave workers the opportunity to do something practically unheard of—attend evening college courses. The union also became active politically, advocating for local, state, and national politicians and their worker-friendly policies.

Min and Bill departed the Wyoming Valley for a new assignment with the ILGWU Union Label Department in 1963, against the protest of their 11,000 members. Though he needed her in New York, David Dubinsky recognized that, because of Min Matheson, the ILGWU "is widely welcomed as an integral part of all community activities in the Wyoming Valley." They returned to the valley in June, 1972, to live their retirement years close to family and friends. Min passed away on December 8, 1992 in Wilkes-Barre's General Hospital. Bill preceded her in death in 1987. Their work in the Wyoming Valley is, however, far from a memory. Min remains very much a local legend—a hero to many—the stuff of folklore. According to one local newspaper editorial, "The memory of Min Matheson should be a permanent part of Wyoming Valley history." Former City Councilman Joseph Williams put it this way: "There should be a statute of Min Matheson on Public Square in Wilkes-Barre for all that she has done for this valley."

Kenneth C. Wolensky is a historian with the Pennsylvania Historical and Museum Commission, and Robert P. Wolensky is a professor at the University of Wisconsin, Stevens Point. Quotations are from the three hundred-interview Wyoming Valley Oral History Project, co-directed by the authors.

Keystone Vignette

Pittsburgh Teachers and
Collective Bargaining

John Tarka

Pittsburgh's Local 400 of the American Federation of Teachers was organized in 1935. Over its first quarter century, led by teachers like Anne Schreiber Leifer, the union waged campaigns on behalf of Pittsburgh teachers. These included the demand that female teachers who married be allowed to retain their positions and an effort to force the school board to open its financial books to public scrutiny. Despite these early positive efforts, membership in the local remained small and no real collective bargaining took place.

By the 1960s, led by educators Joseph Zunic and Albert Fondy, the union began to slowly expand. The AFT contributed support, in terms of staff and finances, enabling a vigorous organizing drive to be launched in 1967. Despite growing support for the union, the school board refused to negotiate or to even permit a union election to be held among the teachers. In a daring step, the union membership voted, in February 1968, to call a strike in support of its request for an election. While only about seven hundred of the district's 3,600 teachers were actual members, over twelve hundred teachers heeded the strike call. After an eleven-day walkout, the school board reluctantly agreed to allow a court-supervised secret ballot election. Local 400 won the election, which was held that May. On Labor Day, 1968 the school board agreed to recognize the union as the representative of "the majority of the teachers."

Some hard bargaining followed, as membership in the local swelled. On September 2, 1969 the Pittsburgh teachers signed their first real negotiated contract. This success was followed by a victory for Local 400 in a second representation election in May 1970, giving the union exclusive bargaining rights for the teachers.

Since the inception of collective bargaining in the Pittsburgh

School District, Federation members have enjoyed tremendous economic and professional gains. The early, adversarial relationship between the union and the district has evolved in such a manner that both groups were presented with the Governor's Labor Management Cooperation Award in 1988.

John Tarka is an English teacher in the Pittsburgh schools and a staff member for the PaFT.

Readings for Chapter Five

Bergman, Daniel. *Death on the Job: Occupational Health and Safety Struggles in the United States*. New York: Monthly Review Press, 1978.

Bodnar, John; Simon, Roger; and Weber, Michael. *Lives of Their Own: Blacks, Italians, and Poles in Pittsburgh, 1900-1960*. Urbana: University of Illinois Press, 1982.

Clark, Paul. *The Miners' Fight for Democracy*. Ithaca: New York State School of Industrial and Labor Relations, Cornell University, 1981.

Clark, Paul; Gottlieb, Peter; and Kennedy, Donald, eds. *Forging A Union of Steel: Philip Murray, SWOC, and the United Steel Workers*. Ithaca: New York State School of Industrial and Labor Relations, Cornell University, 1981.

Crone, Harry. *35 Northeast: A Short History of the Northeast Department of the ILGWU*. New York: International Ladies' Garment Workers' Union, 1970.

Davis, Mike. *Prisoners of the American Dream*. London: Verso, 1986.

Galenson, Walter. *CIO Challenge to the AFL: A History of the American Labor Movement, 1935-1941*. Cambridge: Harvard University Press, 1960.

Harris, Howell. *The Right to Manage*. Madison: University of Wisconsin Press, 1982.

Herling, John. *Right to Challenge*. New York: Harper and Row, 1972.

Higgins, James and James Matles. *Them and Us: Struggles of a Rank-and-File Union*. Englewood Cliffs: United Electrical, 1974.

Hoerr, John. *And the Wolf Finally Came*. Pittsburgh: University of Pittsburgh Press, 1988.

Laslett, John, ed. *The United Mine Workers of America: A Model of*

Industrial Solidarity? University Park: Pennsylvania State University Press in association with the Pennsylvania State University Libraries, 1996.

Libertella, Anthony. "The Steel Strike of 1959: Labor, Management and Government Relations." Unpublished dissertation, Ohio State University, 1972.

Lichtenstein, Nelson. *Labor's War at Home: The CIO in World War II.* Cambridge: New York University Press, 1982.

Lipsitz, George. *Class and Culture in Cold War America.* New York: Praeger, 1981.

Miller, Donald and Richard Sharpless. *The Kingdom of Coal.* Philadelphia: University of Pennsylvania Press, 1985.

McColloch, Mark. *White Collar Workers in Transition.* Westport: Greenwood Press, 1983.

Oshinsky, David M. *Senator Joseph McCarthy and the American Labor Movement.* Columbia: University of Missouri Press, 1976.

Preis, Art. *Labor's Giant Step: Thirty Years of the CIO.* New York: Pathfinder Press, 1964.

Roberts, Thomas. "A History and Analysis of Labor-Management Relations in the Philadelphia Transit Industry." Unpublished dissertation, Pennsylvania State University, 1959.

Schatz, Ronald. *The Electrical Workers: A History of Labor at General Electric and Westinghouse, 1923-1960.* Urbana: University of Illinois Press, 1983.

Seidman, Joel. *American Labor From Defense to Reconversion.* Chicago: University of Chicago Press, 1953.

Tate, Juanita. "Philip Murray as a Labor Leader." Unpublished dissertation, New York University, 1962.

Tyler, Gus. *Look for the Union Label: A History of the International Ladies' Garment Workers' Union.* Armonk: M.E. Sharpe, 1995.

Wolensky, Kenneth. Unity House: A Workers' Shangri-La. P*ennsylvania Heritage* 24 (Summer; 1998): 26-30.

_____. "'We Are All Equal': Adult Education and the Transformation of Pennsylvania's Wyoming Valley District of the ILGWU: 1944-1963." Unpublished dissertation. Pennsylvania State University, 1996.

Wolensky, Robert P. and Kenneth C. Wolensky. "Min Matheson and the ILGWU in the Northern Anthracite Region, 1944-1963." *Penn-*

sylvania History 60 (1993):455-474.

_____. Disaster or Murder in the Mines? *Pennsylvania Heritage* 24 (Spring, 1998): 4-11.

Wolensky, Robert P., Kenneth C. Wolensky, and Nicole Wolensky. *The Knox Mine Disaster, January 22, 1959: The Final Years of the Northern Anthracite Industry and the Effort to Rebuild a Regional Economy.* Harrisburg: Pennsylvania Historical and Museum Commission, 1999.

Wolensky, Robert; Wolensky, Kenneth; and Wolensky, Nicole. *The Knox Mine Disaster,* January 22, 1999: The Final Years at the Northern Anthracite Industry and the Effort to Rebuild a Regional Economy. Harrisburg: Pennsylvania Historical and Museum Commission, 1999.

Chapter Six

Hard Times and New Hopes, 1970-1997

Howard Harris

On October 5, 1976, a beaming Governor Milton J. Shapp announced an official agreement between the Volkswagen Corporation and the Commonwealth of Pennsylvania for the German automaker to assume ownership of and put into operation a half-finished auto assembly plant near New Stanton in Westmoreland County. In return for nearly 100 million dollars in direct and indirect assistance from the state and local governments, VW promised to employ a minimum of five thousand workers to produce over fifty thousand cars a year by 1978. Governor Shapp projected that the new plant would attract other industries to the area, resulting in a gain of nearly twenty thousand jobs in the years ahead. Nearly twelve years later, on July 14, 1988, the last car rolled off the assembly line at the New Stanton plant. Citing declining U.S. sales as a significant factor, Volkswagen announced the permanent closing of its only American production facility. Nancy Albanese, a member of United Auto Workers Local 2055, captured the feelings of many of her coworkers on their last day at the plant:

> We got our final pink separation slip today. We had ten years in the sun. Now it's over due to "Reaganomics" and politics. We put our tools away after the last job and start to embrace one another. With tears in our eyes, we look up the assembly line and see empty carriers coming . . . emptiness and quiet, where production and laughter had been. We have pride in our hearts. We did a damn good job. Farewell, friends at Volkswagen.

None of the workers there that gloomy July day would have dared to predict that just two years later, the plant would reopen yet again, this time to produce picture tubes and televisions for the Sony Corporation. Although the Sony operation had a work force of nearly one thousand people by 1995, there was a major difference between it and Volkswagen—hourly employees lacked union representation.

The changing fate of the Westmoreland County facility epitomizes the economic uncertainty that has plagued working men and women in Pennsylvania during the last three decades of the twentieth century. A period that began optimistically for most wage earners soon turned to one of uncertainty, and even fear, as the Commonwealth's economy was rocked by both internal and external forces that ultimately cost the jobs of hundreds of thousands of Pennsylvanians. The belief of previous decades that workers had finally achieved the "American Dream" received a cruel jolt as an unstable economy led employers to demand wage concessions, close profitable plants and stores, invest in labor-saving technology, and avert unionization of the work force to free themselves from contractual obligations. Decisions made by corporate officials in boardrooms far removed from Erie, Reading, McKeesport, Lock Haven, and Johnstown negatively impacted not only employment but state and local tax bases as well, forcing reductions in many public services. Hundreds of families lost their homes due to their inability to meet mortgage payments. Thousands more used their life savings in an effort to cope with prolonged unemployment. Even in the midst of the gradual and geographically uneven recovery of the late 1980s and early 1990s, many Pennsylvania communities had yet to rebound from the effects of the economic crisis which had swept over them earlier.

The labor movement, along with most Pennsylvanians, had never dreamed that so many of the gains of the preceding two decades could evaporate so quickly. Although the warning signs were apparent, few people, if any, bothered to take them seriously. The Vietnam War, heightened racial tension, the development of the environmental and women's movements, the Arab oil embargo, and the Watergate affair dominated public attention while steadily increasing wage settlements facilitated the entry of both organized and unorganized workers into a consumer-oriented economy. Union leaders responded to the desires of their members by focusing on obtaining immediate wage gains at the bargaining table. While the labor movement continued to engage in political action, education and organizing, its major focus remained the maintenance of a much-improved standard of living for the average trade unionist.

Runaway inflation in the late 1970s and the devastating recession of the early 1980s, combined with broader changes in the demographics of the work force and a general restructuring of the economy, forced Pennsylvania unions to re-evaluate their traditional tactics and goals. Such issues as pay equity for women, employee ownership, affirmative action, labor-management cooperation, and employer-provided daycare became significant agenda items for labor. Moving beyond its primary concern over wages and working conditions, the labor movement joined with other groups to fight for economic development, occupational retraining, women's rights, stricter environmental regulations, controls over rising health care costs, and stabilization of Pennsylvania's unemployment compensation program. Innovative tactics and new technology were brought to bear on organizing and political action, while attempts to link labor's past with its future were strengthened by the revival of Labor Day celebrations in many communities.

More than anything else, the state's labor movement learned that it had to assume a much more visible and public role in the formulation of future economic policy. No longer could rank-and-file workers depend solely on the collective bargaining process to guarantee a decent standard of living. Increased economic globalization meant that garment workers in Waynesburg and Wilkes-Barre, retail store clerks in Beaver Falls, autoworkers in Allentown, and health care workers in Ebensburg had to begin to confront broader forces at work in American society. Meeting such a challenge remained a great source of both hope and frustration for both union and non-union workers alike.

An Economy in Transition

Mack Truck, Piper Cub, Robertshaw, Pullman Standard, WABCO, Bucyrus-Erie, and Colt Industries: at one time such a list might have appeared on the desk of a broker looking for investments in blue chip stocks. For most Pennsylvanians in the 1980s they represented a "who's who" of the manufacturing firms that had shut their doors, throwing thousands of state citizens out of work. The dramatic decline of basic industry in the late 1970s and early 1980s represented the single most important change in the state's economy during the period. Between 1980 and 1994 Pennsylvania lost over 391,000 manufacturing jobs, the highest number of any state in the union. New tax laws and government policies, increased availability of low-wage labor overseas, direct foreign competition, development of microelectronic technology, enhanced financial/investment interests in the corporate decision-making process, erosion of limited import protections once enjoyed by domestic industries, and employer desires to rid themselves of relatively expensive union contracts all contributed to the decision by many firms to close their Pennsylvania operations.

Employment in basic manufacturing peaked at about 1.5 million people in 1965, a number which remained fairly constant throughout the mid-1970s. Increased inflation and declining profits in the latter part of the decade initiated a series of plant closings or work force reductions that continued into the 1990s. Cutbacks reached into all industries and into most sections of the state. The Philadelphia area lost over 50 percent of its manufacturing jobs, primarily in the apparel, textile, machinery, and electrical industries. Southwestern counties experienced nearly the same proportion of loss in the primary and fabricated metals industries. Food, paper, and metals in Blair County; steel and apparel in Lebanon County; electronic equipment in Cameron County; and textiles in Columbia County all expe-

278

rienced sharp declines. Cutbacks in the steel industry in Johnstown, for example, caused Cambria County to lose more manufacturing jobs than any other rural county in the state. Between 1965 and 1983 nearly 65 percent of its 21,450 industrial workers were laid off.

The decline of Pennsylvania steel making became representative in the public mind of the fate of basic industry throughout much of the northeastern and central United States during the 1970s and 1980s. For decades America's automobiles, office buildings, bridges, and armaments had been built with Pennsylvania steel. The long struggle to unionize steel companies and the subsequent gains made through collective bargaining became the model for the progress that industrial workers had achieved in the aftermath of World War II. The apparent prosperity of the industry masked the fact that it had been steadily declining in the state throughout the twentieth century. In the early 1900s, the Pittsburgh-Youngstown-Wheeling region produced 70 percent of the nation's steel and iron. By 1969 the figure had dropped to approximately 28 percent of the national total. Between 1965 and 1983 employment in Pennsylvania's steel industry alone declined nearly 60 percent. In 1983 the production of clothing and related items actually passed the production of primary metals as the state's major industry.

A deteriorating state economy accelerated declines in a number of other industries. Coal mining, despite a brief resurgence in output during the Arab oil embargo of the mid-1970s, continued on a downward path. Even though the number of facilities producing bituminous coal actually increased, the number of working miners decreased significantly. Surface mining, which employed far fewer people and tended to remain in operation for brief periods of time, increased as the number of unionized deep mines dwindled. Poor working conditions and the nonunion status of most surface operations generally led to high turnover rates. Westmoreland County, with its many subsurface mines, was hardest hit by the decline of the state's coal industry.

The decreased demand for Pennsylvania coal proved fatal for anthracite mining in the northeastern region of the Commonwealth. Even during the Great Depression over 120,000 miners labored in the deep mines and open pits of the anthracite region. Yet, the replacement of hard coal as a primary fuel by gas, oil, and electricity after the Second World War drastically reduced employment in the northeast coal fields. The Knox Mine Disaster of 1959 further exacerbated the industry's decline by permanently sealing off millions of tons of coal in the once highly productive northern anthracite field, resulting in the permanent layoff of thousands of miners. As a result of such events, by 1983 only three thousand miners worked in the state's anthracite industry. Of those, some 650 worked in subsurface mines.

The development of garment and textile manufacturing in Scranton, Wilkes-Barre, and other northeastern communities had, for many years, helped to minimize the impact of the deterioration of anthracite mining. Members of mining families and even some miners went to work in mills and garment factories as the coal pits closed. The decline of these two industries in the late 1970s and early 1980s had a severe impact on such counties as Northampton, Lackawanna, and especially Luzerne. Four northeastern counties lost nearly twenty thousand apparel jobs, as well as thousands in the textile industry between 1965 and 1982. While some communities, such as Wilkes-Barre and Scranton, began working as early as the 1940s to diversify their economies, longer term economic decline meant that northeastern Pennsylvania had among the lowest average household incomes in the state by the late 1970s.

The economic downturn of the late 1970s and early 1980s accelerated the movement of Pennsylvania's economy away from heavy dependence on basic manufacturing to greater reliance on services. All sections of the state and most traditional industrial categories experienced considerable job loss during the period.

Expansion in certain specialized types of production during the 1970s and 1980s reflected the changing nature of the state's economy. Manufacturing with ties to the emerging technical and/or service sectors actually grew, although its development was unevenly distributed across the state and it was structured differently from more traditional industries. Employment in the production of technical instruments, advanced electrical equipment, and specialized machinery increased in southeastern sections of the state even as nearby Philadelphia experienced a sharp decline in the number of people working in primary manufacturing. The availability of low-cost, modern machinery facilitated the development of the plastics in dustry, especially in rural areas, where the need for low or moderately skilled jobs was acute. The movement of production jobs out of major urban areas affected some old-line industries as well. Although printing and publishing experienced continual growth, longtime centers of the trade such as Philadelphia actually lost over twelve thousand jobs between the mid-1960s and the mid-1980s. During the same period, nearby Montgomery County picked up over thirty-three hundred printing jobs.

Job Loss, Selected Industries 1965-1983

Industry	Employment, 1965	Employment, 1983	% Decrease
Tobacco	11,100	1,700	84.7
Footwear	31,500	11,200	65.0
Stone, Glass and Clay	56,000	41,000	26.8
Equipment	74,700	56,000	25.0
Electrical and Electronic Equipment	114,000	90,300	20.8
Food (non-farm) Production and Processing	103,000	83,700	18.8

The organization and nature of work in growth industries differed considerably from that found in such mainstays as steel, industrial machinery, and consumer electronics. Most new plants invested heavily in sophisticated equipment, minimizing the need for a large, highly skilled work force. A majority of the high-tech electronic firms in southeast Pennsylvania employed fewer than one hundred people while nearly half the rural-based plastics plants had fewer than twenty full-time employees. Often specializing in one particular product, the state's newer industries were extremely sensitive to even the slightest fluctuations in the national economy. Many of these plants and factories were located in areas with low union representation. Avoiding unionization often meant that employers could remain more competitive and enjoy lower production costs. The fate of wage earners in the highly organized steel or machinery industries became a frequent reminder for employees when manufacturers imposed concessions or attempted to thwart union organizing drives.

An absence of unionization was apparent in Pennsylvania's growing service sector as well. While the number of industrial jobs dropped in the 1970s and 1980s, non-manufacturing employment increased dramatically. By the mid-1980s only one-quarter of the state's labor force was employed in farming, mining, construction, or primary production. The service sector, most of which remained nonunion—with the exception of government employment—accounted for nearly 3.6 million jobs in 1985.

Job Increase, Selected Service Sector Categories 1965-1983

Category	Employment, 1965	Employment, 1983	% Increase
Health Services	120,000	370,000	208.3
Government	487,000*	729,000**	49.7
Wholesaling	194,500	235,500	21.1
Retailing	520,700	731,850	40.6
Finance, Insurance, etc.	160,600	253,712	58.0

* 1964 Figure
** 1980 Figure

While growth in the health care industry attracted many skilled professionals to major urban centers, construction of suburban shopping malls eliminated tens of thousands of less-skilled retail jobs in those same cities. Even as Philadelphia became the only county in the state to experience an overall decline in retail employment, surrounding counties had the biggest increases as new stores and restaurants opened to meet the needs of a more affluent suburban population. In addition to paying low wages and providing few fringe benefits, many service sector firms offered only part-time employment. Grocery clerks, store salespeople, bank tellers, and many office workers rarely worked forty or even thirty hours a week. Such arrangements also meant that part-time employees did not enjoy benefits such as paid holidays, vacations, and medical insurance.

In contrast to employment conditions in the private sector, Pennsylvanians working for the federal, state, or local governments improved their position considerably during the period. Aggressive unionization and the support of sympathetic legislators allowed public employees to make real gains in wages, fringe benefits, safety and health conditions, hours of work, and protection against arbitrary supervision. Letter carriers, teachers, sanitation workers, claims supervisors, police officers, and caseworkers pressured lawmakers into expanding their employment rights, often in the face of hostile public opinion. Not all public workers, however, fared equally well especially during the 1980s. Many local communities, faced with serious revenue losses due to layoffs or plant closings, reduced public services. Clairton, in Allegheny County, was forced to lay off its entire police force, most of its firefighters, and numerous clerical workers in 1983. When these moves did not sufficiently reduce expenditures, city officials resorted to extinguishing street lights.

Overall, however, most public workers made significant gains during the 1970s and 1980s. Yet, changes and reductions in some areas of state and federal spending during the 1990s would raise major concerns among the Commonwealth's public employees about their future job security.

Hospital workers demonstrating for improved health care for working Pennsylvanians. (Pennsylvania AFL-CIO)

Changing Workplaces - Changing Workers

The 1970s and 1980s witnessed not only a change in the nature of Pennsylvania's economy but a change in the ideas and attitudes of its working men and women as well. In the wake of the civil rights and feminist movements, African American and female wage earners actively challenged traditions of job discrimination, while young workers of all backgrounds expressed increased dissatisfaction with the authoritarian structure of most workplaces. Initial disagreements over hair length or clothing styles often escalated into full-scale conflicts over what constituted basic rights of employees in factories and offices. Increased drug use by workers of all ages

284

represented a more negative legacy of the so-called "youth rebellion." While substance abuse both on and off the job became increasingly common, employers responded by instituting drug testing procedures which were often challenged legally and in other ways by workers who felt that their rights were being violated. In addition, growing awareness of the dangers of coal dust, asbestos, PCBs, formaldehyde and other carcinogens led many Pennsylvanians to question their legal obligation to accept work assignments that exposed them to dangerous materials or chemicals. These issues, and others, represented a direct challenge to management and created major problems for union officials who were often unprepared to deal with them.

Affirmative action to correct past racial and sexual discrimination, especially in the construction and steel industries, represented the type of problem with which both organized and unorganized workers had to deal in the 1970s and 1980s. Due to continuing pressure from civil rights groups, highlighted by the 1969 demonstration by black construction workers in Pittsburgh, the U.S. Department of Labor developed the "Philadelphia Plan" to guarantee greater minority participation on building projects receiving federal funds. Rather than set actual employment quotas for selected construction trades with low minority participation, the plan established multiyear goals that contractors had to make a good faith effort to fulfill. Despite the semivoluntary nature of the plan, building trades' unions in Philadelphia and elsewhere attacked the proposal, arguing that it constituted reverse discrimination. They claimed that contrary to government figures, "More than 30 percent of the members employed on unionized jobs within our jurisdiction" were African American. Although general laborers represented over 18 percent of that total, the construction trades pointed out that minority participation in unionized construction work in Philadelphia still exceeded that of most other American cities. Construction unions, contractors, and African American building trade workers in Pittsburgh moved to avoid Labor Department intervention by developing their own "hometown" plan. Rather than placing blacks on specific construction projects, the Pittsburgh Plan wanted to guarantee full union membership for minority workers. By late 1974 nearly 580 African Americans, out of a targeted goal of 1250 had been recruited into building trades' locals. The success of the program was marred by the fact that four of twenty-one Pittsburgh construction locals had to be placed under government sanction for failing to comply with the plan.

In order to forestall the development of a "Philadelphia" plan for the steel industry, I.W. Abel, president of the United Steelworkers of America, and steel company officials accepted a consent decree in 1974 designed to overhaul existing seniority systems. While large numbers of African Americans were employed in steel mills, they traditionally worked as unskilled laborers in dangerous and unhealthy operations. Complex networks of local seniority systems prevented all but a few from moving to better-paying, more highly skilled positions. Spurred on by a federal court ruling covering U.S. Steel's Fairfield Works in Birmingham, Alabama, the union and the steel companies negotiated an agreement that, among other things, allowed for the utilization of plantwide seniority and "bumping" to move African Americans out of lower-paying, unskilled positions. While the plan had the support of top union officials, a number of local leaders as well as large numbers of rank and file workers opposed it, especially where bumping became common.

The 1974 consent decree applied to women as well. Between 1974 and 1980, the number of women employed in maintenance and production work in Mon Valley steel plants, for example, went from none to nearly 10 percent. Most women became steelworkers because of the prospect of earning higher wages. Their decision to seek steel jobs reflected the changing role of women in Pennsylvania's economy during the 1970s and 1980s. As inflation heated up and layoffs and shutdowns increased, female participation in the labor force expanded dramatically. A majority of both married and unmarried women, many of them heads of single-parent households, found themselves channeled into traditional female occupations— nursing, teaching, retailing, or clerical work. Compensation in those occupations averaged 30 or 40 percent lower than in male-dominated employment categories requiring similar training or experience.

Comparative Wages - Selected Job Categories*

Female Dominated Job	Monthly Wage	Male Dominated Job	Monthly Wage
Licensed Nurse	1,362	Driver	1,580
Clerk/Typist II	1,024	Tree Pruner	1,467
Child Care Worker	1,192	Tire Repairman	1,463
Keypunch Operator	1,024	Laborer	1,268
Clerk/Typist I	988	Utility Worker	1,076

*Allegheny County, September, 1984

Employment in the steel industry or in other nontraditional female occupations offered women an opportunity to achieve a standard of living that they could never have reached if they remained clerks or typists. The effort to open up new jobs for women was not easy. In Erie, for example, two women successfully filed a class action suit against the city after they were passed over in favor of two men for appointment to the police force, although they were equally qualified. Even when women did manage to obtain work in predominantly male industries, they often faced rejection or harassment from both supervisors and male employees. Women employed at U.S. Steel's Clairton plant often had to walk a half mile to the one women's rest room in the mill. For two years their locker room had no heat. In one instance, a male steelworker set a newspaper on fire under the feet of a female coworker as a joke. Despite such conditions, many Pennsylvania women thrived in their new jobs, obtaining valuable skills and training. A majority of women, however, continued to work in traditionally female occupations.

The expanded social awareness of the 1970s and early 1980s created other challenges for Pennsylvania workers and their unions. A growing concern over air and water pollution brought some wage

Teachers on strike, Bethel Park. (Carnegie Library of Pittsburgh)

earners into direct conflict with environmentalists. Many mineworkers felt threatened by the strict regulations that were enacted on all types of mining to control water pollution. In a similar fashion, efforts by the U.S. Environmental Protection Agency to require steel makers in Johnstown, Clairton, and Pittsburgh to reduce air pollution levels evoked opposition and hostility from both steelworkers and company officials. Environmental concerns even led to conflicts between some of the state's major labor organizations. In the aftermath of the nuclear accident at Three Mile Island in 1979, a number of Pennsylvania unions, including the United Mineworkers, began to work with environmental groups to explore the development of alternative forms of energy that could provide large numbers of new jobs while reducing the risks inherent in nuclear power. Building trades' unions strongly opposed the effort since many of their members worked at the state's nuclear power plants. At a labor-environmental conference in Pittsburgh, an open confrontation occurred between construction workers and other trade unionists in attendance. Although the furor eventually subsided, tension remained between the need for jobs and maintaining the quality of the environment.

One of the biggest changes and challenges of the era was the growth of collective bargaining in the public sector, a reflection of the increasing importance of federal, state, and municipal workers in Pennsylvania's economy. Public sector bargaining probably had its greatest impact in public education. Primary and secondary teachers had traditionally shunned trade unionism in the name of professionalism and public service. Yet as their already lagging salaries fell further behind those of other municipal workers during the late 1960s and 1970s, attitudes began to change. Although teachers in Philadelphia and some other communities had been bargaining for years, they still did not have the legal right to strike. The passage of Act 195 during the summer of 1970 paved the way for an explosion of militancy among teachers, virtually unmatched by almost any other group of workers in the state. (For more information on public sector collective bargaining, see Keystone Vignette: "Act 195," page 326.)

Beginning in 1970, the summer and fall of each year meant tough collective bargaining between local school boards and teachers' unions. Although some walkouts did occur, most contracts were settled peacefully. Between 1970 and 1983, an average of 36 out of a total of 505 Pennsylvania districts experienced some strike activity each year. These strikes generally lasted less than two weeks. A 1977 strike in Aliquippa extended for forty days. Teachers in the Alle-Kiski school district left their classrooms for thirty-eight days in 1982 while a 1981 strike in Erie continued for more than six weeks. By September of 1981, Philadelphia teachers had been on strike six times while those in Pittsburgh had walked out three times. In response to growing public frustration with such strikes, the courts meted out harsh penalties against teachers' unions. After ignoring a judge's back to work order during a fifty-seven day strike in the winter of 1975-76, the Pittsburgh Federation of Teachers had its offices padlocked. The same judge fined the PFT $25,000 plus an additional $10,000 for each day the union remained on strike. Each

Throughout the 1970s, 1980s, and 1990s Pennsylvania workers struggled to maintain a fair workers' compensation system. (Pennsylvania AFL-CIO)

striking teacher or aide received a fine of $100 per day. During a 1981 Philadelphia walkout, another judge sent two hundred teachers to jail. As both sides became more familiar with collective bargaining during the 1980s, the number of teachers' strikes gradually declined. Between 1983 and 1989, the average number of strikes per year dropped to less than twenty. A major factor in the ability of Pennsylvania teachers to sustain collective bargaining during the period was the important role that the labor movement played in state politics, especially during the governorship of Milton J. Shapp.

Political Fortunes at High Tide

While Pennsylvania workers and their unions had a hard time with such issues as racial or sexual discrimination or environmental pollution in the 1970s, they had considerable success in the area of protective and social legislation on the state level. During the 1960s the Republican Party generally controlled both the governor's office and General Assembly. The threat of a strong Democratic challenge in the 1970 gubernatorial race, however, forced the Republican controlled Senate to moderate its generally anti-labor stance. By the summer of 1970, collective bargaining for public employees became a reality with the passage of Senate Bill 1333.

Enactment of the bill marked the culmination of a fifteen-year struggle. Despite last-minute GOP attempts to appeal to Pennsylvania workers, labor-backed Democrat Milton J. Shapp won the governor's race by over half a million votes. Democrats also gained control of both houses of the legislature. Working closely with Harry Boyer, Harry Block, and Mike Johnson—leaders of the Pennsylvania AFL-CIO—Shapp and his legislative allies developed and enacted numerous legislative initiatives friendly to working people and families. Enacted measures included extension and expansion of unemployment benefits, improved regulation of both surface and subsurface mining, reform of the workers' compensation system, no-fault auto insurance, improvements in the state's occupational disease law, increased aid to black lung victims, a higher minimum wage, and enhanced advocacy for and protection of consumers' rights. Shapp established a Women's Commission and supported efforts to pass equal rights legislation. In addition, a bill to protect high voltage electrical line workers became law after being stuck in the Assembly for ten years. In May of 1971 Pennsylvania became the first state to retain its right to enforce health and safety laws under OSHA, rather than accept federal pre-emption. In response to the efforts of the United Farmworkers Union to reach an agreement with western produce growers, the governor issued an executive order banning the use of all non-union lettuce by state agencies. The order exempted only lettuce grown within the Commonwealth. Shapp also signed a bill six years later forbidding the use of foreign-produced steel on any construction projects initiated by Commonwealth agencies.

Organized labor and Milton Shapp did not, however, agree on every issue. In May 1972, the state AFL-CIO publicly broke with Shapp over his proposal to turn over state health and safety inspections to the federal government. Another constant source of tension was the implementation of the state's new public employee relations legislation, commonly known as Acts 195 and 111. The acts gave public employees full collective bargaining rights as well as a limited ability to strike after they exhausted all other methods of dispute resolution. Pennsylvania workers now had the broadest bargaining rights of any public employees in the country.

As soon as Act 195 went into effect organizers from the Service Employees International Union, Teamsters, American Federation of State, County, and Municipal Employees, and the Retail Clerks fanned out across the state to sign up new members. Wilkes-Barre Hospital workers, office workers in Lackawanna County, road crews in Huntingdon, and state liquor store employees throughout Pennsylvania quickly signed up for union representation. By October of 1972, nearly eighty-two thousand state workers were unionized. Success did not always come easily. Even as AFSCME was attempting to organize and then negotiate a contract for state highway workers, the Shapp administration furloughed twenty-five hundred of them in April of 1972 and another fifteen hundred in August as a result of fiscal constraints. After a considerable amount of fist shaking and name calling, both sides finally agreed to a contract. In addition to providing a 20 percent basic salary increase, the agreement also provided for the rehiring of all laid-off employees. Other unions experienced similar difficulties in negotiations with various state agencies. In 1973, several thousand state store employees engaged in a ten-day strike when contract negotiations with the Liquor Control Board reached a deadlock. The full implications of the new collective bargaining relationship became apparent in 1975 with a major round of new contract negotiations.

Although most state workers had seen significant increases in their wages and fringe benefits, double-digit inflation devalued most of what they had gained. AFSCME and other state unions immediately rejected a state proposal for a maximum salary increase of 3.5 percent. Although negotiations continued, it became clear that only a miracle could avert a statewide walkout on July 1. On that day, approximatley fifty-five thousand AFSCME and SEIU members took to the picket lines to protest the Shapp administration's inadequate wage offer. The state immediately obtained an injunction preventing hospital and corrections personnel from participating in the strike. Two days later AFSCME agreed to a new contract. SEIU members in the public assistance and employment security programs remained on strike for twenty-one days. Many supervisory personnel stayed off their jobs even though they did not have a legal right to strike.

Part of the settlement with both unions was the promise of no disciplinary action against those supervisors who had joined the walkout. Although no other major public employee walkouts occurred during the decade, there were sporadic wildcat strikes over local issues and a one-day "sick-out" of some nine thousand state workers in 1977 protesting difficulties caused by a state budget crisis. While full collective bargaining was an important step forward for public employees, it also opened the door to increased conflict between public officials and organized workers in the state.

Many of the legislative gains of the 1970s remained controversial while some came under immediate fire from various interest groups. Business interests across the state strongly opposed improvements in the state's unemployment compensation system and successfully supported efforts to have the state's new income tax law declared unconstitutional. Workers' compensation remained an issue of consternation, so much so that the state Chamber of Business and Industry worked closely with the Pennsylvania AFL-CIO to develop and spearhead reforms to the system. The insurance industry and trial lawyers mounted a strong campaign against the passage of no-fault auto insurance which stabilized insurance costs for millions of Pennsylvanians.

The combined forces of Pennsylvania trade unionists, the governor, legislators, and sometimes even traditionally non-aligned interests were able to maintain or expand many of the reforms of the 1970s. One thing they couldn't do, however, was influence the national and international economies. Beginning with the Arab oil embargo of 1973, the American economy went on a roller coaster ride in the 1970s and early 1980s. Rapid economic change played havoc with the lives of many ordinary Pennsylvanians.

End of an Era

The country's economic problems profoundly affected Pennsylvania as much as any state in the union. Its workers felt the full impact of layoffs, plant closings, downsizing, and technological displacement. While management and labor organizations in the Commonwealth traditionally engaged in tough collective bargaining, a kind of live-and-let-live atmosphere had emerged by the 1950s and

1960s. This delicate balance began to be threatened with the appearance of inflation in the early 1970s, then recession, then "stagflation" by the end of the decade. Intensifying international economic competition and a stagnant domestic economy upset the relationship between workers and employers and led to an emerging atmosphere of antagonism towards labor.

Traditional collective bargaining procedures and tactics remained intact through the early and mid-1970s. Rising inflation in the beginning of the decade forced organized workers to increase their wage demands as their contracts expired. Major strikes in rail, communications, and steel during the summer of 1971 reflected growing economic pressures felt by working men and women. The federal government's imposition of wage and price controls during the late summer immediately dampened wage settlements in both the private and public sectors. An inability to negotiate acceptable pay enhanced hostilities between labor and management. Other issues such as health and safety in mining and increased automation in the newspaper industry led to conflict between specific unions and employers. Even as the general state of labor relations was beginning to erode in many sectors of the state's economy, some unions and employers attempted to find new ways to deal with such problems. In April of 1973, the United Steelworkers negotiated an experimental bargaining agreement, covering over 350,000 members in the ten largest steel firms. Instead of resorting to strikes or lockouts to settle unresolved bargaining issues, both sides agreed to accept final, binding arbitration. In addition to a one-time lump-sum bonus, the pact insured workers an annual 3 percent wage increase plus cost of living adjustments in each of four succeeding years. While the agreement prohibited company-wide strikes, locals could still walk out over specific plant issues. Although the experimental bargaining agreement was considered a major breakthrough in the field of labor-management relations, few industries adopted the practice.

Aggressive competition from foreign manufacturers and the prospects of cutting expenses and generating greater returns persuaded an increasing number of employers to shut down their Pennsylvania operations in favor of overseas locations. Due to intense competition from often less expensive foreign imports, the American St.

Gobain Corporation in Arnold furloughed 350 members of the Glass and Ceramic Workers Union as well as the Glasscutters Union in June of 1970. Four hundred and fifty International Ladies' Garment Workers' Union members employed in five knitting mills in Philadelphia met the same fate late in 1975 as did 350 Clothing Workers at Cross Country Clothes in Whitehall and Northampton. While imports were a bonafide problem, a number of plant closings resulted from corporate efforts to cut costs. The experience of six hundred members of the International Union of Electrical Workers Local 114, working at the Bendix plant in York, was a good example.

Built in 1952, the plant produced fuses and other electrical components for the U.S. Navy. On June 21, 1971, Bendix publicly acknowledged plans to close the York plant. Although they claimed that they were transferring production to another U.S. facility, it soon became clear that they were shifting work to a new plant in Matamoros, Mexico where the average wage was forty-two cents an hour. For at least six months prior to the official closing, company officials had been secretly moving equipment from the York plant to Mexico. Dismayed by the sudden change of events, one union official commented, "I don't know who they think they are fooling. Relations between the union and Bendix had always been good." Making things worse was the fact that the company reported a 36 percent increase in profits in the second quarter of 1971. Despite the best efforts of Local 114, the leadership of the IUE, public officials, and the media, Bendix refused to reconsider its decision. Over the course of the 1970s and 1980s, the scenario at York was repeated in hundreds of Pennsylvania communities. Between 1969 and 1976 alone, approximately 865,000 Pennsylvanians lost their jobs due to business closings.

Another disturbing trend for workers, especially in the building trades, was the increased use of nonunion firms on major construction projects. In July of 1972, over thirty thousand members of the building trades staged a march in Norristown protesting an injunction against their picketing of nonunion construction sites in the area. Unionized workers from Erie to Scranton to Reading traditionally used such picketing to put pressure on nonunion contractors to deal with local construction unions. The inability of the Philadelphia Building and Construction Trades Council to get the Altemose

Construction Company to pay the union scale on its many construction projects in southeastern Pennsylvania led to a three-year battle that included injunctions, lawsuits, and an attack on a retail construction site outside the city by over one thousand workers resulting in more than $300,000 in damage. Perhaps the most ominous sign for members of Pennsylvania's building trades was that Altemose received legal and financial support from the Associated Builders and Contractors Inc., the National Chamber of Commerce and the National Right to Work Committee.

Even where plant closings or nonunion competition was not an issue, the state's economic problems had a direct and often negative impact on collective bargaining relationships. Pennsylvania, as late as 1981, led the nation in the number of work days lost to strikes. Between 1975 and 1979, an average of thirty-five thousand Pennsylvanians per year walked off their jobs. The majority of public and private sector strikes resulted from deadlocked negotiations over wages and fringe benefits. Both sides accepted the fact that strikes were an inevitable and unfortunate part of the bargaining process. While employers always resented such strikes, they generally refrained from using strikebreakers to remain in operation. The situation began to change as the economy worsened in the latter part of the 1970s.

Nowhere was the change more apparent than in northeastern Pennsylvania. Workers hit hard by the decline of anthracite mining, textile, and garment production, now faced an aggressive antiunion campaign by some area employers. No confrontation was more bitter than in Wilkes-Barre in the fall of 1978, between printing trades' unions and the Wilkes-Barre *Times Leader*, the city's only major newspaper. Facing the expiration of their contract in late September, members of the Printing Pressmen, the Newspaper Guild, the Typographers and Stereotypers, and the Electrotypers grew apprehensive when Capital Cities Communications, a communications conglomerate, bought the *Times Leader* in May of 1978. As the contract deadline approached, the new owners erected barbed wire fences and surveillance equipment around the building while bringing in beds, refrigerators, stoves, and other equipment. When negotiations finally began, Capital Cities demanded concessions in almost every clause of the contract. The company flatly rejected a

Confrontation outside Wilkes-Barre Times Leader, *1978.* (Citizens' Voice)

joint union proposal to operate under the terms of existing agreements, with a slight pay increase. Anticipating a strike vote, the company brought in over one hundred Wackenhut guards as well as replacement workers from as far away as Texas and Missouri. Given little alternative, the 240 members of the four unions authorized a strike. Unfortunately, the disagreement soon escalated into violent confrontation.

Almost immediately, pickets came into conflict with the security guards. Union supporters rushed a printing pressman to the hospital after a guard sprayed his face with a fire extinguisher, while another was hospitalized after a clubbing by guards. Company vehicles hit or ran over five pickets. Community residents not involved with the dispute also ran afoul of the Wackenhuts. Guards sprayed a number of people walking past the plant with a high-pressure hose. Striking unionists retaliated by slashing car tires and spray painting vehicles owned by replacement workers or sometimes resorting to prank phone calls to the homes of those who stayed on the job.

Sensing widespread support from the community in this generally prounion town, the four striking unions decided to publish their own newspaper until the strike ended. On October 9, 1978,

297

the first issue of the Wilkes-Barre *Citizens' Voice* hit the streets. Within forty-eight hours, tens of thousands of *Times Leader* readers canceled their subscriptions and signed up with the *Voice*. Within a few weeks, the all-union newspaper had a circulation of approximately fifty-five thousand of which 95 percent was home delivery. Trade unionists from around the state rallied behind the newspaper workers. Over two thousand community residents, as well as representatives from nearly fifty unions, the Pennsylvania AFL-CIO, and many local labor councils attended a November rally to show their support for printing trades' workers. Despite a drastic drop in circulation, the *Times Leader* refused to budge. What started out as an interim strike paper became a fixture in Wilkes-Barre. Ten years later the *Citizens' Voice* continued to outsell the *Leader*.

Unfortunately, the *Times Leader* strike was not the only incident of its type to occur in northeastern Pennsylvania. In June 1979, Kerr-McGee Corporation moved some twenty strikebreakers into its Avoca railroad tie treatment facility. Forty-one members of the Oil, Chemical, and Atomic Workers Union Local 8642 had walked out earlier that month over company demands for a two-year wage freeze and an increase in employee health benefit costs. The Potlach Corporation took similar action at its Ransom paper products plant three months later resulting in a strike of 350 members of United Paperworkers Local 1448. They struck over the issue of removing seniority provisions from a proposed new contract. Although it refrained from operating the plant, Potlach imported six truckloads of guards from Baltimore, complete with cartridge belts and German shepherd dogs, and surrounded its facility with barbed wire and searchlights.

Other areas of the state were not immune to employer-employee conflict. Members of International Brotherhood of Electrical Workers Local 1448 employed at the Hollingsworth Solderless Terminal Company in Malvern struck in April 1979, in response to company demands for the elimination of the union security and dues check-off clauses in a new contract. Two firms in the Harrisburg area, Capital Baking Company and Morrison Labs, a producer of eyeglasses, refused to deal with the Bakery, Confectionery, and Tobacco Workers and the IBEW after they both won representation elections at the respective companies. In the Morrison case, highly-

Electric-arc furnaces represented one of the few modern technologies adopted by Pennsylvania steel companies during the 1970s. (Pennsylvania Historical and Museum Commission)

skilled workers responsible for the precision grinding of lenses protested the fact that they worked for minimum wage. The head of Capitol Baking publicly stated that he would ignore a National Labor Relations Board ruling directing the company to bargain with the union.

During the same period, Pennsylvania steelworkers, especially in the western part of the state, began to feel the effects of a basic restructuring of their industry that would leave tens of thousands without jobs and devastate their communities. Given its central position in Pennsylvania's economy, the collapse of steelmaking in the late 1970s and early 1980s was to leave an indelible mark on the state.

299

Shuttered Mills - Shattered Dreams

The idea of industrial citizenship, which reflected many of the values and beliefs of Pennsylvania workers following World War II, had its roots in the steel mills of Bethlehem, Johnstown, Pittsburgh, Sharon, McKeesport, and Steelton. Journalist John P. Hoerr clearly identified work in the mills as part of a way of life, not just a means of earning a living.

> For young men in the mill towns of those days, there was a very tangible sense of having to make an implicit bargain with life from the outset. There were two choices. If you took a job in the mill, you could stay among family and friends, earn decent pay, and gain a sort of lifetime security (except for layoffs and strikes) in an industry that would last forever. You traded advancement for security and expected life to stick to its bargain. Or you could spurn the good pay and long-term security, leave your family and community, and take a flyer on making a career in some other field. . . . the very presence of the mill on the riverbank . . . forced you to make this choice.

Although the Commonwealth's overall share of the national steel industry had been steadily shrinking since 1945, it continued to provide employment for most of those wanting to work there, including women and minorities brought in under the 1974 consent decree. The fortunes of hundreds of local businesses and thousands of secondary manufacturers and suppliers across the state depended heavily on the continued health of the industry.The first real indication of problems among major steel producers in the state came in early 1975 when Bethlehem Steel informed USWA locals at its fabricating plants in Pottstown, Bethlehem, and Leetsdale that it would permanently shut the facilities if the unions did not agree to a 10 percent wage cut and a two-year wage freeze. Increased competition from smaller firms, a general decline in highway, office, and bridge construction and sometimes questionable corporate management gave the company no other choice but to make the first demand for concessions in the history of the modern steel industry. Underestimating the resolve of the company, the local unions rejected Bethlehem's demands for give backs. By the third quarter of

1976, the company closed all fabricating shops. Yet the shutdowns did little to improve the economic health of the nation's number-two steel maker. In order to further reduce costs, the company announced major layoffs at its mills in Johnstown and Lackawanna, New York in August 1977. The dismissal of one-third of Bethlehem's 11,400 hourly employees in the Cambria County community was particularly devastating since Johnstown was recovering from a major flood that had killed over seventy people in late July. Not only did the flood destroy hundreds of homes and businesses, it also inundated a number of Bethlehem mines in the region, forcing the layoff of scores of local coal miners. The furloughs and shutdowns did little to immediately help the ailing steel company that reported a net loss of over 480 million dollars for 1977.

The situation at Bethlehem was symptomatic of the broader problems facing the American steel industry in the late 1970s. The industry hadn't undertaken sufficient efforts to modernize, which threatened its ability to compete with foreign producers or domestic mini-mills. In one effort to modernize, Bethlehem built an experimental continuous caster at its Lehigh Valley facility in the 1960s in conjunction with Republic, Youngstown, and Inland Steel Companies. Although the caster worked extremely well, none of the companies believed that they could adapt the process to their particular operations. When Bethlehem finally decided to build a caster, it invested nearly ten million dollars at its Johnstown plant, but later realized that this was probably not an ideal location. Uncertainty as to the benefits of modernization left many domestic steel producers unwilling to adopt basic oxygen furnace technology on a wide scale, thus placing them at a competitive disadvantage.

As long as the worldwide demand for steel remained high, the negative impact of these and other decisions was not readily apparent. Yet, the growth of international competition and the softening of domestic markets created a major crisis for American steel producers and their employees. In addition to the Bethlehem cutbacks, other companies began closing facilities and furloughing workers. In 1977, the Lykes Corporation closed its Campbell Works in Youngstown, Ohio, costing the community over four thousand jobs. In 1981, McLouth Steel of Detroit and Phoenix Steel in Delaware sought protection from their creditors by using federal bankruptcy laws.

Even though the industry employed 435,000 workers at the end of 1979 it was becoming clear that basic steel was in trouble.

The nationwide recession that began during the summer of 1981 inevitably led to widespread layoffs and calls for contract concessions in all segments of the economy. In response to growing financial problems, major steel producers wanted to overturn the Experimental Negotiating Agreement with the United Steelworkers of America that had locked them into wage and benefit increases. Wheeling-Pittsburgh Steel, with plants at Monessen and Allenport, approached the USWA in early 1982 seeking financial relief. Though willing to invest in modern equipment, Wheeling-Pitt found that it could not meet the interest payments on its debts. In order to help the firm, the Steelworkers conceded negotiated wage increases plus two weeks of vacation and thirteen paid holidays over a nineteen month period. The union refused, however, to give up its cost of living adjustment.

By June, 1982, other major steel makers requested a reopening of contracts to deal with the growing crisis in the industry—made apparent by the fact that 111,500 steelworkers had lost their jobs nationwide. Attempts to negotiate an acceptable contract failed in July and again in November. In February 1983, the USWA reluctantly agreed to a forty-one month contract that included cutbacks in hourly pay, vacations, holidays and Sunday premium pay. The agreement did retain a workable cost of living provision, an early retirement plan, and a program to increase aid to unemployed workers. Not only did the negotiations heighten the hostility between the union and the companies, they also created real tensions within the union itself. Many leaders of U.S. Steel locals, especially in western Pennsylvania, resented the company's decision to buy Marathon Oil in March of 1982, even as the bottom was falling out of the domestic steel market. That decision led many of them to actively oppose concessions, even when steel companies could document substantive financial hardship. Negotiations in 1982-83 also marked the end of coordinated bargaining and the Experimental Negotiating Agreement, as individual firms realized that no single strategy could deal with the problems that each of them faced.

Relations between the USWA and U.S. Steel, in particular, continued to deteriorate. Soon after the conclusion of contract negotia-

Fighting for jobs and justice. (Pennsylvania AFL-CIO)

tions, the company announced plans to close the open hearth furnaces at its Fairless Hills plant and import semifinished steel slabs
from Britain. David Roderick, chairman of the company, warned
that although the move would eliminate nearly one thousand jobs,
it would save those of the remaining five thousand production workers. The union immediately condemned the move, launching a massive public relations campaign to mobilize opposition to the plan.
For various reasons, the deal fell through, yet the damage was done.
Increased contracting out, demands for additional concessions, and
a late 1983 announcement of the partial or total closing of twenty-eight
U.S. Steel facilities affecting over fifteen thousand workers soured
relationships between the union and the company.

U.S. Steel's plan sent shock waves throughout western Pennsylvania, especially in the Monongahela Valley where it had its greatest
concentration of steel making facilities. Although the number of
workers employed by the company in the Pittsburgh metropolitan
area had declined from 41,560 in 1979 to a little over 19,000 by

303

1983, many people still believed that the layoffs were only temporary. Roderick's announcement made it clear that a majority of those jobs were gone forever. The closings affected workers employed by the company, as well as tens of thousands of others in the Mon Valley. Department store clerks, teamsters hauling coke, producers of industrial valves and other mill equipment, installers and maintainers of vending machines, suppliers of clothing and protective gear, uniform shops, and utility companies all felt the negative impact of the shutdowns. The plant closings and continuing high levels of unemployment greatly affected the quality of life in the steel towns of western Pennsylvania.

Layoffs, shutdowns, and demands for concessions affected many industries in all sections of the state in the early 1980s. Kroger, one of the largest supermarket chains in the country, closed a total of fifty-four Pennsylvania stores in 1984 when United Food and Commercial Workers Local 23 struck over company demands for wage and benefit concessions of $2 an hour. With one day's notice, the Two Guys department store in the Delaware Valley closed its doors, leaving sixteen hundred people unemployed. Fifteen hundred workers at Marx Toys in Girard, another fifteen hundred at Continental Rubber in Pottstown, six hundred employees of the Armstrong Corporation in Lancaster, one thousand at Robertshaw Controls in Indiana, and 175 wage earners at the Matlack Corporation in Northampton all met a similar fate.

The trend continued. Within four days of an announced plant closing at Anchor Hocking's glass plant in Connellsville, the Glass, Pottery, Plastics and Allied Workers Union called off a strike in return for a six-month moratorium on the proposed shutdown. The company made it clear to the union that the closing would continue after the six months unless the two sides could find ways to increase productivity, reduce costs, and improve in-plant labor-management relations. After agreeing to two previous rounds of concessions, Steelworkers at U.S. Steel's Johnstown works rejected a demand for a $5 an hour cut in labor costs in March, 1984. The company fulfilled a prior warning by closing, then selling the facility. (See Keystone Vignette: "Lock Haven's Last Piper Airplane," page 329.)

The wave of plant and store closings that swept across the Commonwealth in the early 1980s had a major impact on the quality of people's lives, especially in western Pennsylvania. Inhabitants of Aliquippa, for example, experienced a 55 percent decline in real income between 1982 and 1984. The city of Duquesne lost $500,000, or 16 percent of its annual revenue in 1984, forcing serious cutbacks in many public services due to the loss of over one thousand jobs at the local U.S. Steel facility. Dozens of other western Pennsylvania communities found themselves in the same position, as layoffs and shutdowns continued. On a personal level, individual workers had to deal with the prospects of long-term unemployment or permanent job loss. The blow fell particularly hard on the most vulnerable groups of workers—women, minorities, and young people. Lacking the seniority accrued by older white males, they were the first to be furloughed when closings and cutbacks began. African American steelworkers often had a harder time than their white counterparts finding new jobs due to lingering patterns of discrimination. By the mid-1980s hardly a woman could be found working in the remaining steel mills in the Mon Valley. A comparison of the experiences of laid-off men and women who had worked at the Robertshaw Controls plant in Indiana, Pennsylvania, found that 58 percent of the men but only 40 percent of the women had obtained new jobs two years after the shutdown. The latter's wages were 13 percent less than those of their male, former co-workers.

Long-term unemployment took its toll on family life as well. For the first time, many women in steelworker families had to look for work outside their homes, when it became clear that the mills would not reopen. Often without marketable job skills, they found themselves accepting part-time employment in local convenience stores, banks, fast-food restaurants and shopping malls. Their frustration with a lack of benefits and low pay often matched that of their husbands, who were unable to find any type of full-time work. Even with part-time work, many families were unable to meet loan and mortgage payments. This resulted in a significant increase in repossessions and foreclosures. The situation reached a point where fifteen thousand families in western Pennsylvania were at least one month behind in their mortgage payments and another 22,500 were on the verge of delinquency. Government officials in Allegheny and Lawrence Counties declared temporary halts on sheriff's sales and foreclosures in order to give individuals and agencies additional time to find ways for people to keep their homes. Financial problems put tremendous stress on families. Increases in alcoholism, spousal abuse, depression, divorce, and suicide were common among families of laid-off workers. While instances of serious illness increased, many families found themselves without any health insurance.

As was so often the case, Pennsylvania workers attempted to come to grips with the problems facing them, even in the worst of times. After the initial shock wore off, unemployed workers, their families, unions, and local supporters organized food pantries and unemployed committees to address the immediate problems of families in need. Others pushed for legislation to require companies to give advanced warnings of their intentions to close particular facilities. The willingness of employers to shut even profitable operations led to a renewed interest on the part of workers to own and operate their own places of employment. Many of these ideas and individuals coalesced in the struggle to save the "Dorothy Number 6" blast furnace at U.S. Steel's closed Duquesne Works.

Even though the twenty-one-year-old Dorothy Number 6 was one of the newest blast furnaces in the Mon Valley, U.S. Steel announced plans to level the facility in October 1984. A coalition of local union members, community activists, and representatives of the Steelworkers union launched an aggressive campaign to buy the furnace and related facilities to be run as a worker-owned company. With financial support from the union, Pittsburgh City Council and Allegheny County commissioners, the coalition initiated a study to determine if its plan was feasible. The study indicated that a worker-owned firm might succeed if it found the money to modernize and upgrade the plant and if workers were willing to dramatically increase productivity while accepting considerably lower rates of pay. News of the report quickly spread throughout the Mon Valley. Local, state, and federal officials endorsed the plan, while enthusiastic crowds attended local meetings to further develop the project. Members of USWA Local 1256 kept a constant watch on Dorothy Number 6 to make sure that the company did not try to sneak in and demolish the furnace. In early 1986 U.S. Steel issued its own report, prepared by a New York investment firm, that offered clear proof that the original plan would not work given chronic over-capacity in both the domestic and foreign steel industries. The coalition ended its campaign and the company tore down the furnace late in August of 1988. Although the campaign ended in apparent failure, it set an important precedent for workers, labor, and their communities. Joining with government officials, they began to develop new and innovative approaches to the problems faced by wage earners in a rapidly changing economy. While some may have seen the campaign to save Dorothy Number 6 as a last-gasp attempt to preserve the past, it may have been a first step in providing working people with the means to improve their lives and futures.

Cooperation or Confrontation?

At least part of the reason for the upsurge in community-based activism in the early and mid-1980s was a general lack of constructive action by the state and federal governments. The failure of the campaign for labor law reform in 1977, despite the fact that Democrats controlled both houses of Congress, was a clear signal that the labor movement had lost much of its political clout. The national political and economic environment of the early 1980s marked the beginning of efforts to rescind—or a least hold in check—many of the social and economic gains that both organized and unorganized workers had made since World War II. The severe recession of the early 1980s, caused, in part, by federal policies to control inflation, devastated Pennsylvania's economy. As the recession worsened in 1982 and 1983, the federal government claimed that the benefits of deregulation and corporate tax cuts would, in the long term, benefit wage earners. Unlike earlier eras, direct government intervention in the economy was no longer viewed as a politically acceptable solution. General federal inaction on issues such as plant closings, non-competitive foreign trade practices, job creation, and increased or extended unemployment benefits were met with severe criticism by affected people as were federal measures to weaken the National Labor Relations Board and overturn civil rights policy—especially with regard to affirmative action. In the view of many working people, the government's handling of the 1981 Air Traffic Controllers' strike signaled a major shift in federal policy towards labor and organized workers.

The federal government remained unwilling to make any significant concessions to the Professional Air Traffic Controllers Organization (PATCO) over wages and working conditions during the course of contract negotiations in the spring and summer of 1981. After rejecting a final contract offer, the controllers began an illegal strike, convinced that the nation's air traffic system could not operate without them. The president immediately ordered all strikers to return to work within forty-eight hours or forfeit their jobs. Within two days, over eleven thousand of the nation's seventeen thousand controllers were unemployed. The federal government seized PATCO's assets and moved to have it decertified as the bargaining agent for air traffic controllers. Those participating in the strike were permanently banned from working as controllers. Many found themselves on a "blacklist" when they attempted to find work in other government agencies. The trials of Erie and Pittsburgh PATCO officials resulted in six-month suspended jail sentences, $1,000 fines, three years probation, and twelve hundred hours of public service work over a three-year period.

At the state level issues such as workers' compensation, no-fault auto insurance, the political activities of unions, "right-to-work" legislation, consumer rights, and prevailing wage laws took center stage in Harrisburg political circles. A major crisis developed over the state's unemployment program which was deeply in debt to the federal government. In an unprecedented move, state AFL-CIO President Julius Uehlein and the president of the Pennsylvania Chamber of Business and Industry fashioned a reform package that the General Assembly subsequently passed. Although the labor movement and the Chamber had been bitter enemies for many years, both groups recognized that the nature of the state's economic crisis forced them to search out areas where they could work together for the benefit of all Pennsylvanians. They adopted a similar position in relation to a 1984 ballot referendum dealing with a bond issue for statewide economic development.

The Pennsylvania AFL-CIO under the leadership of Julius Uehlein, Robert McIntyre, and Judith Heh, pushed for legislation to aid all Pennsylvania workers. Heh's election marked the first time that a woman held a top leadership spot in the state federation. In addition to working with the Chamber to develop major overhauls of the workers' compensation programs the AFL-CIO lobbied hard for an increase in the minimum wage and for "right-to-know" laws that would inform workers as to the nature of hazardous materials they came in contact with on the job.

The example of cooperation between business and labor on the state level mirrored a growing pattern of cooperation on the local level. In 1978, the state AFL-CIO strongly supported establishment of a joint labor-management-government agency to encourage regional economic development. Composed of top business and labor leaders, the MILRITE Council (Make Industry and Labor Right in Today's Economy) attempted to improve communication between unions and employers by establishing county-based labor-management committees (LMCs). In addition to developing strategies to retain existing jobs or attract new ones, area LMCs tried to bring the idea of cooperation to individual work sites. This paralleled a nationwide trend that had its roots in the troubles facing the steel and auto industries. Many people believed that productivity could be increased, costs reduced, and quality improved if employees and their supervisors worked together to find solutions to workplace problems. This approach would allow American companies to remain competitive with foreign producers. It also represented a direct contrast to the traditional adversarial relationship that was so common in Pennsylvania.

Reactions to and experiences with cooperation varied. Unions such as the United Electrical Workers and the International Association of Machinists flatly rejected the idea while Autoworkers, Steelworkers, the IUE, and Communications Workers actively participated in cooperative efforts. Other unions such as the IBEW, Paperworkers, and United Food and Commercial Workers dealt with the issue on a case-by-base basis. Although most initial employee involvement experiments took place in the private sector, public sector workers and supervisors also began experimenting with labor-management cooperation. Teachers, road workers, vocational rehabilitation counselors, and letter carriers all became involved in participative programs.

The whole idea of cooperation went against decades of experience of Pennsylvania trade unionists. They remained suspicious but, in many cases, were willing to try new approaches to solve seemingly insurmountable problems. While some employers' interest in the idea amounted to little more than a disguised effort to increase output, many genuinely believed that such a change could be beneficial both to themselves and their employees. Even while a new approach to labor-management relations was being undertaken in Harrisburg and other parts of the state, paper workers in Erie and Lock Haven, steelworkers in Braddock, rubber workers in Indiana, transit workers in Philadelphia, grocery clerks in Pittsburgh, and social service professionals still found themselves on picket lines in opposition to wage and benefit cuts. (See Keystone Vignette: "Conflict and Cooperation in the Western Pennsylvania Construction Industry," page 332.)

In one instance Steelworkers at a water meter plant in Uniontown found that their plant was to be sold to a foreign corporation, whose owners intended to shut it down and reopen it non-union—even while they had been working with the original owner, Rockwell Corporation, to establish an employee involvement program. Despite such sporadic setbacks, by the end of the 1980s, more than three hundred Pennsylvania companies and government agencies had some form of formal worker participation.

By 1986, the political winds in Harrisburg shifted with the election of Robert P. Casey, a Democrat from Lackawanna County, to the post of governor. Not long after Casey's election, the General Assembly enacted legislation guaranteeing the agency shop for state employees, an increase in the minimum wage, and effective chemical right-to-know programs. The governor also assumed a personal and highly visible role in attempting to forestall or lessen the impact of plant closings. Workplace participation continued as the Department of Labor and Industry mounted a major effort to bring together representatives of labor and management to explore new possibilities and limitations. The administration would also begin to legislatively explore comprehensive reforms to the statewide health care delivery and financing system, with an eye toward controlling costs and improving access to the uninsured—issues of great concern to working people. Despite what appeared to be a political environment more favorable to the needs of Pennsylvania's workers, major challenges remained.

310

The More Things Change . . .

Even in the face of a national recovery that began in the late 1980s, many sections of the Commonwealth remained locked in the economic doldrums. While the number of plant closings and layoffs had slowed, it was difficult to attract the kinds of major investments that could help offset the massive job loss of the early and mid 1980s. Workers often found that new employment frequently paid less, included few if any benefits, and failed to offer any real prospects for long-term security. A survey of former steelworkers conducted in the Monongahela Valley early in 1990 found that even highly skilled persons had a difficult time finding meaningful employment. Forty percent of the thirty-four hundred workers surveyed were unemployed, while one-third of those with jobs worked part time. Nearly 70 percent of those surveyed said that they would take jobs at $7 to $8 an hour if they could use their existing skills. The experience of Mon Valley steelworkers was part of a broader pattern. Employers had learned to rely on various strategies to reduce their dependence on full-time workers and often utilized independent contractors or increased their use of temporary and contingent workers. Working Pennsylvanians who accepted such conditions juggled multiple jobs in order to provide necessities for their families.

For those who had retained employment during the recession, a reviving economy did not necessarily bring a return to good times. Changes in corporate investment tactics in the 1980s, with a growing reliance on leveraged buyouts and hostile takeovers, saddled many companies with debt. In order to placate stockholders and satisfy creditors, in some cases, they sold off their most productive operations at a fraction of their value. Some new owners offered either minimal improvements in pay and benefits or demanded concessions from employees. Many unionized workers found themselves bargaining to impasse. In a few cases, companies ignored existing collective bargaining agreements altogether.

While public employees had generally fared better during the early and mid-1980s, they now found themselves facing many of the same problems as their counterparts in the private sector. State, federal, and local government agencies experienced budget reduc-

311

tions or changes in funding levels. Plant closings and layoffs in many areas led to reductions in tax revenue, forcing some localities to make further cutbacks in public services. Added to this was a growing popular dissatisfaction with government on all levels. Whether accurate or not, there was a sense that elected officials and public employees were out of touch with the concerns of ordinary citizens. This was particularly true in the area of public education. Even though the number of teachers' strikes continued to decline and educators launched a major effort to reform the operation of primary and secondary schools, many Pennsylvanians believed that the system no longer met the educational needs of their children. They expressed their frustration, in part, by attempting to limit the collective bargaining rights of public educators.

The growing popular ambivalence to electoral politics directly impacted Pennsylvania office holders. Following the tragic accidental death of U.S. Senator John Heinz in 1991, Harris Wofford, state secretary of Labor and Industry, defeated former governor, then U.S. Attorney General, Richard Thornburgh in a special election. Wofford campaigned on the issue of health care reform and had developed strong ties with the interests of working people. Yet by 1994, anti-incumbent sentiment led to Wofford's defeat by Republican candidate Rick Santorum, as well as the election of a Republican governor, Tom Ridge, and majorities in both houses of the General Assembly and in the United States Congress.

Despite an ever-shifting political climate, labor and management in some areas of the state strove toward amicable relationships. Members of Machinists Lodge 175 and Harley-Davidson, the legendary producer of motorcycles located in York, worked together for years to recapture a significant segment of their market that had been lost to imports. Although they still disagreed sharply on many issues, the trust that had built up over time carried over into contract negotiations. In February of 1994, for example, they negotiated a new three-year contract that included a 3 percent raise and lump sum bonuses, as well as improvements in pension and health benefits. While the settlement couldn't compare with those of years gone by, the signing of the contract represented a significant achievement in the context of the 1990s.

Members of Bakery, Confectionery, and Tobacco Workers Local

312

464 had a similar experience with the Hershey Chocolate Company in Hershey. A basic acceptance of the validity of collective bargaining by both sides made it possible for them to constructively deal with new and important issues when they entered negotiations in the fall of 1992. In addition to agreeing on wage increases, the union and the company offered workers a first-year bonus of $175 if they joined a managed health care plan. They also came up with an innovative family leave program that allowed employees to take care of seriously ill children, parents or spouses without penalty. In the second year of the contract, a "family illness" clause went into effect that allowed parents with sick children under the age of fourteen to stay home up to four days to care for them while only being considered absent for one day.

While both Harley-Davidson and Hershey were in better financial shape than many other Pennsylvania companies, their ability to achieve new bargaining agreements with their employees—without lockouts or strikes—was not unique. In any given year, the vast majority of negotiations in both the public and private sectors ended peacefully. In some cases, ongoing cooperative relationships fostered a positive atmosphere at the bargaining table which facilitated quick settlements. Other situations were characterized by tough negotiations—complete with threats of strikes or lockouts—though, more often than not, new contracts were agreed upon just before old ones expired. There were, however, a small number of instances where an impasse was apparent. While such occurrences represented only a tiny fragment of labor-management relations in the state, they had a major impact on workers, employers and their communities.

In 1989, the United Mineworkers of America attempted to organize a surface mine in Osceola Mills. Two weeks before a scheduled NLRB election, mine owners laid off thirteen union supporters. The UMWA subsequently lost the election by three votes. The union appealed the results, and three years later an NLRB administrative law judge ordered the company to bargain with the union. The company contested the ruling all the way to a Federal Appeals Court that upheld the original bargaining order. The huge costs of the ongoing legal battles eventually forced the company out of business. Finally, in the summer of 1995, new owners agreed to a con-

313

Paperworkers on strike, Lock Haven, 1987. (Pennsylvania AFL-CIO)

tract with UMWA Local 1303. The settlement included the rehiring of both the original thirteen workers who had been fired and thirteen other union supporters who had subsequently been let go. The company agreed to pay over $2 million in back pay to the twenty-six men, many of whom had endured considerable hardship during the six-year legal battle.

By the 1990s, declining real wages, weak enforcement of existing labor laws, public ambivalence toward organized labor and, in some instances, stiff employer resistance decisively tipped the scales in the collective bargaining process. Changing times and tactics had made it much more difficult for employees to use the strike threat as leverage in contract negotiations, especially if the central issue was wages. Since union pay scales were still considerably higher than those of unorganized workers, the labor movement could expect little public sympathy if their bargaining proposals focused exclusively on wage and benefit increases. Outside observers took a different view of labor-management conflicts, however, when the issues were health care for retirees or work force reductions. In such

314

Labor demonstrating in support of locked-out Pittsburgh Press *workers, 1992. (Pennsylvania AFL-CIO)*

cases, it became a question of fairness and justice, not personal gain. Workers began to recognize that community support and involvement could be crucial in obtaining equity at the work place.

The need for labor to reach out to the broader community during difficult times was best illustrated by the six-month struggle at the *Pittsburgh Press*, one of the city's two daily newspapers. Throughout the fall of 1991 the Pittsburgh Newspaper Unity Council, composed of the Teamsters, Graphic Communications, Typographical Union, Pressmen, Mailers, Paper Handlers, Service Employees, Electrical Workers, Machinists, and Operating Engineers, had been unsuccessful in attempts to negotiate a new contract. Even after their old agreement expired on December 31, 1991, the sixteen hundred union members stayed on the job in hopes of reaching a settlement. As negotiations dragged on through January and February of 1992, it became clear that the *Press* was unwilling to budge on its proposals, which included no wage increases for the first two years, the elimination of a long-standing medical plan, and reductions in re-

315

Union members fight to save their jobs at Leslie Fay, 1995. (Citizens' Voice)

tiree health coverage and pensions. The newspaper also planned to do away with twenty-two Teamster positions and implement a new delivery system that would have eliminated forty-five hundred youth carriers and threatened the jobs of 450 drivers. The situation was complicated by the fact that the city's other newspaper, the *Pittsburgh Post-Gazette*, was published in the same plant, although it was under different ownership.

The Unity Council, with support from the national AFL-CIO, developed a broad strategy in response. In addition to filing unfair labor practice charges with the National Labor Relations Board, the Council began a campaign to build community support. Public rallies complete with "Stop the *Press*" balloons, meetings with local churches and community groups, resolutions to city council, and efforts to secure the support of local advertisers were all part of the effort. Even after the NLRB issued a complaint against the *Press,* charging it with six unfair labor practices, the issue remained at a deadlock. Finally, on May 17, 1992, the Teamsters struck.

Attempts by federal mediators to resolve the dispute got nowhere. The *Press* continued to publish a scaled-down paper despite

a decline in advertising. On July 28, the company resumed full publication using replacement workers and out-of-state distributors.
Thousands of workers and community supporters responded by
keeping an all-night vigil around the paper's downtown headquarters. The crowd clashed with police when drivers attempted to move
out delivery trucks. Rather than risk more violence and injuries, the
city forced the company to cease operations. Officials in surrounding communities ordered local distribution facilities closed in the
name of public safety. The mayor of Pittsburgh publicly canceled
her subscription, and the city finance director ordered the *Press* to
collect a 1 percent wage tax from out-of-state replacement workers.

Despite the best efforts of state and federal officials, the problems at the *Press* remained at an impasse. Finally in October of
1992, its parent firm, E.W. Scripps Co., announced the sale of the
paper. After plans for an employee buyout failed to materialize,
Scripps sold the paper to the rival *Post-Gazette*. Finally, in December of 1992, the *Post-Gazette* and various unions signed a five-year
contract that included a signing bonus, yearly wage increases, improved health coverage, and retirement incentives. Although the
agreement provided for the elimination of the youth carriers and
some delivery drivers, it guaranteed union security in the new distribution system.

Other Pennsylvania workers were not as successful in confront-
ing the challenges posed by economic reorganization and the rapidly changing global economy. Nearly two thousand members of
the International Ladies' Garment Workers' Union employed at dress
manufacturer Leslie Fay in northeastern Pennsylvania faced an equally
difficult challenge in 1994. Due to a company accounting scandal,
the firm filed for Chapter 11 bankruptcy in 1993. In July of that year,
the union and the company reached an agreement that provided for
major wage and benefit concessions in exchange for guaranteed
employment for twelve hundred workers. Just as the union and
local Leslie Fay officials sat down to negotiate a new contract in
March of 1994, the company announced the closing of all four of its
U.S. plants. It planned to move production offshore, to countries
like Guatemala.

An offer from the Pennsylvania Department of Commerce to
help the company fund a new state-of-the-art facility in the north-

east region drew little positive reaction. The ILGWU launched a nationwide campaign to alert consumers about the impending plant closings. They leafleted shoppers in twenty-five U.S. cities and pleaded their case before executives of such major retail chains as Macy's. With absolutely no progress at the bargaining table, Leslie Fay workers went on strike when their contract expired at the end of May. A thirty-eight-year employee of the company gave voice to the workers' efforts to keep their jobs. They were ready "to take a strong stand against management, stockholders, creditors, and whoever else is involved. They have to be reminded that we built the company. They owe us, and we're not about to let them send us to the unemployment line without a fight."

The union and its supporters staged a rally in front of the company's New York headquarters to demonstrate support for the striking garment workers. State officials pledged every resource at their disposal to keep the jobs in Pennsylvania. Members of the U.S. House Education and Labor Committee held hearings in Wilkes-Barre on the shutdown, and the AFL-CIO put the company on its national boycott list. On June 9, Montgomery Ward announced that it would no longer handle garments made by Leslie Fay. Later that month company officials admitted that the strike was seriously hurting their business. With the help of federal mediator William J. Usery, the two sides finally agreed to a three-year contract, six weeks after the strike had begun. The major feature of the pact was a plan to reduce the work force at the main plant in Wilkes-Barre to six hundred people. The plan guaranteed their jobs through July of 1995 and provided them with a 10 percent raise over the three years. Leslie Fay agreed to establish a $2.3 million fund to help the four hundred or so workers who would lose their jobs. Perhaps the most encouraging aspect of the contract was a plan to establish a joint committee to "forge a new and different relationship in order to achieve both the union's objective of increased employment opportunity and security and the company's need for continued competitiveness and financial stability." The two sides jointly selected Usery to be the program's facilitator. The company also agreed to a corporate code of conduct in relation to the operation of its overseas plants.

Everyone involved in the effort to keep the Wilkes-Barre plant open had high hopes for the new endeavor. Jay Mazur, president of the ILGWU hailed the pact, stating that "This is not only a fair agreement but it is a trail-blazing agreement. It points the way to joint labor-management efforts to preserve American manufacturing jobs even as American companies participate in the global economy." Just ten months later, however, the company announced that it was eliminating all production in the United States as of August 1, 1995. It based its actions on a recommendation from Usery. The facilitator claimed that the company could not manufacture dresses profitably at the Pennsylvania location, thus freeing it from all contractual obligations. Despite efforts by the union and government officials, it was clear that this time there would be no second chance.

The Leslie Fay situation underscored the complexity of economic life in the Commonwealth in the late 1980s and 1990s. Whether rightly or wrongly, many American corporations decided that ongoing reductions in labor costs were the key to continued profitability. It appeared to many that the impact of these decisions on employees and communities was secondary to profit considerations. Unlike earlier periods however, when layoffs and shutdowns affected mainly blue-collar workers, they were now becoming more common for white-collar workers as well.

Mergers and corporate reorganizations in banking, health care, and communications led to the dismissal of middle managers, technicians, tellers, and administrators. The growing sophistication of computer-based technology greatly facilitated such work force reductions. As bank customers became increasingly familiar with automatic teller machines (ATMs), for example, it became possible for major financial institutions to close local branches and lay off employees. Hospitals looked to shed workers by contracting out services or by redefining the duties of existing employees. Doctor's assistants took on many of the tasks formerly carried out by registered nurses who now assumed more administrative duties. Hospitals shifted some basic health care functions to newly cross-trained workers who had previously been classified as clerical employees.

Public sector employers also embarked on concerted efforts to downsize or reorganize their operations by not filling job vacancies and implementing furloughs, early retirement incentives, and contracting out. Even the state government was not immune to such

319

pressures. Due to a financial crisis in the fall of 1991, for example, Governor Casey announced plans to furlough 650 management employees and implement a 10 percent wage cut for ten weeks for another ten thousand state managers. A similar plan that would have affected all city workers in Philadelphia sparked a major confrontation between AFSCME and Mayor Ed Rendell the following summer. Philadelphia, as much as any Pennsylvania community, had to grapple with the results of the decline of manufacturing in the 1980s and 1990s. The city ran deficits for four straight years and earned the worst credit rating of any metropolitan area in the nation. In order to deal with the problem, local officials embarked on a dramatic course in their negotiations with municipal unions in 1992. In February, Mayor Rendell presented a five-year plan to members of AFSCME Councils 33 and 47, calling for $508 million in labor concessions including cuts in health care and retirement benefits, a three-year wage freeze and the right to contract out public services. The two AFSCME Councils, along with Firefighters Local 22, offered an alternative plan to save the city money by closing tax loopholes, improving Medicaid billing, and reducing disability costs through better health and safety on the job. Rendell rejected the proposals and went ahead with the hiring of private contractors to clean city hall and guard the Philadelphia Museum of Art.

The two sides failed to conclude a new agreement before the existing contract expired on June 30. State law prohibited workers from striking and barred the city from imposing a new contract until a neutral fact-finder produced non-binding settlement proposals. Rendell successfully appealed the implementation of fact-finding to the state supreme court. The dispute came to a head on September 23 when Mayor Rendell unilaterally imposed a new contract.

AFSCME members stayed on the job as the two sides continued to talk. Finally on October 6, at 12:01 A.M., they struck. Within fifteen hours they were back at work, having reached a tentative agreement with city officials. The new contract contained a two-year wage freeze, a 2 percent raise in the third year and a 3 percent increase in the final year. The settlement maintained existing benefit levels and the union gained language that prevented layoffs except where the city could clearly demonstrate financial hardship. Most importantly, the new agreement replaced the mayor's plan to unilaterally contract out city services. A provision now required that the union be involved in all such decisions.

By the mid-1990s, many organized Pennsylvania workers finally accepted the fact that the "good old days" were gone forever and that they had to develop new tactics and approaches in dealing with both public- and private-sector employers. As the prospect of unilaterally achieving their goals at the bargaining table became more remote, they began to reach out to other trade unionists and the community at large. Sometimes it meant support from locals of their own international union. In April, members of Teamsters Local 429, working at Lehigh Dairies in Schuylkill Haven, rejected company demands for wage and benefit concessions. After overwhelmingly rejecting the company's last proposal, the workers walked out for the first time in anyone's memory. They immediately set up picket lines outside two other Lehigh plants that had contracts with Teamsters Local 463. Members of that local refused to cross the picket lines. Within two days the company offered to settle, dropping its demands for concessions.

Unfortunately, not all disagreements were settled that easily. During the nationwide strike at Greyhound, which began in the spring of 1990, pickets from a host of unions turned out across the Commonwealth to support the striking drivers. Efforts to block buses from leaving terminals resulted in arrests in Harrisburg, Pittsburgh, and elsewhere. The following year, hundreds of union members joined strikers from SEIU Local 1199P in weekly demonstrations outside Canonsburg Hospital, where the administration had brought in replacement workers. Police arrested dozens of people, including Bill George, president of the Pennsylvania AFL-CIO, and other labor leaders, for engaging in civil disobedience. At one of the rallies, seven hundred people sat down in front of the hospital, directly violating a court injunction. The mayor of Canonsburg, other town officials, local clergymen, and area legislators all condemned the hospital for attempting to thwart the union. As a result of five months of sit-ins and public demonstrations, the union and hospital finally agreed to a contract.

Changing times and economic circumstances also led unionized workers to experiment with alternative strategies to protect their jobs. Members of Paperworkers Local 1303 in Spring Grove,

*Over seven hundred unionists protested the hiring of replacement
workers at Canonsburg Hospital, 1991. (Pennsylvania AFL-CIO)*

for example, developed an "in-plant" campaign when their employer
demanded concessions during contract negotiations in 1990. Rather
than walk out, members of the local stayed on the job after their
contract had expired in January. They demonstrated their solidarity
by conducting T-shirt and button days. After rejecting three "final"
offers from their employer, the Paperworkers and their supporters
staged marches through the town. According to Local 1303 President Bob Smith—since company officials lived in Spring Grove—
"They didn't like us demonstrating in town. The company is
family-owned and I guess an unhappy bunch of workers is not the
image they want to wear. But it sure helped us at the bargaining
table." The union also instituted a "workers' safety" campaign that
guaranteed that everyone strictly followed all health and safety rules.
Although it took nearly seven months, the local eventually negotiated a new agreement with the company.

Pennsylvania trade unionists used in-plant strategies, worker
involvement programs, corporate campaigns, labor-community coa-
litions, and grassroots political organizing to deal with the economic

uncertainties of the 1990s. The recognition that workers and their unions had to develop new approaches, rooted in traditional values and beliefs, permeated the labor movement. In the fall of 1995, the first contested election in the history of the national AFL-CIO produced a new administration committed to rebuilding the labor movement through aggressive organizing. Many construction unions developed their own organizing strategies based upon the principle that they should represent the interests of all workers in their trades, regardless of their current membership status. The labor movement began a fundamental re-examination of the role of local central bodies in order to determine how they could play a more dynamic part in mobilizing labor's resources on a regional basis.

The Pennsylvania AFL-CIO, under the leadership of Bill George and Rick Bloomingdale, developed an aggressive political agenda to try to redress some of the economic inequities that had developed in the Commonwealth during the 1980s and 1990s. In November of 1997, 20,000 union members rallied in Harrisburg to call for a renewed commitment on the part of state officials to guarantee good jobs at decent wages for the state's working men and women. The demonstration, among the largest ever held at the state capitol, was organized by the state AFL-CIO and the Pennsylvania Building and Construction Trades.

Perhaps the biggest challenge facing Pennsylvania workers as the twentieth century drew to a close was the relentless pace of change. Fostered by an unprecedented and prolonged period of economic growth and increased international competition, a new wave of corporate consolidations and mergers took place which resulted in a further erosion of employment in manufacturing. A continuing push to deregulate public utilities threatened the jobs of thousands of workers in the natural gas, telecommunications, and electric industries. While unprecedented growth in the stock market helped to create considerable wealth for those at the top of the income pyramid, many Pennsylvania wage earners did not fare nearly as well. In 1996, one-third of all full-time workers in the state made less than the official poverty rate for a family of four, or $8.25 per hour. Between 1995 and 1996, the average earnings for African American men declined by $1.17 per hour. Wages in Pittsburgh and surrounding counties in the late 1990s were $1.75 less per hour than they had been in 1979.

Organized workers and their employers responded in a variety of ways to these challenges. Recognizing an urgent need to retain jobs in already unionized sectors of the economy, labor and management continued to search for common ground through joint processes in Lewistown textile factories, Philadelphia bakeries, and on construction sites in western Pennsylvania. Employees in the electric utility industry found themselves working with their employers, other unions, consumer groups, environmentalists, and retirees to deal with the potential pitfalls of rapid deregulation. Unions and employers in the steel and telecommunications industries jointly developed extensive training programs to provide workers with new skills to help them adapt to a rapidly changing work environment. In other instances, unions and employers continued to follow the more traditional path of adversarialism and confrontation.

In October of 1996, 4,500 steelworkers from Ohio, West Virginia, and Pennsylvania went on strike against Wheeling-Pittsburgh Steel, primarily over the issue of pensions. The union had made major wage and benefit concessions to the company when it plunged into bankruptcy in 1985. Although Wheeling-Pitt returned to financial health by 1990, it continued to resist union proposals for a more equitable sharing of economic gains. The result was a ten-month strike, the longest ever in basic steel. An intensive corporate campaign that adversely impacted the value of the company's stock finally forced its officials to reopen bargaining with the Steelworkers in the summer of 1997. In early August, both sides finally came to an agreement.

Relations between the Beverly Nursing Home chain and the Service Employees International Union were even worse. A long history of antagonism between the company and the union resulted in a major confrontation that began in the Spring of 1996. Some union members had been working without a contract at Beverly facilities since 1994. Finally, in April of 1996, SEIU Local 1199P conducted a three-day strike at fifteen Beverly facilities. The company responded by permanently replacing nearly one thousand workers. Even after the National Labor Relations Board found the firm guilty of numerous unfair labor practices and ordered the immediate reinstatement of all discharged workers, Beverly flatly refused to hire nearly one-half of its former employees. The NLRB pursued legal remedies through the courts. SEIU launched an extensive campaign to pressure the firm into signing a contract and restoring its members to their jobs. In January, 1997, a district court agreed with the NLRB, and ordered all union members reinstated. By April, eighty former strikers had not been rehired, and nearly one-half of those rehired had not been given the same amount of working hours as prior to the conflict. It took the combined pressures of a federal court ruling and the direct intervention of Governor Tom Ridge to finally bring about a settlement. By the summer of 1997, the two sides agreed to a four-year contract.

As in the past, workers in Pennsylvania in the 1990s found themselves between two familiar poles. While earning a decent living for themselves and their families was their top priority, they also expected fair and equitable treatment on the job. Despite many setbacks and challenges, trade unionism remained the most effective means of achieving those goals. As in the past, the overwhelming number of disputes between wage earners and their employers were resolved peacefully: strikes occurred only when both sides exhausted all possible avenues of settlement. The difficulties inherent in winning strikes and the continued erosion of organized labor's base in manufacturing forced unionized workers in Pennsylvania to take a hard look at themselves in terms of their tactics and goals. At the same time, a cautious sense of optimism began to grow among workers and their unions that the long years of retreat had ended, and that the labor movement would, once again, reclaim its place as the largest, best organized voice for economic and political democracy in the United States.

Keystone Vignette

Act 195

Harry Boyer

Let me begin by saying that Act 111 and Act 195 have functioned extremely well in the relatively short span of time since they have been in effect.

Obviously, the hundreds of thousands of public employees at state and local levels of government which have been organized for collective bargaining purposes have most directly benefited from this legislation. However, we believe that the public as a whole has also benefited from public employees' labor relations laws. The resulting stability in the labor force serving our state and local governments has led to a development of expertise and skills, resulting in increased efficiencies. And, contrary to the popular myth that the government cannot afford unionized employees, I respectfully point out that since the early days of collective bargaining under Act 195, state taxation rates have actually decreased not increased.

While the Pennsylvania AFL-CIO believes that Act 195 and Act 111 have indeed worked well, this is not to say that we do not have suggestions for improvement. The first amendment to the law which we believe to be of paramount importance would be to provide for the right of a public employees' union to negotiate for an agency shop. Under agency shops union membership is not required, but non-members must pay their fair share of the costs of collective bargaining. The Public Employee Relations Act now allows public employees to enjoy all the benefits obtained by the collective bargaining agent which is working in their behalf, but permits these employees to refuse to contribute to its support. The idea of an agency shop for public employees is not a new one. The Hickman Commission, appointed by Governor Raymond P. Shafer in 1968 to study the then existing Public Employee Law, recommended that a new public employee law be enacted permitting an agency shop.

We furthermore believe that the law should be improved insofar as it applies to first-line supervisors. First-level supervisors groups can only meet with their employers to discuss job-related problems. We submit that everybody covered by Act 195 should enjoy full collective bargaining rights. However, in making this recommendation, we also tell you that it has been our experience that there may have been mixed into certain units of first-level supervisors some who are truly management-level employees. Therefore, we would not oppose a review of the units of first-level supervisors to insure that all those granted full collective bargaining rights under our proposal be actual bargaining unit personnel.

My final two comments here today have to do with amending provisions of the Public Employees Relations Act insofar as it pertains to strikes. Initially, I feel compelled to state that, not withstanding what the press would have us believe, and not withstanding what the misinformed public may believe to be the case, it is the experience of the Pennsylvania AFL-CIO that the amount of time which its public employee affiliates have spent on strike has been infinitesimal. Contracts covering literally millions of worker days have been negotiated and renegotiated with either no work stoppages or minimal lost time. Unfortunately, these settlements seldom make the headlines.

We believe that two changes regarding strikes would be in order. First it has been our observation that the courts have been all too ready to issue an injunction against a public employee strike on the ground that it creates a clear and present danger or threat to the welfare of the public. We urge that injunction against public employee unions should be issued only in those rare circumstances in which there is an immediate and irreparable harm or threat thereof to the public health or safety.

Furthermore, once the direct, irreparable and immediate threat to the public health and safety has been determined and an injunction has been issued, we believe that the law should provide means in which the collective bargaining process can be meaningfully continued. When a union is deprived of its right to strike, it has lost its bargaining position. Unless some alternative bargaining routes are available, it has no way to go. Such post-injunction procedures that you might consider would include mandatory fact-finding, round-the-clock negotiations, and the like. Finally, sometimes during the course of a strike a union or a striker is fined or a union leader is imprisoned. The governmental unit which had sought the injunction may be most willing to recommend to the court that the fines or imprisonment be remitted, but very often the court will ignore this recommendation. Thus strike settlement is impeded. Therefore, we believe it would encourage speedier settlements if the law contained stronger provisions for remission of fines and imprisonment upon recommendation of the governmental unit involved.

In summary, Act 111 and Act 195 have provided the basis for successful labor-management relations in the public sector. The passage of time has revealed certain deficiencies which need correcting. It is imperative, however, to resist attempts to substantially dismember these laws, which can only assure a return to the chaos which preceded their enactment.

Harry Boyer was president of the Pennsylvania AFL-CIO from 1960 to 1982. The full text of this article appeared in the *Pennsylvania AFL-CIO News* 17, No. 11, April 1977.

Keystone Vignette

Lock Haven's Last Piper Airplane

Howard Harris

As a twin-engine Piper Mojave lifted off a small Pennsylvania airfield on the morning of August 14, 1984, headed for Florida, an era came to an end in the borough of Lock Haven. Home of the Piper Aircraft Company since 1937, Lock Haven's experience mirrored that of dozens of other small Pennsylvania communities during the 1980s. Dependent on one major employer, they had to face the task of rebuilding the local economy when that firm decided to pull up stakes and move production elsewhere.

Similar to many Pennsylvania companies, Piper was a family-owned business for much of its history. Founded by William T. Piper in an old silk mill, at its peak it employed over two thousand local residents out of a total population of approximately eleven thousand people. The International Association of Machinists, which organized the plant during the late 1930s, had maintained a good working relationship with the company. The workers in Lock Haven developed a reputation for turning out high quality work and felt a genuine sense of loyalty to the firm.

In the late 1940s Piper opened a research and development center in Vero Beach, Florida and a new production plant in Lakeland, Florida as the commuter aircraft industry boomed after World War II. While it also opened parts plants in Renovo and Quehanna, Pennsylvania and an engineering center in Lock Haven, the company did little to upgrade its main production facility in the town. Piper's continued growth attracted considerable outside interest. After a number of deals had fallen through, the Piper family sold its stake in the company to Bangor Punta Corporation, which also produced Smith & Wesson firearms and parts for recreational boats. Shortly after Bangor took over, floods resulting from Hurricane Agnes left the Lock Haven plant knee-deep in mud. In the aftermath of the flood, the company moved one whole product line to Florida. Looking back, one Piper employee observed, "We should have wised up. When they were sitting over there in the flood mud they were at our mercy. We should have had them sign something saying that they would not move anything else out of the plant." While the plant did reopen, the floods marked the beginning of the end of airplane production in Clinton County.

Piper continued to boom, employing seventy-eight hundred people at its various facilities by the end of the decade. The nation-wide recession in the early 1980s spelled trouble for the company. Piper sold 956 planes in one four-month period in 1981. During the same period in 1982 the figure dropped to 433; a year later it stood at 252. Wholesale layoffs began both in Pennsylvania and Florida. By 1984, only 650 people worked at the Lock Haven plant, with an additional 200 at Quehanna. As Bangor Punta's debts continued to pile up, the company became a takeover target. Late in 1983, Lear Siegler Corporation bought out Bangor, including its Piper Aircraft division. In February of 1984, Piper officials declared that "When you have four facilities running at less than 30 percent capacity each, it makes sense to study how you could combine operations. We have not made a decision to close any facilities. . . . We also have not identified which would be closed if we do decide to con-solidate our operations." Two months later the company made up its mind. On Tuesday, May 1, officials announced the closing of both the Lock Haven and Quehanna facilities and the moving of all production and corporate activity to Florida.

The announcement devastated the community. With an unem-ployment rate of at least 15 percent, Lock Haven could ill-afford a major plant shutdown, especially one with an $8 million payroll. Members of Machinists Local 734 felt particularly bitter. They had recently agreed to a new contract that included a wage freeze and had attempted to work closely with company officials to improve the plant's competitive position. As Jim Young, secretary of the local put it, "We, the people of Lock Haven, built Piper and now they're giving it all away to the people in Florida." The move was particu-larly upsetting because the company's southern operations were nonunion. Union members, community leaders, local politicians, and government officials mounted a major campaign to save the plant, all to no avail. All that remained after the last Mojave left for Florida was to dismantle the plant. John Cebulka, a forty-five year employee observed, "It's heartsickening, loading the parts. The guys are packing the crates and saying, 'There goes my job, There goes my job.'" On a broader scale, the closing of Piper demonstrated how changing and uncertain economics pitted people in a Pennsylvania community against people in Florida.

Although the union negotiated a fair severance agreement with the company and Piper provided resources and space for a job placement center, many former aircraft workers had a difficult time. "Jobs are hard to get around here," said one thirty-five year veteran while another fifty-nine-year-old former employee mentioned that, "I'm too old to get a job and too young to retire." The shutdown also affected many town businesses. A bar and diner next to the factory usually served six hundred people a day; once the factory closed there was often only one or two people in the place at the end of the day shift. Although some Lock Haven residents decided to move south with Piper, most workers stayed, finding full-time or part-time jobs at greatly reduced wages. Numerous attempts to find new tenants for the plant failed.

Unlike many Pennsylvania communities, however, Lock Haven did have some cause for hope. In 1987 Stuart Millar bought Piper from Lear Siegler and turned it into a privately held corporation. Two members of the Piper family joined him and began to explore the possibility of returning to aircraft production. In December, 1989, Governor Robert P. Casey, with the approval of the General Assembly, made $10 million available to Piper North to reopen at least part of the plant. In addition to producing new airplanes, the firm hoped to obtain contract work from such major companies as Boeing. Former Piper workers greeted the news with guarded enthusiasm. Bernard Hill, who spent thirty-three years with the company, summed up many people's feelings. "I'm glad they'll be building airplanes again there. I'd like to think they found out they had better workers here than in Florida. It's really going to help the economy. I put thirty-three years in and it kind of grows on you."

Ultimately, attempts to revive aircraft production in Lock Haven failed. Today, all that remains of the Piper Aircraft Company in town is a museum dedicated to the history of the planes that were once built in this Pennsylvania community.

Keystone Vignette

Conflict and Cooperation in the
Western Pennsylvania Construction Industry

Howard Harris

"Union Marchers Tie Up Downtown" read the November 4, 1986, headline of the *Pittsburgh Post-Gazette*. On the previous morning approximately forty-five thousand construction workers and supporters from throughout the region staged one of the largest labor demonstrations ever held in Pittsburgh. Called to protest the continued use of nonunion workers on major local construction projects, the march snarled downtown traffic. The massive public display forced the closing of many building sites, as organized craftsmen joined their fellow construction workers. The immediate target of the demonstration, the old Pennsylvania Station, had been the site of bloody confrontations between strikers and troops during the great railroad strikes of 1877. Now, a little over one hundred years later, a new battle was raging at the same location. Although the weapons and tactics differed, the major issues remained the same—steady work and decent wages.

For years, a tacit agreement existed between the building trades and area contractors. The unofficial pact guaranteed that major, downtown construction projects would be unionized. In return, unions refrained from actively opposing the nonunion status of smaller projects undertaken outside the city. This understanding started to unravel in the early 1980s as the anti-union Associated Builders and Contractors association began to bid on major construction and renovation projects. ABC members consistently underbid union contractors. By 1986 nearly 60 percent of the eighteen-thousand members of the Pittsburgh Building Trades Council were on layoff.

Even as they attempted to negotiate with the contractor on the

Pennsylvania Station project, local union leaders recognized a need to take more aggressive action. According to Leo Puma, head of the Building Trades Council, "Unions are not dead in Pittsburgh. We were just asleep. . . . Those ABC guys have come onto our turf and we're taking them on. They're not going to get away with paying hungry, jobless steelworkers $5 an hour . . . and eroding our livelihoods. . . . The firms we work for are going to be hurt. The next thing you know, they'll be squeezed so bad that they'll want to go open shop."

Although the two sides actually reached an agreement on the station project the day before the protest, the demonstration put local builders on notice that they had a choice to make. They could either risk an open public confrontation with the building trades or they could attempt to work with them in the creation of a more positive labor environment. The latter approach bore fruit two-and-a-half years later. On April 4, 1989, the *Post-Gazette* ran an editorial entitled "Labor Peace at the Airport." The editorial applauded a Project Stabilization Agreement that guaranteed labor peace at the $567 million Midfield Terminal Project underway at the Pittsburgh International Airport. At stake were nearly ten thousand construction jobs on western Pennsylvania's biggest public works project ever.

Twenty-seven trade unions and the county of Allegheny agreed that all contractors at the site had to "pay prevailing wages, make proper contributions to workers' compensation and follow safety procedures." They also had to guarantee "affirmative action hiring, apprenticeship, medical, and pension programs." While the pact did not prevent nonunion contractors from working on the terminal, it took away their ability to underbid union contractors. In return the unions pledged not to call any work stoppages, allowing the project to be completed on schedule. They also agreed to submit all jurisdictional disputes to a three-member committee for resolution.

Had the building trades not demonstrated their willingness to fight in November of 1986, there would probably have been no Stabilization Agreement in 1989. A correspondent to the *Pittsburgh Press* of November 9, 1986, Linda Lewis, summed up the importance of the demonstration. "Not only did they make an impact on the issue they set out to address, they sent a very important message signed by the American worker. . . . The unions were established and grew strong because people like them cared about the quality of the work and the conditions in the workplace. . . . And they can only stay that way if the American worker cares enough, and is ready to show his or her support when necessary toward the same kind of movement that took place on the streets of Downtown Pittsburgh on Nov. 3."

Readings for Chapter Six

Bensman, David and Robert Lynch. *Rusted Dreams: Hard Times in a Steel Community.* Berkeley: University of California Press, 1988.

Camp, Scott D. *Worker Response to Plant Closings: Steelworkers In Johnstown and Youngstown.* New York: Garland Publishers, 1995.

Chaikin, Sol. *A Labor Viewpoint: Another Opinion.* Monroe: Library Research Associates, 1980.

Clements, John. *Pennsylvania Facts: A Comprehensive look at Pennsylvania Today, County by County.* Dallas: Clements Research Inc., 1987.

Cornwell, Gretchen, et. al. *Pennsylvania's Changing Labor Force: Women and Their Families; A Background Report for the Governor's Conference on Responses to Workforce 2000.* University Park: Population Issues Research Center, 1990.

Dublin, Thomas and George Harvan. *When the Mines Closed.* Ithaca: Cornell University Press, 1998.

Hathaway, Dale A. *Can Workers Have a Voice?: The Politics of Deindustrialization in Pittsburgh.* University Park: Pennsylvania State University Press, 1993.

Hertzenberg, Stephen and Howard Urial. *The State of Working Pennsylvania.* Harrisburg: Keystone Research Center, 1996, 1997, 1998.

Hoerr, John P. *And the Wolf Finally Came: The Decline of the American Steel Industry,* Pittsburgh: University of Pittsburgh Press, 1988.

Magda, Matthew S. *Monessen: Industrial Boomtown and Steel Community, 1898-1980,* Harrisburg: Pennsylvania Historical and Museum Commission, 1983.

Milke, Ray M. A Survey of Unemployed Steelworkers in the Mon Valley. Master's thesis,University of Pittsburgh, 1984.

Miller, E. W. *Pennsylvania: Keystone to Progress-An Illustrated History*. Northridge: Windsor Publications, 1986.

Pennsylvania AFL-CIO News, 1970-1996. Harrisburg.

Serrin, William. *Homestead: The Glory and Tragedy of an American Steel Town*. New York: Times Books, 1992.

Singh, Vijai. et. al. *The State of the Region: Recent Economic, Demographic and Social Trends in Southwestern Pennsylvania*. Pittsburgh, 1984.

Strohmeyer, John. *Crisis in Bethlehem: Big Steel's Struggle to Survive* Pittsburgh: University of Pittsburgh Press, 1994.

Tyler, Gus. *Look for the Union Label*. Armonk: M.E. Sharpe, 1995.

Wolensky, Kenneth. "Diamonds and Coal." *Now and Then - The Appalachian Magazine*, Winter, 1997:20-24.

Conclusion

The Keystone of Democracy

Howard Harris

I n many ways, the Volkswagen plant at New Stanton stands as a
symbol of the problems facing Pennsylvania wage earners as
they look with uncertainty toward the future. Globalization of
the world economy, rapid technological innovation, shifting political and social values, and changing work force demographics all
played crucial roles in altering the traditional economic landscape
of Pennsylvania in the last third of the twentieth century. As employment declined in steel, textiles, electronics, coal, and apparel,
new jobs developed in banking, retailing, and health services. Breath-
taking developments in microelectronics led to an explosion in both
the personal and business use of computers. Supermarket scanners,
word processors, robots, computer-aided design and manufacturing
equipment, and laser printers removed much of the drudgery from
common workplace tasks. Women and minorities gained access to
new jobs and careers as old stereotypes slowly faded. A growing
awareness of the threats posed by hazardous substances at the work
site, as well as in the air and in the water, raised the possibility of a

safer, healthier environment for future generations.

Not all Pennsylvania wage earners, however, were in a position to take advantage of the changes. While many new plants and offices sprang up in southeastern Pennsylvania, Philadelphia continued to lose entry-level manufacturing jobs that often provided the first step out of poverty for inner-city African Americans and Latinos. Computer software or clerical jobs in Pittsburgh's shiny, new office towers offered little to a forty-five-year-old former steel worker in Homestead with a high-school education who hadn't had a full-time job in many years. Although employment opportunities for women in Altoona, Hazleton, and Meadville may have improved, most jobs remained in traditional female occupations with wage rates significantly lower than those paid to men for comparable work. A lack of quality child care in many areas made it difficult for women who wanted to work to enter the job market. While new microelectronic equipment provided lucrative employment for people with the related skills and training, it also led to reductions in hours or dismissal for thousands of store clerks, telephone operators, and bank tellers.

Some people believed that unions constrained economic growth in Pennsylvania. A significant body of research, however, demonstrates that union labor was generally more productive and cost-efficient in the long run. Yet economic pressures led many employers to continue to demand wage and benefit concessions or institute two-tier wage systems which widened the earnings gap between new hires and veteran employees. Some employers threatened to close facilities and a few followed through on such threats. Unresolvable differences sometimes led to strikes. Intricate NLRB and PLRB legal procedures hampered potential organizing drives. Mergers and buyouts forced many corporations to sell off productive units in order to maintain their financial integrity. New owners sometimes refused to honor the terms of existing collective-bargaining agreements. This was the labor-management environment during the final years of the century.

Organized workers and their unions responded to these challenges by continuing to fight for the rights of working men and women in the Commonwealth. They experimented with new approaches to organizing and began reaching out to people employed in the rapidly expanding service economy. Such issues as child care, sexual harassment on the job, part-time employment, lack of adequate health insurance, and work-related stress all came to the fore as important issues affecting all wage earners. Unions began to explore the possibility of assuming a different role in the workplace that went beyond their traditional concentration on wages and benefits. When A&P decided to close its Philadelphia operation, for example, members of the United Food and Commercial Workers bought a number of the stores, turning them into worker-owned supermarkets. While other efforts to buy and run meat processing plants, bakeries, glass plants, and steel mills proved less successful, the general idea of worker ownership and control became an important part of labor's thinking. The willingness of trade unions to work with other community groups over plant closings, nuclear power, environmental pollution, or health care costs marked another significant development during the period.

Perhaps the union members at Volkswagen expressed it best when the plant was closed in 1988. "We have pride in our hearts. We did a damn good job." Throughout the history of the Commonwealth its working men and women have continually struggled to make a better life for themselves and their families. Always proud, rarely boastful, they believe in their ability to overcome any challenge whether natural or manmade. From the anthracite mines of Pittston to the garment shops of Philipsburg, the classrooms of New Castle, the railroad yards of Hollidaysburg, the candy factories of Hershey, and the Erie waterfront, Pennsylvania workers have never lost sight of the idea that they are free and equal citizens of a democratic republic. Through good times and bad, they retain their faith in the "American Dream" tempered by the reality that there is often a heavy price to pay to retain one's freedom. Workers paid the price in Lattimer, Homestead, Pottsville, Pittsburgh, Tioga and Cambria Counties, and elsewhere. They paid the price so that future generations might live securely with pride and dignity. It is a heritage which all Pennsylvanians should remember.

Acronyms

AAISW – Amalgamated Association of Iron and Steel Workers

AASERE – Amalgamated Association of Street and Electric Railway Employees

ACTWA – Amalgamated Clothing and Textile Workers of America

ACWA - Amalgamated Clothing Workers of America

AFL - American Federation of Labor

AFSCME – American Federation of State, County, and Municipal Employees

AFT – American Federation of Teachers

CIO - Congress of Industrial Organizations

FEPC – Fair Employment Practices Commission

HERE – Hotel and Restaurant Employees

HUAC – House Un-American Activities Committee

IAM – International Association of Machinists

IBEW – International Brotherhood of Electrical Workers

IUE – International Union of Electrical Workers

ILGWU – International Ladies Garment Workers

IWW – Industrial Workers of the World

MILRITE – Make Industry and Labor Right in Today's Economy

MLAA – Miners and Laborers Amalgamated Association

NIRA – National Industrial Recovery Act

NLRA – National Labor Relations Act

NLU – National Labor Union

NWLB – National War Labor Board

PATCO – Professional Air Traffic Controllers Organization

SEIU – Service Employees International Union

SWOC – Steel Workers Organizing Committee

TWOC – Textile Workers Organizing Committee

UE – United Electrical Workers

UMWA – United Mine Workers

URW – United Rubber Workers

USWA – United Steelworkers of America

WLB – War Labor Board

Index

340

Humphrey, Hubert H., 245
Hungarians, 106
Huntingdon, 40, 292
Huntingdon County, 100
Hurricane Agnes, 329

immigrants, xii-xiii, 7, 11, 22,
38, 44-45, 55, 56, 62, 66,
69, 70, 88, 91, 100, 103,
106, 108, 110, 115, 118,
123, 133, 134, 138-39, 140,
144, 149, 153, 161-62, 173,
177, 178-79, 180, 233, 263,
265
income, 228-29, 231, 239. *See
also* minimum wage
indebtedness, imprisonment
for, 52
Indiana, Pa., 304, 305, 310
Indiana County, 178
Indiana Democrat, 64
industrial citizenship, 215, 221,
227, 230, 231, 232, 263,
257, 300, 338
industrial democracy, 213, 310.
See also employee ownership
industrial revolution, xii-xiii, 41,
43, 45, 57, 66, 240
Industrial Union Councils, 193
Industrial Union of Marine and
Shipbuilding Workers, 219
industrial unionism, xiii, 192-93,
218. *See also* Congress of
Industrial Organizations
Industrial Workers of the World,
133-34, 138-40, 165
Inland Steel Company, 198, 209
innkeeping, 21

insurance business, 217, 220
International Association of Fire
Fighters, 320
International Association of
Machinists, 145, 199, 309,
312, 316, 329-30
International Brotherhood of
Electrical Workers, 242,
298, 309
International Brotherhood of
Teamsters, 199, 225, 243,
245, 248, 250, 292, 315-16,
319, 321. *See also* teamsters
International Ladies' Garment
Workers' Union, 190, 216,
228, 237, 243, 244-45, 246,
255, 265-69, 295, 317-19
International Longshoremen's
Association, 241
International Typographical
Union, 72, 316
International Union of Electrical
Workers, 242, 246, 248,
254, 295, 309
International Workingmen's
Association, 70
Ireland, 7, 24, 88
Irish, xii, 25, 55, 56, 62, 63, 65,
64, 70, 91, 92, 149, 150, 259
iron, 3, 8, 39, 40, 42, 44, 45, 66,
67, 86, 99, 143-144, 167,
187
iron and steel, 87, 88, 89, 97,
102, 106, 192
Irwin, 143
Italians, 154-55, 180

Jackson, John Price, 146
James, Charles Tillinghast, 57

steelworkers, 110, 123, 124,
125, 146, 169-70, 191, 198,
218, 221, 222-24, 232, 236,
242, 286, 288, 299, 311;
strike of 1919, xiii, 167-70,
175, 183; strike of 1937,
200; strike of 1946, 222-24,
263; strike of 1949, 228;
strike of 1959, 240, 242,
255; strike of 1955-56, 243
Stokley, William S., 96
Stone, William, 120, 121
Stowe Township, 174
strikebreakers, 66, 72, 85, 88,
101, 105, 108, 109, 112-13,
116, 124, 133, 136-37, 138-
39, 142, 143, 147, 169, 170,
183, 194
strikes, 31, 50, 53, 54, 59, 60,
61, 74, 87, 86, 90-92, 96-97,
99, 100, 101, 103, 104, 107,
109, 113, 115, 116, 119,
123, 126, 133, 135, 136,
138-39, 142, 143-44, 147,
150, 155, 170, 173, 178,
185, 191, 193, 195, 199,
200, 219, 225, 228, 240,
242, 248, 250-51, 253, 267,
270, 289, 290, 292-93, 297,
304, 314, 318, 320, 321,
324, 327, 332; sit-down,
263. *See also* no-strike
pledge
strip mining, 239
Stuart, Edwin S., 144
suburbanization, 238
suffragists, 72
Sullivan, William, 54

Sun Shipbuilding Company,
218-19
Sunbury, 4, 242
Superior Tube, 247
Susquehanna Boom Company,
75
Susquehanna Depot, 89
Susquehanna River, 75, 77, 157,
252
Swissvale, 144, 233
Sylvania, 60
Sylvania Electric Company, 216
Sylvis, William, 61, 62, 63, 64,
65, 66, 70, 72

Taft-Hartley Act, 157, 224, 226,
242, 245, 251, 252, 260. *See
also* Little Taft-Hartley law
Tamaqua, 91
Tarentum CIO, 247
Taylor, Frederick W., 133, 145,
177
Taylors Company of Philadelphia, 29
teachers 250-51, 270-1, 288,
289. *See also* American
Federation of Teachers
teamsters, 17. *See also* International Brotherhood of
Teamsters
telecommunications, 323-24
temperance, 52, 53
ten-hour day. *See* workday
Textile Machinery Works, 247
Textile Workers Organizing
Committee, 199
Textile Workers Union of
America, 199, 221
textiles, 21, 42, 43, 48, 54, 55,

57, 59, 60, 70, 87, 103, 104-
5, 106, 123, 134-35, 146,
164, 175, 180, 181, 187,
241, 280, 296. *See also*
company and union names
Thomson, J. Edgar, Works, 101,
108, 146
Thornburgh, Richard, 312
Three Mile Island, 288
Times Leader. See Wilkes Barre
tin, 40
Tioga County, 65, 89
Titusville, 65
Towanda, 43
Towne, Benjamin, 34
Trainmen's Union, 92, 94, 95
Transit Workers Union, 219,
310
transportation, 40, 41, 184, 230.
See also company and
union names
Trautmann, William, 139-40
Trbovich, Mike, 254
trolley lines, 136-37, 140, 146
Turner, Samuel G., 79
Two Guys Department Store,
304
Typographers and Stereotypers
Union, 246, 296

Uehlein, Julius, 308
UMW Journal, 208
unemployed committees, 306
Unemployed Councils, 187; of
New England, 261
unemployment: insurance, 187;
relief, 187-90, 192, 195,
306; compensation, 206,
223, 225, 244-45, 261, 277,

291, 293
Union Switch and Signal Company, 233
unionism, xii-xiii, 28-31, 37, 43,
46-47, 49-52, 54, 55, 61-63,
65, 66-74, 79, 85, 86, 90,
91, 99, 100, 101, 104, 107,
108, 109, 113, 120, 122,
133-49, 161-209, 213-71,
276-77, 279, 282, 287, 290,
308, 314, 322, 323, 325,
337. *See also* company
unionism
Uniontown, 236, 310
United Anthracite Miners of
Pennsylvania, 158
United Autoworkers of
America, 309
United Company of Philadelphia for Promoting Ameri-
can Manufacturing, 31
United Electrical Workers, 216,
223, 227, 233, 242, 248, 309
United Engineering and
Foundry Company, 217,
221
United Food and Commercial
Workers, 304, 309
United Garment Workers of
America, 170
United Mine Workers of
America, 106, 114, 116-21,
124, 126, 135, 143, 146,
149, 151, 154-57, 167, 170,
171, 175, 181-83, 190, 192-
94, 195, 197, 205, 208-9,
220, 230, 242, 243, 252-54,
259-60, 267, 288, 313-14
United Office and Professional

Whig Party, 52, 62
Whitaker's Mill, 49
Whitehall, 295
Wiggans Patch, 184
Wilkes-Barre, 96, 146-47, 153, 236, 252, 268, 280, 296-98, 318
Wilkes-Barre *Citizens' Voice*, 298
Wilkes-Barre General Hospital, 269, 292
Wilkes-Barre Industrial Union Council, 246
Wilkes-Barre Railway Company, 146
Wilkes-Barre Times, 151
Wilkes-Barre *Times Leader*, 296-98
Wilkes College, 269
Williamsport, 75, 77, 247
Willingboro, 238
Wilmerding, 144
Wilson, William B., 126
Wilson, Woodrow, 169, 171
Wingohocking mills, 106-7
Wise, C. A., 139-40
Wise Potato Chip Company, 247
Wissahickon, 8
Wofford, Harris, 312
women, 5, 8, 9, 13, 19-22, 24, 30, 31, 38, 45, 46, 53, 55, 56, 57, 60, 61, 66, 68, 70, 71, 72, 98, 105, 124-25, 126, 129, 132, 134-35, 144, 166, 173, 177, 178, 181, 185, 197, 199, 230-32, 250, 263-64, 276, 284-85, 286-87,

290, 305, 308, 337
workday: ten-hour, 49, 50, 53, 54, 59, 60; eight-hour, 71-73, 104, 108-9, 135, 146
workers' compensation, 133, 134, 206, 261, 290, 291, 308-9
working class, 19, 22, 24-26, 47-74, 127, 162, 165, 174, 180, 182, 185, 231, 237-38
Working Women's Association, 72
Workingmen's Benevolent Association, 66, 71, 72, 74, 78, 90, 91
Workingmen's Party, 51-52, 96
Works Progress Administration, 194
World War I, 147, 162-67, 201, 203, 208
World War II, 174, 203, 214, 230, 232, 234, 243, 257
Wyoming anthracite region, 96, 119
Wyoming Valley, 147, 237, 265-69

Yablonski, Joseph "Jock," 253-54
Yale and Towne, 248
York, 7, 16, 41, 261, 295
Youngstown Sheet and Tube, 198

Zunic, Joseph, 270